DRESS
YOUR BEST
LIFE

ABOUT THE AUTHOR

Dawnn Karen is a pioneer in the field of fashion psychology. A graduate of Columbia University and a former model, Karen is currently a professor in the social sciences department at the Fashion Institute of Technology, in addition to maintaining her private therapy practice, Fashion Psychology Success, and her online classes, the Fashion Psychology Institute. Dubbed the 'Dress Doctor' by *The New York Times*, Karen has been featured by *Cosmopolitan*, the *Wall Street Journal*, *Glamour Italia*, *Good Morning America*, the *Daily Mail*, *Lorraine* and many others. Karen is Caribbean American and lives in New York.

Author website: fashionpsychologysuccess.com
Twitter: @dawnn_karen
Instagram: @dawnn_karen
Facebook: FashionPsychologistDawnnKaren

DRESS YOUR BEST LIFE

Harness the Power of
Clothes to Transform
Your Confidence

DAWNN KAREN

PENGUIN LIFE

AN IMPRINT OF

PENGUIN BOOKS

PENGUIN LIFE

UK | USA | Canada | Ireland | Australia
India | New Zealand | South Africa

Penguin Life is part of the Penguin Random House group of companies
whose addresses can be found at global.penguinrandomhouse.com.

First published in the United States by Little, Brown Spark, an imprint of
Little, Brown and Company, a division of Hachette Book Group, Inc. 2020
First published in Great Britain by Penguin Life 2020
001

Printed and bound in Great Britain by Clays Ltd, Elcograf S.p.A.

A CIP catalogue record for this book is available from the British Library

ISBN: 978–0–241–41413–2

www.greenpenguin.co.uk

MIX
Paper from
responsible sources
FSC® C018179

Penguin Random House is committed to a
sustainable future for our business, our readers
and our planet. This book is made from Forest
Stewardship Council® certified paper.

To Rosa-Lee "Baby Cooper" Cooper

CONTENTS

DRESS
YOUR BEST
LIFE

MY STYLE STORY

We delight in the beauty of the butterfly, but rarely admit the changes it has gone through to achieve that beauty.

—*Maya Angelou*

What if I told you fashion was a readily available, solidly reliable way to feel more in control of your life? That there are ways to match your clothing to your mood, to use accessories to conjure comfort, to reduce anxiety through color and fabric choices, to project power when you need it most? Clothes can help us maintain our cultural identity even when our environment demands we assimilate. Conversely, they can help us fit in when doing so is advantageous. With everything I've discovered about Fashion Psychology, I can't wait to help you break out of style ruts, create uniforms when useful, prevent the dreaded "I have nothing to wear" feeling, curb compulsive shopping behaviors, and avoid trends when they won't work for your lifestyle or your budget. What if I told you clothes can help you lift yourself up out of despair? Fashion is not meaningless. Far from it. Fashion is the voice we use to declare ourselves to the world.

The first time it occurred to me to practice psychology within the framework of fashion, I was twenty-one, working toward dual master's degrees (a Master of Arts and a Master of Education) in the Counseling Psychology Department at Columbia University's Teachers College. As a

3

recently graduated psychology major from Bowling Green State University in Ohio, I had spent my entire life in the Midwest. But when I arrived in New York for grad school, I hit the ground running. In addition to taking classes, I quickly achieved some side-hustle success as a runway model and fashion PR assistant. Though I served up fierce "lewks" on the runway, the truth is I'm an introvert and a keen observer of those around me. I was awed by the kaleidoscope of styles I encountered on the subways and streets of my new city. As I clocked the outfits of my fellow students, other models backstage, and everyday New Yorkers, I just couldn't get this question out of my head: *What do your clothes reveal about your psyche?* This idea was the seed from which Fashion Psychology (as I came to call it) would grow. I knew back then by instinct what I know now from academic research and clinical experience: People express their emotions, their well-being, even their trauma through their clothes. And clothes, in turn, can be a powerful tool for healing. I know this because I've lived it.

From the moment I set foot in Manhattan, I was home. The rhythm of the city just felt right. I was already accustomed to a rise-and-grind lifestyle, ready to balance rigorous academic demands with my creative passions. Growing up, I was a singer, studying opera and musical theater at the Cleveland School of the Arts. I had always excelled in my classes — even skipping the fifth grade — thanks to my curious mind and unending desire to please my parents. Achievement meant a lot in my family, especially to my father, a Jamaican immigrant who worked as a middle school janitor. My mom was an administrative assistant in a hospital, raising my brothers and me largely on her own, because my parents were never married. My twin brother and I shuffled back and forth between our parents' homes — the weekdays at our mom's and the weekend at our dad's. (My baby brother has a different father, whom he visited separately.) Studying hard and being onstage gave me an identity — "the performer" and "the risk taker" — that helped me distinguish myself from my shyer, more reserved siblings.

But life in the spotlight definitely created some tension between my peers and me. In middle school I was bullied for my appearance (I was tall and thin with glasses) by a guy who, fifteen years later, asked me out on Facebook. One girl in particular (a "best friend" who was anything but— know the type?) loved to talk about her designer clothes and would ask me pointedly about mine. I owned none. My father felt fancy labels were wasteful since, he reasoned, you could buy the same quality item—minus the brand name—for a fraction of the cost. In high school I was targeted for having an operatic voice and not a "church" voice. In college a sorority sister relentlessly made fun of me for deciding to shave my head and later, in colder weather, for experimenting with head scarves similar to the hijabs worn by Muslim women. Insecure as all of this made me, I always felt a deep urge to challenge norms with my look. Being creative with my style, utilizing whatever I had in my closet, was a major source of joy for me. It still is. Good grades and cheering audiences were external affirmations that I belonged where I was, and that I wasn't as out of place as my bullies would have me believe.

So when I started grad school at Columbia, I followed my trusty formula. I studied hard, worked hard, and said yes to every modeling gig that came my way. In my downtime, I designed and hand-made dramatic pearl and feather jewelry and christened my line Optukal Illusion (#truth). I made some fierce new friends, and they modeled my creations for promotional photos. I also volunteered at the Barnard/Columbia Rape Crisis Anti-Violence Support Center. It was work that felt like a calling, and it would become meaningful in a way I could not have foreseen. I was what my professors might call an ambitious self-starter. Being one of only a handful of black students in my program and from a lower-middle-class background, I felt I had everything to prove.

I was motivated, focused, and firing on all cylinders. I enthusiastically approached several professors for guidance, pitching this idea I had to practice Fashion Psychology, hoping they could help me find a job. But the field, as far as I could tell at the time, didn't seem to exist. One professor acknowledged that my résumé seemed to be a fifty-fifty split, with half my experience rooted in the world of fashion and the other half in the world of Freud. She urged me to seek an entry-level position assisting a renowned celebrity stylist. The stylist, however, had an infamous reputation for tearing down clients before building them back up with a makeover. Her approach just didn't sit right with me. Nor did it seem forward-thinking, given the messages of self-acceptance, body positivity, and inclusivity that were beginning to bubble up in pop culture, though they hadn't yet reached critical mass in the fashion industry at the time.

Still, even though the type of work I believed in wasn't easy to find, I couldn't let go of the notion of styling from the inside out. It seemed obvious to me that you should acknowledge a client's humanity — exploring her emotional history, her family background, her self-esteem, all that personal stuff that drew me to psychology — to understand how it affected her look. I wanted to be up in everybody's business and also help them gain confidence with great clothes. People *and* fashion fascinated me in equal measure.

I began to do this combination of talk therapy and wardrobe assessment on my own, first with family friends, then with friends of friends. Word of mouth spread, and my Rolodex of clients slowly began to grow. But my road to success hasn't been smooth. My idea to create this new psychological subdiscipline continues to rattle the academic establishment, with some of my colleagues calling me a "pop psychologist." But as powerful women now say: Nevertheless, I persist. After all, you can't learn persistence without resistance. And I always remember that the people to whom I'm truly accountable are the ones I'm here to help: my clients, my students, and now you. They — and you — are my North Star.

My time at Columbia was instrumental in helping me hone my message and clarify my mission. I came to define Fashion Psychology as the study and treatment of how color, beauty, style, image, and shape affect human behavior while addressing cultural sensitivities and cultural norms. The cultural angle? My classes taught me that. I learned how a patient's racial-ethnic background is an essential contextual consideration in therapy—a notion that was routinely emphasized by my professors. See, my teachers were cutting-edge academics, global citizens, savvy about the latest research, "woke." Though I was a minority in my program, the coursework seemed designed to acknowledge my reality. As future therapists, we were taught always to be aware of how different cultures respond to emotional difficulties, and how they feel about people seeking help for their problems. We were taught how a client's cultural background could shape her view of therapy, sometimes even more than socioeconomic class. For example, in collectivist Asian cultures, an individual's personal troubles may be perceived as a reflection on her family as a whole. Losing face, admitting weakness, seeking help for mental health issues will more often than not bring shame. Opening up to a therapist—a stranger—is simply not done.

Similarly, with African or Caribbean American individuals, like myself, there is a stigma surrounding going to therapy. Where I come from, unpacking your baggage in front of some random person is akin to blasphemy or defamation. Most of my family members would rather self-medicate than talk to somebody to expose and evaluate their trauma. In an article for *Psychology Today,* clinical psychologist Dr. Monnica T. Williams cites a 2008 study published in the *Journal of Health Care for the Poor and Underserved:* "Among Blacks... over a third felt that mild depression or anxiety would be considered 'crazy' in their social circles. Talking about problems with an outsider (i.e., therapist) may be viewed as airing one's 'dirty laundry,' and... over a quarter felt that discussions about mental illness would not be appropriate even among family."[1]

I really relate. My dad is my champion. My rock. My ride or die. But to this day, if I cry on the phone with him, he tells me to hang up, pull myself together, and call him back once I'm composed. If anything bad happens in my family, we have an unspoken rule: Don't speak about it. Ever the rebel, I opted *not* to follow that rule when a personal crisis upended my life. A year and a half into grad school, in the spring of 2011, my then-fiancé came to New York from Ohio to visit me for the weekend.

We'd met in college. We had been dating exclusively for two years. We loved each other. And he raped me.

The weekend of my rape began and ended with clothes. Knowing my fiancé would be arriving from Ohio on a Saturday, I picked out my favorite LBD for dinner that night. We were growing apart—a fact that gnawed at me, though I tried to bury it. I was evolving in grad school, incubating in my various industries. My fiancé was still living in Ohio, working as a restaurant server, supposedly saving enough to eventually join me in the Big Apple after we were married. That was my plan, at least. Even as I strutted down catwalks and went on go-sees, I was never enticed by the "models and bottles" club scene that sucked in and spat out so many of the girls I met backstage. It was different for me. *I can't tonight, I have class tomorrow* was my go-to excuse to stay home and hang out with my own introverted self. I was on a path. And I could see it leading in only one direction: up. I had it all figured out. I went over my fantasy mentally every day, like a mantra. I even illustrated my goals on a mood board: I would be living in Manhattan, married to my college sweetheart. We would have 2.5 children and a dog. And I would have a thriving career as a psychologist in private practice. I devoted my spare time to planning my wedding. *My* wedding. Not our wedding. That's how caught up I was in this vision of how my life was supposed to play out. He filled a role: the groom half of a wedding cake topper on a Pinterest page. Did I truly know him? I certainly had not a single clue that my partner would become my perpetrator.

He arrived in the afternoon. As we headed out to a restaurant near my apartment uptown, I was giddy—consumed with invitation ideas, comparing reception venues, debating color combinations, stewing over bridesmaid drama. It all spilled out of me as I blabbered a mile a minute between bites. He seemed despondent and distant. He drank more than usual. But...we were celebrating. I was buoyant. He seemed bored. He never was the loquacious one in the relationship, I told myself. Still, I was perplexed about what could have driven such an obvious wedge between us. Looking back, I think I was so busy chasing my future, I had failed to acknowledge my present. We were already over. In an essay about women and power for *New York Magazine,* author Lindy West wrote: "Women are conditioned to subsume our own needs to the needs of others and to try to make everything okay for everyone, emotionally and practically. And that becomes really insidious when women aren't conditioned to prioritize their own safety and even their own sense of self."[2] I didn't have that awareness yet. But I agree with her now. Now that I know what true powerlessness feels like.

When we got home that night, I couldn't take the tension anymore. I got emotional and questioned him about what was going on. He became totally agitated, which was so unlike the guy I knew. Alarm bells started going off left and right in my head. Why wouldn't he open up about what was bothering him? This strange mix of insecurity, anxiety, and irritation in the air was almost palpable. We had history. We had shared a warm, intimate life together for years. Later that night, he initiated sex. I refused to consent unless we communicated. In his book *The Gift of Fear, and Other Survival Signals That Protect Us from Violence,* security expert Gavin de Becker writes, "When it comes to danger, intuition is always right in at least two important ways: 1) It is always in response to something. 2) It always has your best interest at heart."[3] That night, my intuition sought to protect me from the man I already considered to be my husband. It was confusing as hell. My intuition wasn't enough. My fiancé raped me. My best friend violated me. The counselor in training, the mental health advocate, the empath had become the victim. According to the Centers for Disease Control and Prevention, "About 1 in 4 women and nearly 1 in 10 men have experienced contact sexual violence, physical violence, and/or stalking by an intimate partner during their lifetime."[4] I became a statistic. I actually passed out from shock. Shut straight down.

In the middle of the night, I woke up and my fiancé started to apologize, saying that he regretted what he had done. His acknowledging the reality of what had happened made something in me snap. I ran out of the apartment in a panic and called my parents back in Ohio. Each of them asked me what I wanted to do. I didn't want to file a report, I told them. I just wanted to finish my studies and adjust to a life without him in it. What I really wanted was to rewind time. I raged at myself. How could I not have anticipated this? I was stunned. How could I reconcile love with such brutality? I felt isolated. Who would believe that my fiancé raped me? How could I call the police and send another black man to prison?

I went back home, kicked him out of my apartment, and told him never to come near me again. I don't know where I found the strength. He packed wordlessly and left. A few hours later there was a knock at my door. I thought it was him. I didn't even hesitate to open the door. But it was the campus police. One of my parents (to this day I still don't know which one; I've never asked) had called them so I would have to file a report. I walked two officers through the details, feeling like I was floating outside my body. And then, with my ex-fiancé already on a bus back to Ohio, I officially declined to pursue the matter further. As soon as the police left, I told myself that I was going to move on with my life. I spent Sunday in bed. I didn't eat. I didn't shower. I barely moved. Then on Monday morning, I woke up and opened my closet.

On went a body-skimming 1950s-style dress, reminiscent of Audrey Hepburn's iconic Givenchy silhouettes. Church gloves. A wide-brimmed hat. Full makeup. Bold lipstick. My giant handmade feather earrings. I figured if I felt good in my outfit, I would feel good, period. In the months that followed, I kept upping the ante, fashion-wise. I wore gowns to class. Other students, in their jeans and t-shirts, gave me side-eye. I didn't care. Getting dressed in the morning was the one bright spot in my day. My apartment became my atelier, where I was in complete control. Selecting my clothes and accessories, I could tap into the creativity of my childhood, my sense of fun, of play. What some might cast as power dressing, I called dressing up my pain. I've since come to think of it as dressing from the heart. All I know is, after my rape, I clung to my clothes like a toddler to a teddy bear, like a drowning person to a life raft.

In a series of interviews conducted by researchers for a book called *Appearance and Power*, survivors of sexual assault were asked how they chose to dress in the aftermath of their attack. More than half changed the way they dressed as a result. Some dressed to avoid attention, to self-protect, to deter comments on their appearance. Others, however, changed up their style to communicate indomitable power.[5] That was me. Years later, I discovered even more research describing this type of behavior and read it with my mouth open, feeling like I was reading my own damn diary. At the University of Queensland Business School in Australia, marketing lecturer Dr. Alastair Tombs determined that women associate positive feelings with certain clothing items and negative feelings with others, on the basis of their previous emotional experiences and memories of wearing those items. After extensive interviews with thirty women, Tombs concluded, as he told the *Sydney Morning Herald,* that "outfit choices are made to match mood and as a form of self-expression, but we've also found that clothing is used to control or mask emotions."[6] Bam! There I was: controlling, masking, and attempting to transform my emotions with my outfits. And it helped a little—it really did.

I came to define this behavior as Mood Enhancement Dress—when you use clothes to elevate or optimize your emotional state, to cheer yourself up. You know how there's that saying "Don't dress for the job you have, dress for the job you want"? Well, we can translate that idea into emotion. With Mood Enhancement Dress, you dress to evoke the feelings you want to feel. Wearing brighter colors to bring myself joy, tall heels to feel powerful, and makeup to feel polished and put together—these were all acts of Mood Enhancement. They were ways of investing in myself when someone I loved and trusted had just shown me he didn't think I was worth much. It's been said that "Looking good is the best revenge," which today has morphed into the popular hashtag #RevengeBody. But I wasn't dressing up for him. Not anymore and never again. I was shoring myself up to face the world. Dressing well was my first step toward reclaiming my life.

It wasn't enough, of course. You don't need to be a shrink to figure out that recovering from intimate partner violence takes a lot more than a pencil skirt and strappy sandals. Over the course of that summer and fall, my looks got more and more outlandish, but ironically, I was increasingly withdrawn—a shell of my former self. My professors took notice. (Honestly, the way I was dressed, how could they miss me?) In a series of closed-door meetings, summoning all of my courage, I told them everything. And though they were aware of my situation, with my culture's mental health stigma baked into their curriculum, in December they advised me to take a leave of absence from my program. They had determined that I "lacked the requisite empathy to be a therapist."

Looking back, I believe I was probably suffering from some sort of post-traumatic stress, unable to connect fully with patients or peers as I went through the motions of my daily life. This is not an excuse for what happened. It's simply important to me to clarify that deep down, beneath the surface, *I* knew I was still the same empathetic, sensitive, intuitive person I had always been. I was simply cut off from that part of myself. I couldn't seem to find a way to pull it up and belt it out to the back of the room. I was just five credits shy of earning my second master's degree in education for counseling psychology when I was effectively kicked out of Columbia. I walked away with my Master of Arts and was officially a trained therapist. In the years since, I've let any resentment go. I firmly believe that when faced with a closed door, you have two choices: Give up, or find a different door.

So there I was, twenty-three, and in the midst of a full-blown existential and emotional crisis. I had lost the structure of school. I had lost my fiancé. Going home to lick my wounds wasn't an option, even if I could have afforded the plane ticket back to Ohio. I felt so alone, like my insides had been hollowed out. If only I had known that I was in good company. According to a 2009 survey by the American Psychological Association, 87 percent of psychology graduate students reported experiencing anxiety, 68 percent depression. It's no accident that the study of psychology is jokingly called "Me-Search" — because people who gravitate toward mental health professions commonly wish to address their own issues (while also helping others).[7] And, man, did I have issues.

As with so many other people, I find that many of the themes that have emerged in my life stem from my upbringing. As I mentioned, my father worked as a middle school custodian. But that's not the whole story. In a way that parallels my grad student by day/model by night way of life, my dad too had a sort of double identity. When I was thirteen, he was convicted of a federal drug crime, for which he served two years in prison. My mother's struggles with substance abuse became acute during this time. We've since reached a happy ending of sorts. Both of my parents have, in recent years, put themselves through college. This fills me with a pride words can't express. But that period took its toll — on all of us. Leaving Columbia, I felt lows I hadn't experienced since my teens, when my father was incarcerated. And yet I could no longer blame my troubles on my parents. The predicament I found myself in wasn't my fault, but it was mine to handle alone. I was in uncharted territory.

In the past, my reaction to tragedy, heartbreaks, or setbacks had always been to work even harder and push myself to overachieve. My mission was to make everyone proud, to steal the spotlight and thus take the heat, to make up for my parents' missteps. I learned early that hard work could help you dig yourself out of almost any hole. My father's sister was the first in his family to emigrate from Jamaica. She worked as a maid, cleaning floors, eventually earning enough money to bring him over to join her in the United States. I was the first person in my family to go to college, let alone an Ivy League university. So when the powers that be told me, in essence, that I didn't belong there, it was a gut punch, not only to myself but also to my family. My father's take? "You were born here in the States. And you're setting us back two, three generations." I felt like a failure. I was supposed to be better than this. I was going to be the one to save us. Instead, my disgrace radiated outward, like a ripple effect, staining my already fragile family with shame. Was this reaction fair or merited? Is the role of family savior one I still wish to play? These are questions I continue to wrestle with in therapy to this day.

A die-hard work ethic wasn't the only thing I inherited from my family. I've been told that when my maternal grandmother attempted to speak out about her own sexual assault, she was placed in a mental institution. As a group, black women have been collectively holding this stuff in—brutal racial prejudice, sexual violence, everyday abuse or micro-aggressions—for generations. It's a devastating legacy. No wonder we "pop off." No wonder we are reluctant to seek help. Scientists working in the field of epigenetics are exploring whether we inherit trauma—theorizing that psychic wounds may be passed down genetically from one generation to the next.[8] UC Davis biological scientist Lawrence V. Harper writes in the *Psychological Bulletin,* published by the American Psychological Association: "Currently, behavioral development is thought to result from the interplay among genetic inheritance, congenital characteristics, cultural contexts, and parental practices as they directly impact the individual. Evolutionary ecology points to another contributor, *epigenetic inheritance,* the transmission to offspring of parental phenotypic responses to environmental challenges—even when the young do not experience the challenges themselves."[9] In other words, our lived experiences are possibly seared into our genes. Trauma, some scientists contend, may be heritable.

After my rape, I decided to break this cycle of quietly burying abuse. I spoke out so that my future daughter wouldn't be born burdened by my pain—by my grandmother's pain. And I kept talking. After opening up to my parents and professors, eventually I sought therapy. More recently, I gave a TEDx talk about it. Shame thrives in silence. So I got—and stayed—loud.

But in the immediate aftermath of my assault, there was only the practical matter of my survival to worry about. To stay in New York and keep myself afloat financially, I took a job as a nanny. It felt like a huge step backward, a defeated retreat from my goals. At first, the position seemed no different from cleaning floors and scrubbing toilets, just like the jobs my dad and my aunt had to take as new immigrants. But I had no resources. I knew no one outside my program. It was either nannying or working at McDonald's. If my life were a movie, however, this would be the time to cue the redemption montage set to tearjerker music. The child I cared for was a truly amazing seven-year-old boy with special needs. Being with him, nurturing him, slowing myself down for him turned out to be the best therapy I could have hoped for. Following my assault, a chasm opened up between before and after. The Dawnn I used to be became the Dawnn I would never be again. I relived that night over and over in my mind. Yet as many sexual assault survivors will tell you, when this happens to you, the world doesn't stop to notice. We are the invisible walking wounded, standing in line at coffee shops, shopping at the supermarket, staring at the pavement as we pass you in the crosswalk. "There is an unacknowledged battlefield," tweeted the singer Liz Phair about survivors of sexual violence, "and we are the undecorated veterans."[10]

Back at Columbia during those months when I felt so vulnerable, my sharply tailored dresses made me feel bulletproof. They were my armor. My cover. My way of telegraphing to the world that I was not simply okay, I was *fabulous*. But in addition to masking my suffering, besides wearing crisp, clean clothes to put the lie to my mess of a life, I was also trying desperately to lift myself up. This wasn't madness. It was methodical. To actually heal from my rape took time. Years. You know what? I'm still healing. Self-examination, plenty of pajama days, therapy, the support of my friends and family, my own openness—and, yes, even public speaking—about my assault: These have been the cornerstones of my rebuilding process. So was working with that little boy. (With him, I wore sweats.) We would ride the subway, pretending to be astronauts. Neither of us had any idea what we were going to be when we grew up. I see now that this meant my vision of the future was open to modification. Together we went underground. We let our imaginations take us to infinity and beyond. In the period after my rape, the contents of my closet made me feel weighted to the earth. Clothes were the only tangible, physical things I had that connected me to the self I feared was lost forever.

"Not all storms come to disrupt your life," tweeted the novelist Paulo Coelho. "Some come to clear your path."[11] I also like this quote by author Katherine MacKenett: "Mountains do not rise without earthquakes." I read that one on Instagram. My father, in his desperate pursuit of a better life, took risks, made certain choices, and paid the consequences. My mother, to cope with heartbreak, numbed herself with substances. (She is now in recovery.) I like to think I learned from their struggles, used what I gleaned, and transcended my history to forge a different future. I'm convinced that feeling my feelings and helping other people — showing by example that your past doesn't determine your future — has enabled me to finally achieve what my parents always wanted: the American Dream.

Seven years after my rape, the *New York Times* called me "The Dress Doctor" and described my intersecting passions as "the relationship between attire and attitude: not just how clothes make you look, but how they make you feel."[12] My mother has recently been driving for Lyft to make extra money. When the *Times* article came out, she overheard two passengers discussing it in the backseat of her car. Bursting with pride, she told them I was her daughter. They didn't believe her.

Six years after I became a nanny, I became a contributor to CNBC. Nearly a decade after my professors shrugged at the idea of Fashion Psychology — a term I have since trademarked — a journalist for *New York Magazine* called it an "explosively popular tool" that helps "explain the world we live in."[13] If you had told me a decade ago that I would go on to give a presentation on the field for an international Women's Empowerment Conference backed by the United Nations, I would have laughed to keep from crying.[14] Over the years, client by client, I have built a reputation — and my own educational institute — through word of mouth. One chance encounter with a journalist led to TV appearances in thirty-five countries. I became the first black female psychology professor at the Fashion Institute of Technology — the famed training ground for designers including Calvin Klein and Michael Kors. Hired in my mid-twenties, I was also one of its youngest. In a few short years, I have built the holy grail of millennial career goals: my own brand. Now you know I had to climb through hell to get here. And dammit, I climbed in heels.

I still have my critics, of course. Some of my fellow academics doubt Fashion Psychology can be feasible in clinical practice and question its legitimacy as a scientific pursuit (more on that in chapter 1). But I am here to tell you that it *does* work and its lessons *are* actionable. For everybody. If you ask me, the doubt stems from this notion that fashion itself is superficial or frivolous. That it isn't serious. In our current climate, I can't help but wonder if anything so closely associated with femininity makes it vulnerable to slings and arrows. To venom and derision. To disbelief. And so, to marry "silly," "girly" fashion with a field as esteemed as psychology seems to be falsely elevating the former while cheapening the latter. If I may be so bold: F that. I contend that from an emotional and economic perspective, fashion is not frivolous. It is big, serious business.

And style — the way we use fashion to say something about ourselves — is one of the most important elements linking our private lives to our public personas. Our clothing is the connective tissue between the physical and the emotional. It's what protects our truest, most tender selves, like a shield from an often harsh world. When Melania Trump or Kim Kardashian wears a duster coat draped over her shoulders like a superhero's cape, obscuring her arms and her hands, she is sending a message: Look but don't touch. In our day-to-day lives and careers, we are not permitted to wear our heart on our sleeve, so to speak. In polite society, we are trained to cover up our feelings and layer our emotions. To keep it cool. But even when we succeed at hiding our feelings, we are still sending out subliminal messages with our clothes.

As I look back on my journey, I often think about the Monday morning after my rape. Why did I choose to wear one of my best outfits on a day that could reasonably be described as my worst? Why were *clothes* so essential, so inextricably bound to my will to live? I've come to realize that style is proof of our humanity. A tasteful, carefully considered outfit is evidence that you are a high-functioning member of society. Your clothes have the power to get you noticed or, conversely, to conceal whatever it is you wish to keep hidden. We are all walking around in some sort of pain. When you face struggles due to family issues, financial strain, or mental health challenges, you are still required to look presentable. You still have to show up at school or work. You still have to *show* up; to show yourself— or some version thereof. Getting dressed is the great equalizer. As they say, we all put our pants on one leg at a time. They also say that clothes make the man (and woman). Why not use something that's at your fingertips—a real, physical tool you already have right there, in your closet—to soothe, strengthen, and empower yourself? The idea is simple: If I can open your eyes to WHY you choose to wear what you wear, I can help you make better choices.

And what you wear is, above all, a choice—even if it's one you don't realize you are making. You may opt to look glamorous, to be comfortable, to be practically invisible, or to demand being seen. What you wear is who you are, for all intents and purposes. It's who I am too. My clothes. My armor. Dressing up not only helped me walk out the door and go to school that terrible Monday morning; it set the course for the rest of my life. I am not here to ask you to completely transform the way you dress. I don't believe in "style rules." I have none to offer. But I do know that what I wear has a major impact on how I feel. This knowledge is power. Power that's yours to possess.

Chapter 1

FASHION PSYCHOLOGY 101

Clothes... change our view of the world and the world's view of us.
—*Virginia Woolf*

Feeling anxious about what to wear or disconnected from the way you present yourself? Welcome. As a Fashion Psychologist, I find that my clients represent the full spectrum of ages, races, ethnicities, genders, and nationalities. Clients from all walks of life seek me out to address a variety of concerns, from personal development to shopping addiction to dating advice to career advancement. I counsel c-suite executives and new moms recovering from C-sections (and some women who are both!). Some people want help polishing their online profiles, others with navigating their exploding closets. One client going through a custody battle even wanted to know how to dress so that the family court judge would be sympathetic to his side. While none of your problems is unique, all of the solutions are, because they lie within you. Now let's go find them together.

Did you know your clothes are talking? Mine are too. One recent morning I had to get up to teach class after having basically pulled an all-nighter writing an article for a news site. I lay in bed and assessed my mood. I was grouchy and exhausted with a side of the midwinter blahs. I wanted to reach for my go-to comfort outfit: a matching pair of sweats. Still, I anticipated that as I would be getting up in front of my FIT students to give a lecture, I would need to adjust my attitude and seriously boost my energy level. Fashion dilemma moment. So I added a leopard-print trench coat, some leopard heels, and you know what? I felt so much better! Combining the ease of sweats with the stylishness of the jacket and heels really did lift my spirits. And my students seemed to perceive me as on-point and au courant, appreciating my sleek spin on the popular athleisure trend. By dressing in this eye-catching way, I was sending them a message: I see you guys as creative, visually oriented, trend-savvy fashion students. I communicated to them that while I was in a position of authority (high heels), I also didn't take myself too seriously (sweats).

In this moment I was also combining two of my essential Fashion Psychology philosophies: **Mood Illustration** and **Mood Enhancement Dress.** In a nutshell, Mood Illustration is when you dress to honor or match your mood; Mood Enhancement is when you dress to change it for the better. I was honoring (or illustrating) my emotional state by self-soothing with soft, effortless sweats. And I was simultaneously amplifying my mojo (or enhancing my mood) with outerwear and shoes that popped. We'll delve deeper into these mood-based styling concepts in chapter 5. But for now, I want you to get a taste of how they apply to real life — to understand that your clothing really does connect to your emotions.

There's also a second, equally important dynamic at play when you get dressed: the one between you and other people. What I wear sends signals to you, my perceiver. And what *you* wear sends signals to me, which I interpret. This unspoken dialog happens between us as we cross paths and silently scan each other for visual clues. Whatever we infer about each other sets the stage for our social interaction. Much of this happens on an unconscious level, almost instantly. Now, if other people react strongly to your fashion statements, you may want to insist that you haven't even *said* anything. But with fashion, the message is already woven into the medium. When others look at you, size you up, and consider what you have on, they're gathering information about who you are. It's inescapable. Unavoidable. Your clothes are talking. They can't be silenced. We watch this dialog unfold every day in the public sphere. In the era of social media, political polarization, and the rapid-fire, headline-hungry news cycle, Fashion Psychology is more relevant than ever. Obsessed with our likes and followers, we are all putting ourselves on display and reading each other 24/7. What are you wearing? Who made it? How much did you pay for it? Who are you? Where do you come from? Where do you stand?

In Fashion Psychology, politics, religion, race, gender, nationality, age, class, and culture collide, whether we're talking pussy bows or pantsuits, a black teenager's hoodie or an $895 Balenciaga sweatshirt emblazoned with street graffiti worn by Taylor Swift. (Yep, that happened.)[1] What does a burkini trigger in us? How about Yeezy Boosts? Why did Steve Jobs wear the same outfit every day? Why did his would-be successor Elizabeth Holmes? What are rappers saying with designer logos and diamond grillz? How do we feel when Kim Kardashian matches her neon latex dress to her neon luxury car? How does Instagram influence retail? Do Kylie Jenner's selfies make young people want cosmetic surgery? I have been asked to discuss these topics and more by international heads of state, students at FIT, executives at major fashion labels, *Good Morning America,* and many others. Here's what I tell everyone: Once you understand how powerfully fashion drives perception, you can take the wheel.

But first, back to those snap judgments. One important study published in the journal *Psychological Science* revealed that we determine someone's attractiveness, likability, trustworthiness, competence, and aggressiveness within *one hundred milliseconds* of seeing them.[2] That's all it takes. Bolstering this point is a great quote from drag performer Trixie Mattel. "In society," she told the *New York Times Magazine,* "we are what we're dressed as."[3] If you're in a police uniform, you're a cop, she explains, a person in a position of power. If you're in scrubs, you're a doctor, an intelligent, caretaking authority figure. If you're in head-to-toe Lululemon, you're a privileged wellness fan who perhaps lives a life of leisure. We rarely question what our eyes tell us, or the soundness of these assumptions. And instinctively, we are pretty convinced our first impressions are spot-on. They aren't always. But they certainly can be. For example, when people are under stress or really going through some drama, it can seem like they're wearing their heart on their sleeve. They say your eyes are a window into your soul; I say your *clothes* are. When a depressed person wears drab, unkempt clothing, this too is an example of Mood Illustration Dress. After all, your clothing selections reflect the full range of emotions, and that includes some unhappy ones. This was the situation my client Jim* found himself in. Let's meet him.

CASE STUDY:
WHAT BECOMES OF THE BROKENHEARTED?

When I first met Jim, he was in his mid-forties and in the process of divorcing his husband, with whom he shares children. Though Jim was a very accomplished legal professional, at that moment in his life, emotional turmoil was his middle name. Despite his overwhelming personal crisis, he felt compelled to keep up appearances at work. And yet every time we met, I noticed he had missed a button or two on his dress shirt, or it would be partially untucked. When I gently addressed his rumpled appearance, his anxiety would spike and his self-esteem would plummet. It seemed to him that an untied shoelace was proof that his life was unraveling, and worse yet, that others were aware. His untidy style was an outer symptom of his inner despondency. Jim did not have the mental bandwidth to worry about the small things. Looking in the mirror was a reminder of who he had become—a divorcé, disconnected from the people he loved most, untethered to the person he used to be—so he avoided them. But ignoring his

---

* All Case Studies in this book have been included with the permission of my clients. In some instances, when indicated by an asterisk, I have changed their names to protect their privacy.

appearance only added to his anxiety and further diminished his sense of self-worth.

Style Rx

So how did I help Jim? I didn't tell him to go out and buy a new Ralph Lauren suit (though he could have afforded one). Instead, during our third session, I tried a bit of cognitive behavioral therapy. I asked him to put all of his focus on his shirt, taking his time to slowly and carefully fasten each button. Then I asked him to thoughtfully and methodically tuck it into his suit pants, in a 360-degree motion. Next, I asked him to check, loop by loop, to make sure his belt was fastened correctly. To his surprise, performing these **small acts of mindfulness** and self-care helped him regain a feeling of control. As he momentarily turned every ounce of his conscious attention to his attire, he was unable to think of anything else. He was forced to be present, instead of letting his thoughts spiral. And in this small way, I showed Jim that he was still capable of quieting his mind, of attending to himself and treating his appearance as a priority.

Over the months I worked with Jim, I also guided him toward **labeling his feelings.** Instead of his saying, "My life is a disaster," I encouraged him to describe his emotions more specifically: "I'm worried I'll be alone forever. I feel deep sadness when I think about missing my kids' milestones." From there, we worked to **identify concrete steps he could take to empower himself** (by making lunch plans with his brother, by signing up for complimentary personal training sessions at his new gym, etc.). Taking the time to carefully pull his appearance together offered him a tangible, actionable way to move forward through his crisis instead of being immobilized by it.

- - - - - - - - -

*   *   *

Self-expressing through clothes is not a new thing. In fact, it's a tale as old as time—or at least as old as the Middle Ages, when historians say people first started wearing clothes that designated their position in society.[4] The fact is, we've been using clothes to declare our gender identities, our group memberships, our class, our unconscious feelings and desires for a *loooong* time. Pulitzer Prize–winning fashion critic Robin Givhan once said: "As soon as man emerged from the cave, clothes took on a social significance. I don't think there's ever been a period where a shirt was just a shirt!" Throughout history, people have used clothes to signify their tribe, their wealth or status, their position in the social hierarchy. "Those things have always been wrapped up in fashion," Givhan notes, "whether we consider the era of the French courts or even the emergence of hip-hop."[5]

Now this is some cerebral stuff! But when you boil Fashion Psychology down to its essence, we're simply looking at how clothing affects human behavior. So what does any of this have to do with what you're supposed to wear to work tomorrow? First of all, my mission is to convince you that your clothes can be utilized to make people respond to you in the way you'd like, as well as to make you feel your best. No more getting dressed on autopilot. Those days are done. (See "Have a Mindful Morning" on page 33.) Next, I want to help you define your fashion personality and home in on your signature style (aka your personal brand). I'll help you break unhealthy retail habits and bust out of style ruts—all using Fashion Psychology techniques.

Once you have a clear-eyed sense of your own ideal style and a savvier awareness of what triggers you to shop, we'll explore different, more simplified ways to approach getting dressed. My goal is to help you streamline the process to reduce stress. You'll learn to be more conscious of your mood before you set foot in your closet, to identify clearer goals for how you want to feel each day and for what reactions you hope to inspire, and then to actualize those goals by wearing items you already own. I'll give you all the tools you'll need, like a time-saving Capsule Wardrobe, anti-anxiety jewelry, and power colors to improve your look *and* your outlook.

This book will not include "Dos & Don'ts" lists or sidebars on the perfect little black dress (which is not a solution for every sartorial situation, no matter what experts say!). Instead, I will teach you how to maintain your cultural identity anywhere, anytime, to level up your Instagram game, to prevent the dreaded "I have nothing to wear" feeling, to sidestep trends when they won't work for your lifestyle (keep it moving, bike shorts!), and more. By sharing Case Studies featuring real people I've counseled (like Jim), I will illuminate how your style habits and beliefs are either helping or hurting you. And I will prove to you that you are not the only one with issues. I have lots of motivating, thought-provoking exercises up my sleeve (ahem). They're the same ones I offer my clients, and they'll help you get to work right away. But before I do all that, I'd like to tell you a little bit more about what I will *not* do.

WHAT ON EARTH IS A FASHION PSYCHOLOGIST?

Here's the deal: I am a professor and a therapist with a background in and a passion for the fashion industry. I am skeptical of rules, flash-in-the-pan trends, retail therapy, and paint-by-numbers styling advice. I want to know how you *feel* in your clothes so I can help you find clothes that make you feel phenomenal. I also believe fashion can be a catalyst for social change. Whether I am chatting over tea with abaya-clad clients in Dubai or developing curriculum on "Trayvon Martin and the Hoodie Effect," I am deeply cognizant of the way cultural stories play out through our clothes. I have always been, and remain, voraciously curious about people. How you dress is just one aspect of who you are, but it is a significant one. If you've got style questions, I've got answers. I'm just going to ask you to do some soul-searching first.

I can help you dress and feel better. But I am not a stylist, at least not in the traditional sense. A stylist, image consultant, or personal shopper tells clients what to wear on the basis of the latest trends, what's new and now on the runways and racks, and what *she* thinks will make them look their best. In Hollywood, dressing celebrities is a full-blown industry with its own exclusive ecosystem. A star's "personal style" is generally bought and paid for, though usually not by the star. Instead, it is the creation of a team of professional artists, known as a glam squad. It is their job to bring glamorous fashion fantasies to life. *My* job is to improve your real life — and, yes, ideally make it a little more glamorous.

I've worked with my share of boldface names, but one reason being a celebrity stylist isn't #goals for me is the lack of inclusivity in the industry. Stylist Jason Bolden, who works with Mindy Kaling, Serena Williams, and Taraji P. Henson, among others, has described the racially charged roadblocks he's encountered on the way to the red carpet. When he has approached A-list fashion houses seeking dresses for a sample-size Oscar nominee who happens to be a minority, their answer has been "'Oh, no. Pass,'" he told *New York Magazine*'s website *The Cut.* "But then I see them work with someone [white] who has no career, no fashion profile. It's bizarre."[6]

Size-ism also comes into play. Stars who do not fit into size 00 sample gowns tend to be shut out of the designer garment game. You may remember when *Saturday Night Live* comedian Leslie Jones couldn't find a designer dress to wear to the 2016 premiere of her film *Ghostbusters.* She tweeted: "It's so funny how there are no designers wanting to help me with a premiere dress for a movie. Hmmm that will change and I remember everything."[7] While fashion houses often cite legitimate reasons for producing collections in only a limited number of sizes (cost, engineering, etc.), this "You can't sit with us" mean girls shtick is starting to feel old. Not only do I not play this game, I never even set foot in the arena.

In my world, whatever body type you are, whatever skin tone, whatever nationality, whatever generation, whatever is in your bank account, I am here to help you examine your life and reimagine your relationship with your clothes. I'm laser-focused on how people use fashion either as a means of empowerment or as an emotional crutch. Stylists may be amazingly skilled, but their primary concern is optics. They care about how their client *appears*. I care about how you *are*. In the fashion industry, in the world of Instagram influencers, and in Hollywood, authenticity counts, but image counts more. My job is to help you connect what you wear on the outside with how you feel on the inside. For a stylist, the client's inner life is a secondary, incidental consideration, *if* it ever comes up at all. You would probably find it pretty inappropriate and unprofessional if your stylist started asking probing questions about your romantic situation, your past traumas, your family dynamics. Girl, that's where I begin.

A Fashion Psychologist *starts* by excavating what's beneath the surface, hence my motto "styling from the inside out." I want to know why the person sitting in front of me chooses to dress the way she does. So I ask. I ask questions about her love life, her racial-ethnic-religious-cultural background, her family history, her self-esteem, her body image, her lifestyle, her relationships, her fears and insecurities, her challenges and strengths—long before we ever consider changing a stitch of clothing. I typically meet with a client for three sessions of talk therapy before I look at her wardrobe. Now, because this is a book, I can't come and see your closet. But I can teach you to *style yourself*, using clothes and accessories you already own.

So let's get to where the rubber meets the road. How does Fashion Psychology actually work? In the following Case Study, you'll see Fashion Psychology in action and begin to understand how it can help you.

CASE STUDY:
IT AIN'T BROKE, BUT WE CAN STILL FIX IT

- -

My client in this case was an Australian fashion editor in her mid-twenties named Tracey. She has a busy life, a vivacious personality, and is often unsure about what to wear to the various social events, celebrity interviews, and professional meetings on her agenda. I would describe her personal style as fashion forward and eclectic. She makes bold choices. She doesn't hesitate to wear a white faux croc-embossed bomber jacket, a blue-and-black leopard-print silk t-shirt, or white snakeskin pumps—all at once. But somewhat incongruously, she favors relaxed essentials (tops, pants, jackets) in slouchy silhouettes. She is a bit all over the place.

Tracey has great style instincts but lacks a cohesive vision for who she is and how to communicate it. As a result, during the morning rush, she tends to take a "kitchen sink" approach, throwing on a bunch of trendy, disparate statement pieces all at once, then trying to balance them out with too casual basics (like worn-out, baggy boyfriend jeans). She tends to get dressed in such a flurry that she doesn't give much forethought to how everything works together, or how she will feel as her day goes on. Tracey's innate creativity and energetic personality combined with her high-pressure job (a fashion editor has to dress the part) create anxiety, leading her to lean into looks that overwhelm her. She has it going on; she just has too much of it.

As Tracey and I talked through her social calendar, I advised her on how to simplify her style for a variety of upcoming pressure-cooker situations. Let's see if you can apply some of my advice to your own life.

Performance Review

Especially in corporate environments, women often get the message that they should dress to emulate those in power. That would usually be men. Working at a magazine, Tracey could have easily pulled a "business suit" from her office fashion closet, or headed out to a fast-fashion retailer like Zara to buy something "professional"-looking for her big meeting. But after a long conversation, we determined that putting on a slick new suit with sharp shoulders and constricting trousers would hurt her more than it would help. If she doesn't feel natural in her look, she'll feel like a fraud (#ImposterSyndrome) and her anxiety will flare.

Style Rx

I suggested Tracey wear a soft silky button-down shirt she feels great in and has worn on successful workdays in the past—one she therefore associates with feeling empowered. She already owns several such tops featuring delicate prints or piped edges, details that can subtly set you apart.

Next, we selected trim black pants with some stretch (think cigarette pants to balance out the volume on top), a classic black jacket, and pointy-toe pumps. These are all fail-safe yet comfortable components of a polished look.

My goal for Tracey was that she feel like herself in all important meetings. So I advised her to start elevating her work style ahead of time, wearing these types of outfits on the days before she sets up a meeting to lobby for a promotion. **Road test your outfits!** As I told Tracey: "You'll get used to seeing yourself as a power player, and so will anyone else who's watching. Dressing like you've already got the job—and owning that look— will program your higher-ups to visualize you in the role."

Flying Solo at a Wedding

You may feel vulnerable showing up at a wedding alone. But as I told Tracey, it is better to feel your feelings than to drown them at the open bar. As she contemplated what to wear to an upcoming summer wedding, I asked her to imagine interactions with other guests and **anticipate the kinds of comments that could unravel her confidence.** Then I advised her to dress to get the kinds of compliments she would hope to hear.

Style Rx

Tracey already owned a few dresses with sleeves, a cinched waist, and a kicky A-line skirt. These tend to be universally flattering silhouettes that satisfy most dress codes and, given their breathability, work in many climates. If the wedding calls for black tie attire, statement accessories like bold jewelry, embellished heels, and luxe outerwear can boost the formality factor.

Next I advised her to **consider color.** Red is a sex magnet (see chapter 6). Blue is calming. Black will help you blend in. If the mother of the bride says, "Wow, that dress is a showstopper!" would Tracey hear "My, you're looking thirsty these days"? It's not about dressing to please others, I explained. It's about knowing what kind of feedback might knock you off your game and dressing to avoid it.

A Tinder Date

First dates are awkwardness bombs just waiting to detonate. Like so many of us, Tracey tends to get goofy, overshare, or clam up when she's nervous. I explained that her clothes can pick up the slack and send clearer, more self-assured messages. Tops with sheer or delicate lace accents show a sliver of skin without being overly revealing. Anything boxy, baggy, or too fashion forward could obscure her allure. (Those who are into the Man Repeller aesthetic may disagree!)

Style Rx

I advised Tracey to ask herself **how she wants to feel** with this person — sexy (red dress, architectural neckline; metallic heels and clutch), fun (denim on denim with statement sandals), energized (summery dress in citrus hue with white sneakers), relaxed (maxi skirt, t-shirt) — then pick from her closet accordingly.

- - - - - - - - -

*   *   *

As you can see, I didn't suggest Tracey alter her style dramatically or max out her credit card on a special occasion investment piece. All the "new" looks I prescribed were made up of outfit elements she already owned. As you'll hear me say repeatedly, I don't do makeovers. Makeovers don't stick. They're like the style equivalent of a juice cleanse: dramatic initial results, impossible to sustain. In fact, sometimes the wardrobe changes I suggest to clients are so subtle, no one else ever even notices them!

Makeovers entertain us because they play into our deepest desires for beauty, glamour, escape, transformation. We binge-watch shows to see how clothes can create (and re-create) identities. Think of the heart-pounding "big reveal" moments on *Queer Eye, What Not to Wear, Say Yes to the Dress,* and countless others. On those shows, the subjects morph—frequently via bandage dress—from drab to fab, their new look the key to happily ever after. Glam squads with red carpet résumés swoop in, work their magic on hair, makeup, outfit, and voilà! Heretofore hidden confidence is uncovered and, usually, true love acquired.

But you know how those stories end. The effects evaporate once the director yells "Cut!" The clock strikes midnight and the star-for-a-day turns back into the wallflower dressed in rags. You're too smart to fall for that fairy-tale formula. In this day and age, we've all been forced to grow up. We are no longer willing to be spoon-fed the same tired old tropes. Today, gender is more fluid, yoga pants are more popular than jeans, and lifelong singlehood is a viable version of happily ever after.[8] If you hit the job market after the 2008 recession, you probably care more about how to dress for an informational interview than you do for a date. Fashion Psychology is the natural next step as we evolve beyond the passé makeover mindset. I'm betting you are ready to approach your look—and your life—from a more intentional place.

My role is to help you get in touch with who you are, with how you are feeling underneath it all. If you want to rethink your look or reform your shopping habits, I'm down. But the first step in getting where you want to go is examining where you are coming from. Clothes are simply a vehicle to empower you on your path. Or in some cases, stumbling blocks to be cleared from it.

More things I don't do:

- Dress you according to your "body shape" or compare your body to produce. For the record, I have yet to meet a person whose self-esteem was improved by identifying as "pear-shaped."
- Take you on *Pretty Woman*–esque shopping sprees. In fact, I rarely shop with clients at all.
- KonMari your closet. I could watch Marie Kondo fold t-shirts all day (#SparksJoy). And I do have tips about how to edit your closet and create a Capsule Wardrobe (see page 120). But your junk drawer is none of my business. And there's *no way* I'm showing you mine.

When I work with clients, we talk—*really* talk—about the psychological motivations behind their wardrobe choices. And you're about to meet a bunch of them who were brave enough to bare their secrets. I bet you'll relate to many. And I hope they'll inspire you to think more deeply about your own story and how it drives you to dress. I'm interested in helping you reconnect with your truest, most authentic self. I firmly believe you cannot look good until you *feel* good. I have a hunch that whatever is stopping you from dressing your best is an emotional wound in need of healing. Once you address it, you'll be ready to project a healthier self through your style. Here's a great first step.

HAVE A MINDFUL MORNING

Does this sound familiar? The alarm goes off. You rush through your morning routine and then it's time to confront your closet. You're already late, anxious AF, running through your mental to-do list, stressing about that combative co-worker or disapproving teacher, defeated before you get started. Soon you'll have tried on a dozen outfits, trashing your room, but none will be quite right. You'll have a mountain of clothes strewn all over the damn place, and you'll still have nothing to wear.

What if you took just a minute to lie in bed and, before your feet even hit the floor, ask yourself: How do I *feel* right now? What's on my agenda today? And most important, how do I *want* to feel for the next eight to twelve hours? Just lie there and breathe. Do your best to honor this sacred time. You've just woken up. This could still turn out to be a fantastic day! Focus on this private time and space (your bedroom, your closet, your sanctuary) with the reverence they, and you, deserve.

Doing this type of daily self-check-in has changed my life and helped me dress so much better. I set my alarm five minutes early just to lie in bed and ask myself, *How do I feel right now?* I even keep a picture of myself on my wall as a reminder to connect with myself first, before I think about plans or pleasing other people. For real! And I get it—even a minor act of mindfulness may feel ridiculous at first. But it really can pave the path to calm.

Say you woke up feeling groggy, a bit out of it, heart racing over the stressful day ahead, not your best self. This is important information. Sit with it. Acknowledge it. Now might not be the best time to squeeze into a skintight leather pencil skirt and trendy but itchy fuzzy sweater. Instead, maybe you reach for stretchy, forgiving leggings, a soft cashmere sweater, your favorite boyfriend jeans, or a monochromatic joggers-and-t-shirt combo you can dress up with chic loafers, a quilted handbag, and a camel coat.

Taking your emotional temperature *before you get dressed* means you are feeling your feelings instead of pushing them down or denying them. Your anxiety will diminish if you first accept it and then take positive, meaningful action. Try this every day for a week, and see if you feel more comfortable during your days.

In this moment of mindfulness, one of two things may happen:

- You may decide to stay within your comfort zone. You may feel less interested in pushing your sartorial boundaries once you realize doing so won't serve you. This is another example of **Mood Illustration Dress:** when you thoughtfully assess your emotional state and then dress to respect or match it. The goal here is not to transform or challenge yourself with clothes but to embrace, accept, and honor yourself exactly where you are.

- Creative inspiration may strike, as it so often does once we quiet our minds. (It's why we get our best ideas in the shower!) Pairing patent-leather going-out pants with a black sweater, trench coat, and leopard slip-on loafers? For work?! Go on with your bad self. This is an example of **Mood Enhancement Dress:** when you use clothing to lift up your emotions, putting yourself into a different, more optimal, or heightened state of mind.

BACK IT UP: THE HISTORY BEHIND FASHION PSYCHOLOGY

One of my idols, supermodel Veronica Webb, wrote on *The Root* that Fashion Psychology is "an idea whose time has come."[9] Well, Veronica, it was a long time coming! My fashion philosophies are built on the foundation of psychology's founding fathers, namely, Sigmund Freud and William

James. As Freud expert and Wesleyan University president Michael Roth remarked in an interview with *Gizmodo:* "Freud says human beings can keep no secrets. They reveal their innermost selves with their clothes, with their twitches, with their unconscious mannerisms; that whatever we do, we're expressing things about ourselves, for people who have eyes to see and ears to hear."[10] Preach, Sigmund!

William James was a Harvard psychologist who lived in the nineteenth century, but he was as fashion focused as an Instagram influencer. Dude was obsessed with clothes. In other words, he was highly attuned to their impact on behavior. James believed that our physical experiences or acts cause emotions, as opposed to believing that we feel an emotion (like sadness) to which we then react physically (we cry tears).[11] Of course those physical actions include putting on clothes. When James was traveling abroad in Berlin in 1867, writing letters home to his wife, he described the people he was hanging out with by first detailing their outfits. "James relies on the importance of dress to the social self" before offering more details about an acquaintance's character, job, or likability, writes Cecelia A. Watson (then a PhD candidate at the University of Chicago) in her analysis of these letters. "The clothes enter first, and gradually, over the course of his description, James fills them in with pieces of the personality they express."[12] Woomp, there it is. *The clothes enter first.* Say it with me: The. Clothes. Enter. First. They did then and they do now. Your clothes not only cause you to think, feel, and behave a certain way; they also walk into the room and tell people who you are before you ever even open your mouth.

James believed that by choosing the clothes you put on every day, you are choosing what information to convey about yourself to others. But here's another thing he noticed: Clothes, he said, are like an extension of your body. Not only do they tell other people who you are, but they also tell YOU who you are and dictate how you feel. The sensation of clothes on your skin sends you a message about how to think and act, kind of like how your brain sends a message to your muscles to move. Anyone who has ever tried on prom, wedding, or (Lord help us all) bridesmaids' dresses understands this. Imagine how you'd react—how your posture, mood, comfort level, and attitude would change—if you tried on a long-sleeve sequined floor-length evening gown...Now imagine a slinky, revealing slip dress...Now an off-the-shoulder body-con bandage minidress... Now a linen Jackie O–style button-down shirtdress. As you envision yourself spending an evening in the various dresses, how do the fabrics and silhouettes shape your fantasies?

History shows us that clothes have captivated the world's leading intellectuals for centuries. *The Language of Fashion* is a collection of essays by French cultural critic Roland Barthes, who in the 1960s wrote extensively on topics like hippie style and the power of jewelry. Its publisher calls it "an essential read for anyone seeking to understand the cultural power of fashion."[13] In their book *The Social Psychology of Dress*, scholars Kim K. P. Johnson and Sharon J. Lennon look at the way clothes influence relationships: "We can use dress to identify others in terms of their social position, as well as other possible identities and group memberships they may indicate using their dress, and shape our interaction with them accordingly."[14] Your Christian Louboutin heels with their unmissable red soles tell me you're wealthy, status-conscious, and proud of it. His muscle-baring tank top and track pants mean he's into fitness and possibly narcissistic. Her neat cashmere twinset and string of pearls tells me she's prim, proper, and perhaps a little bit of a control freak. Look, all of these assumptions are subjective, hypothetical, and very possibly erroneous! Two people looking at the imaginary strangers I've just described may have totally different reactions and perceptions of their personality characteristics. We are all influenced by our own histories and biases, which we then project onto others. But there's no doubt about this: Even as we pass each other on the street in silence, our clothes just had a conversation.

FASHION PSYCHOLOGY AND POLITICS: COSTUMES
FOR THE WORLD STAGE

There is almost no place in the world where clothes speak louder than in Washington, DC. If, as some critics might argue, clothes are insignificant, if they truly are meaningless, superficial, and silly, why are they such a hot-button issue for the most powerful people in the world? Why do we focus so much in particular on what female politicians wear? Let's look at some examples. In an effort to discredit a claim New York congresswoman Alexandria Ocasio-Cortez made about her financial circumstances, a male journalist tweeted (in response to a photo taken of her from behind, without her knowledge or consent) that her jacket and coat "don't look like a girl who struggles."[15] When Massachusetts Democrat Ayanna Pressley was elected to Congress, she asked in her victory speech, "Can a congresswoman wear her hair in braids, rock a black leather jacket and bold red lip?"[16] Though not an elected official, Melania Trump has been slammed for wearing a Zara jacket with the words "I Really Don't Care Do U?" across the back to visit children separated from their parents at the US-Mexico border, and Manolo Blahnik stilettos to visit Texas after Hurricane Harvey. *Newsweek* wondered why so many women in President Trump's orbit frequently wear stilettos. "High heels thrust out the buttocks and arch the back into a natural mammalian courting—actually, copulatory—pose called 'lordosis,'" pointed out anthropologist Helen Fisher. "It is a naturally sexy posture that men immediately see as sexual readiness. [Heels] are a 'come-hither' signal."[17] Clothes make the man. It seems that in politics, so do those of the women in his entourage.

Bloggers and late-night talk show hosts once again shook their heads when Mrs. Trump wore a pith helmet—a porous white hat historically associated with European colonialists—while on safari in Kenya. It was a sartorial choice CNN called "appallingly offensive to many Africans." One academic likened her headwear choice to "showing up on an Alabama cotton farm in a confederate uniform."[18] I am not here to pile on. I have never met Mrs. Trump and can only guess at her intentions. My job is to point out that in the absence of other information, our clothing choices will speak for themselves. Look, Mrs. Trump doesn't give many interviews. She doesn't show much emotion on her face, as is her right. And she is in a singular position where everyone is dying to know what she's thinking. Against the backdrop of her silence, her clothes practically shout.

One could make the case that Mrs. Trump's clothes are unfairly critiqued and deliberately misinterpreted. Ironically, this frustration is shared by her husband's former rival Hillary Clinton. In 2010, then Secretary of State Clinton was asked by a journalist to name some of her favorite fashion designers. Her response? "Would you ever ask a man that question?"[19] As Mrs. Trump herself told the press in Africa, "I wish people would focus on what I do, not what I wear."[20] Oooh, but that's just it! What you choose to wear IS a thing that you do. Regardless of politics or party, clothes are the one area where it's impossible for people in the political sphere—and particularly for women—to mute themselves. Secretary Clinton once famously tried to draw attention away from her looks by wearing nondescript clothes, making pantsuits iconic in the process. See, even "boring" clothes still make a certain kind of statement. Writes *New York Times* fashion columnist Vanessa Friedman of Mrs. Trump: "The clothes are a symbol of the actions and the actor. Is it superficial? No more than paying attention to any kind of symbolism is...All clothes are costumes we assume to play ourselves."[21] This observation applies to us all. Style is the platform for the stories you share with other people about who you are (just like Instagram!).

So what's the takeaway for you?

1. Your clothes are talking. Whether you're aware of it or not, whether you wish it were so or not, they are the costumes *you choose* to act out the story of your life.

2. They are sending messages to others that may or *may not* accurately convey what you want to say.

3. Other people will react to your clothes. Of course you can wear whatever the hell you like and deserve safety and respect no matter what. But on a practical level, think carefully about what you want from other people when picking out your outfit. How do you want them to respond to you? Do you want them to see you as authoritative or as open and approachable? Serious or fun? Do you want to show them who you are and where you're from, or do you prefer to remain more anonymous? Do you want to make a splash and get attention? Or do you feel like being left alone, going unnoticed? These desires can change day to day. Assess your mood and ask yourself these questions when you approach your closet.

HOW CLOTHES IMPACT YOUR EMOTIONS

Dressing well is both an art and a science. Maybe you just read that sentence and thought, *Hold up: Is the* science *of getting dressed really a thing?* Some would say no. But Fashion Psychology *is* grounded in legitimate scientific research. And I'm not the only expert who relies on it. Brand consultants, renowned anthropologists, and marketing executives regularly employ scientific methods and strategies to try to figure out what drives us to buy clothes. From primal mating signals to political theater, our clothes speak for us. And at the heart of our relationship to clothes is human emotion.

As we've established, what you wear impacts your mood, performance, and behavior. Let's get into some research that proves it. In 2012, Northwestern University psychologists Hajo Adams and Adam D. Galinsky published a groundbreaking study called "Enclothed Cognition." In it they concluded that "clothes systematically influence wearers' psychological processes." Through a series of tests and experiments, they found that a white lab coat is "generally associated with attentiveness and carefulness." When study participants were wearing a lab coat, they exhibited better attention and focus. This occurred, however, only when the subjects were told it was a *doctor's* lab coat. When a different group was told it was a painter's coat, it had no effect on their attention and focus. As Galinsky explained, "The wearer takes on the symbolic value of the clothes they wear."[22] I know someone who lives this truth every day. Let's meet him.

CASE STUDY: JUDGING A BOOK BY ITS COVER

I have a friend who is a high-powered judge. As an African American man in his position, he has an interesting perspective on the criminal justice system. Every day he sees those who share his race (but not his educational background or social status) meet fates dramatically different from his own. This experience influences both his emotions and his clothing choices. He tells me that when he wears his robes in the courtroom, he commands respect and carries himself accordingly. He feels strong, secure, capable. But, he confesses, when he takes off his robes to go home, his authoritative air evaporates and he feels uncomfortably vulnerable.

He thinks a lot about what to wear during his commute on the subway and in public spaces in general. He deliberately wears a suit and tie every day, even on weekends, even in his own neighborhood. Because of his job, he is hyper-aware that as a black man walking around New York City, were he to wear a hoodie or sweatpants, he could easily be mistaken for a homeless man or a thug and find himself on the other side of the bench.

What's the universal lesson here? First of all, we must acknowledge that minorities face a second set of considerations related to their appearance while moving through public spaces. Wearing crisp, conservative attire and European hairstyles can have a very real effect on our safety, the tenor of our social interactions, and the levels of professional success we achieve. It is my role as an educator to raise awareness about this—and to question it. And I'll get way deeper into these topics in chapter 10. But in general, I want everyone to know it's worthwhile to put serious thought into how you present yourself. Like a superhero's suit, your clothes have the ability to empower you and help you command respect. Use them.

MIND THE GAP: DRESSING OUR FANTASY SELVES

When I work privately with clients, one of my missions is to "bridge the gap between perception and reality." What I mean by "the gap" is the disconnect between who *we* feel we are and who others see. We've all heard a version of this from our loved ones. Hell, you've probably said it yourself: *Wear whatever you want! You do you. As long as you're happy, it doesn't matter what other people think.* If only things were that simple. Sometimes being misunderstood by others due to your appearance can lead to your unhappiness.

CASE STUDY: PREPARE FOR THE PERCEPTION

I once worked with a journalist named Kristen who dyed her hair purple. She viewed her look as avant-garde and fashion forward, not Manic-Panic-throwback. Yet she found that her hair color caused some people to make incorrect assumptions about her. It wasn't quite clear to her why there was such a disparity between the way she saw herself and the way others seemed to see her. In an article about our work together, she wrote: "I style and wear [my hair] in a way that I believe is more high fashion than Hot Topic, but as soon as I leave New York City for any sort of vacation or travel, the looks I get (not to mention the comments from guys) instantly indicate that others think I'm goth, a freak, or

in the case of a recent visit to Paris: a prostitute. At the same time,
I think it's a lot of fun to play with different fashion personas — and
even empowering to wear something one may be afraid to try."[23]

*Kristen was experiencing what I call **Fashion Incongruence**, in*
which her intentions didn't match other people's perceptions. She
knew full well that purple hair might draw some attention, and she
welcomed it. But she was not expecting, nor did she deserve,
derogatory comments. She was surprised to be so misunderstood.

Style Rx

I explained to Kristen that some people won't accept her hair
color — and that's okay. My only advice was that she think ahead
about how she might want to handle unwanted comments.

- - - - - - - - -

Kristen decided to keep her purple hair, a choice I supported. Remember:
no makeovers. But I did ask her to weigh adhering to beauty norms versus
adhering to her own aesthetic. Everybody can benefit from doing this. If
you want to push the envelope with your look, then find yourself in a
scenario where doing so might incite questions, comments, and, worst-case
scenario, insults, think about what's motivating your choice and whether
the consequences are worth it. If you find yourself in a situation like Kristen's, you might role-play some possible interactions and come up with
some prepared responses so you feel less anxious when faced with other
people's remarks. I love to wear dark-blue, deep-purple, and even black
lipstick. It makes me feel like Grace Jones. The looks I get from strangers
on the subway bother me less than bold lip colors please me. If an uncon-
ventional look makes you happy, then there are positive ways to respond
in the face of scrutiny. For example, if someone asks a belittling question
about your appearance, you might politely turn the tables with "Why do
you ask?" If someone says something borderline offensive ("Nice purple
hair. Are you in a band?"), take a pause and think before you reply. Often

using humor or finding common ground defuses tension. You might say, "I'm not in a band, but I *did* fake-play the clarinet for three years in middle school orchestra. How about you?"

It's great to honor your vision, just as long as you are mindful of—and prepared for—the perception. Like it or not, how others perceive us matters, especially at work. To quote former *Seventeen* magazine editor in chief Ann Shoket: "As much as we want to think our clothes or our shoes shouldn't matter as much as what we have to say, the truth is your look can amplify—or undermine—your best ideas...If you want to be seen as smart, or authoritative or creative...your clothes should say those things about you before you even open your mouth."[24] Once again: The clothes enter first. That's just reality.

But here's an interesting twist: Sometimes the disconnect between perception and reality has less to do with other people and more to do with *you*. Many of us shop for the people we *wish* we were, and neglect, deny, or hate on the people we actually are. This is a recipe for low self-esteem, incongruence, and style ruts. I've met with many clients who shop endlessly for a fantasy version of themselves while their actual selves wear the same rotation of tired, uninspired looks (more on Repetitious Wardrobe Complex in chapter 4). Buying clothes for your fantasy self almost always leads to that dreaded "I have nothing to wear" feeling. You may have a ton of clothes, but they are for "her": the person you long to be, the person you used to be, the lady who once wore that fuchsia sheath to her niece's wedding. Her clothes are not for you. Maybe "she" is ten pounds lighter. Maybe "she" is you during your semester abroad in college. Maybe "she" goes to lots of fancy parties and wears glittering sequined camisoles, while you go to your kids' soccer games and crash into bed every night by 9:30. Either way, how can you expect to find anything decent to wear in *her* closet?

If the fantasy self you shop for is an idealized younger version of yourself, you may be buying (and buying...and buying) clothes you associate with being in your prime, regardless of whether those clothes still suit you. Those looks may be outdated or no longer age appropriate. Worst of all, you already own duplicates! Writer Helena Fitzgerald captures this predicament beautifully in her essay "All the Lipsticks I've Bought for Women I'll Never Be": "My lipstick purchases are governed by a part of my brain that cannot accept the difference between who I actually am, and who I imagine myself to be. I buy lipsticks for imaginary selves."[25] *What Not to Wear* star Stacy London has also written about fashion as fantasy fodder. In a viral essay for Refinery 29, she described descending into near financial ruin as a result of compulsive online shopping, kicked off by a series of personal crises (spinal surgery, a breakup, depression). She described the hours she spent shopping online as "magical thinking." During these retail binges, she would envision the fabulous parties she'd attend and the fabulous people she'd meet there—just as soon as she had the perfect bag, jewelry, or shoes to wear to them: "I realize now it was just a fantasy future, to distract me from an agonizing present."[26]

In these examples, women use fashion to tell themselves a story. Clothes and makeup are intertwined with who they used to be, who they wish they could be, with the way they imagine their lives might yet unfold. Their style is tied up in their past, their future, their dreams. Their actual present realities though? Not so much. You may choose to dress in a way that is body-con or loose and flowy, statement-making or quietly minimalist. But whatever you wear, *you must dress for the life you are actually living.* Only then can you improve it.

Remember: Incongruence and inauthenticity are the enemies of confidence. The key to looking and feeling better is to seek alignment between who you are, how you feel, and who the world sees. It won't be easy at first. You may still feel clueless and lost. Do not get down on yourself. Almost everybody struggles with this! In fact, over coffee the other day, a friend asked me: What's the most common problem people come to you with? My answer: They always feel like they don't fit in or can't quite get it right when it comes to clothes, no matter how much they shop. They worry they're either too boring or too weird. If they're older, they fear their look is stale and irrelevant, that they are invisible. If they're younger, they worry that they look ridiculous and everyone is staring (and laughing) at them. They want me to come over and go through their closets and say, *All right, yes, no, yes, no.* But here's what I tell them: I don't have any authority to tell you yes or no because I don't know psychologically what those clothes mean to you. Who am I to tell you what's psychologically salient to you when I haven't lived your experience?

That's when I start asking questions, like: Well, tell me how you feel about this item? You've held on to this thing since 1995. What does it mean to you? Why can't you get rid of it? Why is it still here? Do you like the color? Do you like the texture? The fit? Even though it's no longer trendy, it's clearly still relevant to you. That's when the clothes start to tell the story. Maybe you won't part with your blush-pink prom dress because you love the color, the Empire waist, or the soft silk fabric. That's information you can use now! Maybe you're struggling to get rid of your work shirts even though you're now officially a full-time stay-at-home mom. Perhaps you're not ready to give up that part of your identity. Why not try pairing those work shirts with jeans for a grocery run or a PTA meeting? See how you feel.

Then my friend asked me something else: What's the best piece of advice you give clients? That's simple, but it isn't always easy to execute: Find your favorite color, pattern, fabric, shape, whatever it is that speaks to you, and wear it. Whatever you love, WEAR IT. Regardless of the weather, the occasion, what's in style — wear whatever makes you feel good. For me, it's leopard prints. Even if it's just a scarf or a skinny belt, I always feel better when I incorporate animal prints into my look. For one of my clients, it's Breton stripes. For another client, it's anything sparkly or glittery. For you it could be a leather motorcycle jacket, floral prints, or anything ocean blue. It seems obvious but it's worth saying out loud: Your clothes can enhance your life only if you put them on.

THE BOTTOM LINE

KEY TIPS AND TAKEAWAYS FROM CHAPTER 1

- **Your clothes are talking.** Style and appearance influence human behavior. Your clothes are sending messages both to you and to other people. It is essential to recognize your clothing choices as deliberate, to have a mission in mind when you get dressed, and to like what your clothes are saying.

- **No more getting dressed on autopilot!** Have a mindful morning. Your emotions are your cues for what to wear. Label your feelings with words, then look for clothes to meet your needs, whether that means honoring or lifting your mood.

- **Dress for your real life.** Wear clothes that suit who you are now — not who you used to be, or who you fantasize about becoming.

- **Wear your favorite things.** Don't save your best clothes for a rainy day or a special occasion or because you're afraid to ruin them. Carpe diem. Seize the day. Wear what you love!

Chapter 2

WHAT'S YOUR STYLE STORY?

Fashion you can buy, but style you possess. The key to style is learning who you are, which takes years. There's no how-to road map to style. It's about self-expression and, above all, attitude.

—*Iris Apfel*

When did clothes first start to matter to you? If I had to pinpoint a moment when I "woke up" to fashion, it would be my freshman year of high school, in the walk-in closet of a cousin around my age. My cousin and her mom were very into labels. She wore brands like Tommy Hilfiger, Guess?, the Gap, even Valentino head to toe. I remember thinking she was so privileged. My mom, by contrast, would take me vintage shopping at Goodwill or thrift shops. She was all about finding unique things, as opposed to the most expensive brand, which dovetailed nicely with my dad's insistence that labels were a rip-off anyway. I can still hear him railing against Polo shirts in his Jamaican accent: "You're buying these t-shirts with the horse on them when you could buy the same one at Value City and it costs much less!" Every season, my cousin would bring over several huge Hefty bags full of hand-me-downs for me. If it was winter, I would get her old fall stuff. If it was summer, I'd get spring.

One day I wore a Tommy Hilfiger purse she had given me to school. As I walked in late to algebra class, I passed by the desk of my bully (let's call her Sabrina*). I heard Sabrina and her sidekick (we'll call him Dave*) whispering: "Oh, that must be a fake Tommy bag." Sabrina persuaded Dave to come over and examine my bag, to check the logo for authenticity. I was humiliated. But then something interesting happened. I was still relatively new to the school and had initially been pegged as an awkward loner. But by tenth grade, thanks to my cousin's generosity, I began to become known as the girl with the labels. I was devastated when Sabrina and Dave examined my purse, in large part because I knew it wasn't truly mine. In order for me to feel cool or accepted, I thought I needed these labels. And yet I felt like a fraud because they had been passed down to me. It was my first lesson in **Fashion Incongruence.**

As my stress around this issue built, I found myself back in my cousin's bedroom, where, one afternoon, she casually said, "Oh, here, you can have this," and tossed some article of clothing at me. I don't think she intended to shame me, but in that moment I felt subservient to her. I went home and told my mom, "I am never taking her clothes again." I can't control the students at school, I decided, but I *can* control this situation.

Looking back, I realize that was the moment when I began to consciously incorporate my parents' philosophies into my own point of view. I concluded labels don't count, but your own sense of style does. It's not about how much clothes cost; it's about how you uniquely wear them. And yet, to this day, even in my most casual sweats, I'll always make sure I'm carrying a nice handbag. It *has* to be a nice bag. No matter what. I can trace that need, that insecurity, directly back to Sabrina and Dave in algebra class.

When I refused to take my cousin's hand-me-downs, I drew a line in the sand, and it made me stronger. I was beginning to assert my style identity. I deemphasized external value markers in favor of my own creativity. I put more stock into how I styled my clothes than into which fashion house made them. I used to cut up old Hanes t-shirts, fold the shredded seam inside to create an off-the-shoulder neckline, and secure it with safety pins, transforming a Walmart staple into a punk rock statement.

And then, to my surprise, lots of other girls in my grade started wearing off-the-shoulder shirts. I began to see myself as a trendsetter. I realized my power lay not in how I conformed but in how I individuated. If I feel good about myself, I discovered, people will be attracted to my confidence. This became a point of pride. As time went on, I tapped into my rebellious nature more and more, shaking up style norms, and never looked back. Unless of course I'm in therapy, in which case I rake over the past with a fine-tooth comb (LOL).

WHAT TYPE OF DRESSER ARE YOU?

Okay, your turn. Now it's time for you to look at your past and ask yourself, *Why do I wear what I wear?* I'm here to help you make sense of your own style history and label your behaviors. Once you understand what you're doing when you get dressed and how you formed those habits, it will be easier to change them, should you choose to. Are you an emotional dresser, a Fashion Identification Assimilator, a Situational Code Switcher, someone with a Repetitious Wardrobe Complex or Fashion Incongruence? Maybe you have traits from a few different categories. I will help you zoom in on the *why* behind what you wear, which is typically rooted in emotion. Then we'll spend the rest of the book getting into exactly what you can do about it.

You see, after years of working with all kinds of clients, I've begun to notice certain patterns or recurring modes of behavior. When people get stuck in style ruts, their stories tend to follow a formula. Each of these Fashion Psychology behaviors can be recognized and diagnosed. I am not in the business of prescribing blanket "cures." My advice to every individual is customized. But I can facilitate bringing your issues to consciousness by drawing what's buried to the surface. If your style behavior is impeding your emotional well-being, I have solutions to explore.

First, let's get you familiar with some terminology you'll notice me using throughout the book. In psychiatry (the medical treatment of mental illness), there is something called the *Diagnostic and Statistical Manual of Mental Disorders,* or the *DSM* (now in its fifth iteration). As defined by the American Psychiatric Association, the *DSM-V* is "the authoritative guide to the diagnosis of mental disorders."

Here, in a similar vein, I have outlined a Fashion Psychology Glossary of terms. To be clear, I am not equating style behaviors with mental disorders. I merely think it would be helpful for everyone to have universal definitions, so we can all help ourselves.

FASHION PSYCHOLOGY GLOSSARY

Decision Fatigue Also known as the paradox of choice, this occurs when you are faced with too many options for what to wear or buy. It often results in feeling overwhelmed and paralyzed, and in making decisions you later regret (buyer's remorse, discomfort with your outfit).

Fashion Identification Assimilation When you use style to fit in with or blend into a cultural or social group.

Fashion Incongruence When your ideal dress and perceived dress are incompatible.

Fashion Situational Code Switching When you alternate between different styles, depending on your cultural and social situations. You may dress a certain way with one group or in one context, and a different way with/in another.

Focal Accessory An item that holds psychological value and may be worn repeatedly.

Mood Enhancement Dress Dressing to modify your mood for the better. Doing so optimizes or elevates your current emotional state.

Mood Illustration Dress Dressing in a way that expresses and perpetuates your current emotional state.

Repetitious Wardrobe Complex Wearing the same clothes — or versions of the same clothes — over and over again.

HELP ME HELP YOU

When it comes to style, the possibilities are endless (and, yes, that in itself can feel paralyzing). The only one-size-fits-all thing about clothes is that we've all got issues. Everyone — *everyone* — is grappling with some sort of fashion pathology. No one is immune. That awful feeling of having a closet full of clothes but nothing to wear? The outfit regret that hits you midway through your morning commute? Simply feeling uncomfortable in your own skin as you go about your business, counting the hours till you can go home to your pajamas and Netflix? These feelings do not discriminate. And you are not alone. In fact, these style hang-ups are so common as to be ubiquitous. Like wallpaper. Or the traffic noise I hear outside my window. They're so universal that we all just accept them as something we have to live with. We don't!

I believe Fashion Psychology is having a moment because it helps us define or diagnose behaviors we're all performing every day but don't have names for. Don't get me wrong. Tons of airtime, blog posts, and glossy magazine features have already been devoted to teaching us "How to break out of your style rut once and for all!" But style ruts — aka Repetitious Wardrobe Complex — are rarely resolved with escapist infotainment. You'll have to dig a little deeper than that.

Here is a quiz designed to help you identify your Fashion Psychology behaviors, followed by my advice on how you might change up your look to change your life.

Let's get started.

Fashion Psychology Quiz

What's Your Style Story?

1) When you approach your closet to get dressed in the morning you feel...

   A) Like you need to go shopping immediately. How is it possible that you have so many clothes but absolutely nothing to wear?!

   B) Pumped to put together a cute outfit. You envision walking into an event or meeting, all eyes on you.

   C) Worried about how the people you'll be seeing will perceive you. Ugh, you're never going to get it right. Why bother trying?

   D) Rushed and annoyed, wishing you didn't have to bother with this BS. Obsessing over your looks is shallow, not to mention a total waste of time and money. So you just pull on the same jeans and sweater you always wear. Done and done.

2) The idea of going shopping for a new outfit makes you feel...

   A) Stressed AF. You'll probably love it in the store but hate it once you get home. Just like the last ten thousand times.

   B) Like it's Christmas morning. Joy. To. The. World.

   C) Bummed out. Like you'd rather do literally anything else, including your taxes.

   D) Frustrated. Why would anyone walk into an actual store when you can just shop online for stuff you already know you'll like?

3) You are going through your jewelry box and come across a necklace your grandmother gave you when you were younger. You...

   A) Lock it away in a secure location. In fact, maybe you should rent a safe-deposit box... If you lost it, you'd be heartbroken and never forgive yourself.

B) Build an outfit around it! It would look super-cute with that LBD you saw on Insta.

C) Put it back. It doesn't go with anything you have. No shade intended, Nana!

D) Decide to wear it 24/7, 365. It's like wearing a hug from your Grams all day long.

4) If I asked you *What's your signature style?* you would say . . .

A) I have no clue. Why do you think I'm reading this book?

B) On-trend, fashion forward, All the likes.

C) Next question.

D) Sensible. Jeans and t-shirts all the way, every day.

5) You just won $500 and you're encouraged to spend it on clothes. Where will you shop?

A) Net-a-Porter, Shopbop, Moda Operandi

B) Fashion Nova, Target, Century 21, H&M

C) Nowhere. It's going into my 401k.

D) Amazon, Ann Taylor, the Gap, Banana Republic

6) When you get feedback from friends, family, and colleagues on your look, it tends to make you feel . . .

A) Confused and a little embarrassed. Their comments are totally at odds with how you see yourself. What just happened?

B) Noticed. In fact, when no one comments on your look, you feel kind of deflated. You are dressing to impress, after all.

C) Like you have failed to please them yet again. Is nothing you do ever good enough for these people?

D) Neutral. You are dressing to not be naked. If they judge you for what you're wearing, it's their superficial problem. You keep it moving.

If you got mostly A's...

You may have fashion anxiety.

Somehow the vision you have for yourself never quite matches up with the way others perceive you, no matter how much money you spend on designer clothes. While you love fashion as a fan, you fear you're never getting it quite right IRL. If only you had the easy-breezy attitude of those cool girl models or street style stars on Instagram. They always seem to know exactly what to wear. Their risks pay off. Yours inevitably fail. You get all excited about an outfit you bought for a wedding or a party, but then once you arrive, you get hit on by the wrong people or get strange reactions from friends and relatives. (You were going for "pretty," they're calling you "hot tamale.") No wonder getting dressed is stressing you out! **Fashion Incongruence** is the name of your game. (And don't worry, we've all played it.)

Style Rx

You may benefit from simplifying your approach. Consider creating a Capsule Wardrobe—a collection of outfit elements that can be remixed and repeated. (Yes, there is an upside to **Repetitious Wardrobe Complex;** *see chapter 4.) Spend a week wearing only the items that make you feel 100! and notice what they all have in common. Are the shirts all soft to the touch? Are the pants all a certain cut? Do you love joggers but loathe jeans? Assess color: Do you feel most confident in chic neutrals, pretty pastels, or striking primary hues? Put the animal print and embellishments on ice and try spending a week in whatever makes you feel fail-safe. Sites like Cuyana and Everlane take the guesswork out of cool minimalism. See if starting with simple, soothing basics and toning things down gives your confidence a lift.*

If you got mostly B's . . .

You may be fashion fixated.

Chasing trends can be exhausting and financially draining. Doing so may be taking up too much of your precious time and energy. Worse yet, your shopping habit—online, in store—may be stealing your focus from other, more productive aspects of your life, like your work, health, or relationships. Are you slavishly hyper-trendy? Do the latest fast fashions seem to jump magically from Instagram straight into your closet, regardless of whether they're flattering or affordable? Real talk: How do you react when you read this sentence? *Insta likes > IRL compliments.* If you feel like looking good takes up an inordinate amount of space in your mind, bank statement, or calendar, think honestly about what emotions you may be trying to evoke or escape when you shop.

Maybe you feel you need lots of outfits because you are performing **Fashion Situational Code Switching** (corporate job, baller nightlife), but the key word is *performing*. You might benefit from balance and a firmer grip on your authentic identity. **Mood Illustration Dressing** can help. This is when you meditate (briefly) in the morning before approaching your closet. Ask yourself how you are feeling today, and how you want to feel after you are dressed. Then, rather than conjuring the image of someone you are not (a celebrity, a social media star), your goal is to dress like the best version of you. Was there an event or occasion recently when you felt awesome, like everything was just flowing? What were you wearing?

Style Rx

This week, try replacing some of the time you spend scrolling and shopping with mindfulness and healthy productivity. Instead of walking around the outlet mall, take a walk in the park. Nurture your relationships instead of filling up your feed. Meet up with a friend for a movie or coffee (not to go shopping). Turn off alerts from your Instagram influencers for a designated few hours each day. Volunteer to help someone less fortunate, whether at an animal shelter or a political action campaign. Visit a relative. When you feel the urge to shop online, touch the clothes you own, or reach out and touch someone. (Call your mom or your sister.) Virtually window-shop. I know plenty of women who fill up online shopping carts but rarely actually complete their purchases. Surprisingly, doing this can scratch the itch and satisfy your craving for novelty. Little by little, try to tip the scales away from retail therapy and toward self-care.

If you got mostly C's . . .

You may be fashion avoidant.

You may recognize yourself as someone with **Repetitious Wardrobe Complex** or **Fashion Incongruence** and likely feel intense **Decision Fatigue** when shopping. You might benefit from the soothing powers of a **Focal Accessory** and could feel significant uplift from **Mood Enhancement Dress**.

Style Rx

To select a Focal Accessory, start small and simple. Perhaps you have a family heirloom like a single bangle bracelet, a cocktail ring, a delicate necklace, or even the chain of a necklace without the pendant, from your mother or grandmother, sitting in your jewelry box. Try slipping it on and wearing it with your everyday clothes. If it makes you self-conscious, road test it on a weekend rather than wearing it to work. Notice if it makes you feel connected to your family. Imagine it has the power to envelop you in a cocoon of love and protection. Wear it in that spirit.

*If you wish to try some **Mood Enhancement Dress**, shoes are a low-risk, high-reward place to start. They offer a foolproof way to add a pop of color and a hit of fun to your look.*

Speaking of shoes, now is a great time to note that they alter not only your physical stance but also your emotional state. Naomi Braithwaite, a UK marketing and branding expert, writes, "Shoes, by the very intimate relationship they hold with the body, are . . . key to constructing identity and meaning for the wearer."[1] They also speak loudest to others. A study published in the *Journal of Research in Personality* called "Shoes as a Source of First Impressions" showed that participants accurately judged the age, gender, income, and political persuasion of shoe owners solely on the basis of pictures of their footwear.[2] Shoes = minimal effort, maximum impact. Carrie Bradshaw was right! Change your shoes, change your life.

Style Rx

You could shop for a new pair of statement sandals or simply wear shoes you already own in a new way (e.g., heels with your favorite sweats or joggers; tough boots with a feminine dress). I recently wore sandals with multicolored pom-pom toe straps. I paired them with a simple outfit (a denim shirtdress and solid black leggings), and they dramatically improved my mood and my look.

If you got mostly D's . . .

You may be a repeat offender.

You have committed to your uniform, but are you steady — or stuck? Do you avoid anything sexy like the plague? Are your clothes always baggy? Are you trying to deflect attention? Seeking to bury memories of body shaming or bullying? Some of us disconnect from our bodies or hide ourselves in clothes as a way to cope with trauma. (See Case Study: The Vanishing Girl on page 67.) Are you somebody who refuses to dress up or down, no matter the occasion? Some of us buy the same item over and over and over without realizing it. Maybe you've been wearing the same look for years — happily, you might insist! But let me ask you this: Is there any chance you adopted your signature style during the years you considered to be your prime? How do you feel about change? How would you say you have evolved in the past decade? Does your look reflect that evolution? Where do these inquiries lead you? Just questions. No judgments.

If you suffer from **Repetitious Wardrobe Complex,** then you might benefit from **Mood Enhancement Dressing.** This could mean injecting something new or barely worn into your wardrobe. Start by taking a tiny style risk (see page 145). If you aren't sure where to begin, I suggest icon identification. Hear me out: There's a reason why fashion designers, art directors, and stylists create mood boards to execute their visions for collections or campaigns.

Style Rx

Identify a famous person — the bigger the celebrity, the more photo options available — and screen-grab a shot of her every time she looks amazing. If you can't get enough of Kate Middleton in her timeless classics or Zoë Kravitz in her edgy downtown essentials, pop those shots up on your Pinterest board. Sites like RIXO, Mango, and Nasty Gal specialize in celeb copycat couture. Shopping with #goals and a guideline in mind will keep you on the right path and help you avoid **Decision Fatigue.** *You don't need to reinvent the wheel; it's great you are already comfortable with your foundational uniform. But I promise you can branch out just a little and still look refined, not ridiculous.*

PARENTS, PEERS, AND POP CULTURE: HOW OUR FASHION IDENTITIES FORM

I hope by now you have a better idea of your style behaviors. But along with the "dead dresses" in your closet (i.e., the items that haunt you because you never wear them), you've got to clean out the skeletons! To look forward to a better-dressed future, you need to understand — not be defined by—your past. Only once you confront any issues that are bothering you can you grow beyond them with grace.

How did your upbringing teach you style lessons that still impact your life today? Did you watch in awe as your mom got glammed up to go out at night? I wonder if you now associate intense emotion with looking "fancy"? Did you decide you're a real grown-up only if you wear a dress, jewelry, and full makeup? Can you still smell your mom's perfume? What was she wearing? Do you own anything like it?

Do you still have vivid memories of wanting to buy whatever it took to be accepted by the popular kids? Do you still shop with a certain squad in mind? Did you recently buy something because everybody else was wearing it? When we talk about your personal style, what we're really talking about is your identity. Even though your looks, needs, desires, and priorities evolve with age, you may still be hanging on to style biases, habits, and beliefs you picked up when you were much younger. These predilections can be good! For example, someone with a big, dynamic personality may have always loved flamboyant colors and campy prints to reflect her sassy, brassy sense of humor. Or someone nostalgic for her '90s glory days can nod to them with the skinny sunglasses or choker necklace trend. No harm done. But often, old habits die hard, and they can hold you back. Raise your hand if you still have jeans from high school in your closet. It may be time to let them go, along with the style myths you adopted when you first wore them.

Let's take a walk down memory lane, back to your childhood.

- What stories did loved ones tell you about your looks or style? Were you always a princess? Always a rough-and-tumble tree-climbing tomboy with skinned knees? How were you labeled growing up?
- How did clothes play a role in the way you separated from your parents as an independent individual? Did you have a rebellious fashion phase?

- How have you used clothes to cement (dressing to fit in) or disrupt (dressing to stand out) your relationships with others?
- Do you still wear any of these "important" types of clothes today?

As Kate Spade once said, "Playing dress-up begins at age five and never really ends."[3] When I meet with clients, I ask about how their relationship to fashion *began* to help me understand where it is now. When I inquire about a client's past, it's sort of like Fashion Psychology's spin on the classic analyst's question: "So, tell me about your mother..." (More on mothers in a minute.) How do we begin to use this particular form of communication—style—in our lives? When do we first start to "read" the messages other people's clothes send out? And when do we start to craft those messages ourselves? Who teaches us to "speak" with our appearance—to ourselves, to others? And once we've learned to do so, can we learn to speak differently?

Let's listen in on a session I had with a client (a black college student we'll call Lisa*) that powerfully demonstrates how our families influence our self-perception—and how we can rise above that influence. She came to me with the goal of building up her confidence. During our conversation, I helped her begin to see herself as remarkably resilient. It turned out she didn't want or need to change a thing about her style (so you won't see a **Style Rx** below). She just needed some light shined on her strength.

CASE STUDY: AVATAR

Dawnn: *You started to say something about your hair?*

Lisa: *When I was younger, chemically straightened hair was a big deal. Everyone got their hair straightened and my mom was one of those people. She was like,* You have great hair and it's really long, but it would look even better straight. *The thing is, I never liked heat in my hair because I'm tender-headed. My [scalp] is just really sensitive. So I would always cry when*

I got treatments. My sister always had better hair than me because hers was straight. My hair was so thick and curly that even when I got it professionally done, it would frizz up two hours later. I had so many insecurities about this as a child. I remember being so upset on picture day. I'd be like, Why can't my hair be like my sister's? So when I finally got control of my hair as a teenager and stopped getting it straightened, I was so happy. Things were bumpy at first, because I didn't know how to deal with my hair. But then once I figured it out, it got fun.

Dawnn: *And now natural hair is in! Has the natural hair movement helped you accept yourself more?*

Lisa: *Right! Yeah, when natural hair started to become more accepted, I just smacked tradition to its side. My mom is really traditional. She's the authoritarian parent, so anything she says goes. She's just strict like that. She doesn't want me to date outside my race. But I'm a free spirit. I'm like, Eh, I kind of don't care what you think. We clash because of that. It's funny how it all comes back to hair. Ever since the natural hair movement caught on, I kind of stopped caring about beauty norms in general. I'm like, One day, someone's going to think I'm cool regardless of whether we are different races. So I just push away all those old-school beliefs. You've just got to find out what you like about yourself.*

Dawnn: *And have you always known what you like about yourself?*

Lisa: *No. When I was younger, I was bullied because I have a birthmark. I would be called "Avatar" [a reference to the blue aliens in the James Cameron movie]. My mom and my other family members would joke around and call me names too. They'd be like, We're just preparing you for the future so you heard it already. If you hear it from us, it's not going to hurt* as much when other people say it. *And I was like, Okay, well, that's kind of true. But still, I'm sensitive. So when I would get name-called or made fun of for my skin discoloration, I'd be like, Okay, that's interesting. Besides having straighter hair, my sister also has a more curvy figure. People close to me would also joke around about that. They'd be like, Why does she have more boobs than you? And I'd joke back and be like, Because she stole my boobs. I just kind of got over all that with time. I got some distance from it.*

Dawnn: *So you used humor to stay positive, as a coping mechanism, as self-defense?*

Lisa: *Yeah.*

Dawnn: *It's interesting because in these situations, your family members are the ones evaluating you. They are absorbing our culture's beauty norms about straight hair, about curvy bodies, about "perfect" skin, and then teaching them to you, enforcing those standards. This isn't coming from magazines or movies. The criticism is coming from those closest to you.*

Lisa: *Yeah. We're all following the same trends. We're all just following that hype train.*

Did your heart ache when you read how Lisa's own mother made fun of her looks, under the guise of toughening her up? It reminds me of that horror movie line: "The call is coming from inside the house!" Did you relate? What's the takeaway for you? No matter what scars you bear from your past, it is within your power to accept and embrace the things about yourself that make you different and therefore special. Once you feel worthy inside, you'll feel deserving of looking your best on the outside. Lisa hits the nail on the head: "You've just got to find out what you like about yourself."

- - - - - - - - -

OKAY, NOW TELL ME ABOUT *YOUR* MOTHER

Not surprisingly, our very first fashion role models tend to be our moms. One of my earliest, happiest memories is my mother allowing me to cut up an old t-shirt to design clothes for my Barbie and Melanie's Mall dolls. (Once a fashionista, always a fashionista.) London College of Fashion psychologist and consumer behavior expert Kate Nightingale emphasizes the role our mothers play in shaping our style. As she told *Grazia,* our mothers are often with us—unconsciously—when we shop. We are more inclined to buy clothes in shapes, colors, and fabrics we were exposed to as children, because they will inspire positive feelings when we encounter them, even decades later. We will *think* we like something because it feels familiar, confusing memory with preference, nostalgia with good taste. "For example, if your [mother] was wearing a particular shape of jacket, you'll have a higher inclination towards it," explains Nightingale. "There's an element of attaching emotional security to old representations of the times when you felt comfortable and secure."[4]

Fascinatingly, this works both ways. As daughters grow up, the shoe is on the other foot, and they begin to strongly influence their mother's style. A study in the *Journal of Consumer Behavior* demonstrates how mothers become their teen daughters' "consumer doppelgangers." Researchers theorized that because middle-aged moms are spread so thin with family and work obligations, they don't have time to stay on top of what's hip in youth culture. So they copy their daughters' style as a sort of shortcut to coolness. (If you're fifty-five going on fifteen, this may be news you can use!) The study also illuminates the concept of "cognitive age"—i.e., the age we *feel* we are as opposed to the age we *actually* are. (Incongruence alert!) Researchers discovered that their subjects' cognitive ages tended to be ten years younger than their actual ages. The moms interviewed "sought to project a more youthful identity through their possessions."[5]

What does this mean for you?

1. It may be time to reexamine the myths and messages your family members conveyed to you about your style or appearance. Maybe with the best of intentions, someone important to you told you "ladies wear skirts" when you'd really prefer pants. Maybe someone mentioned you look great in red, and you hate it but keep buying it. Maybe it's time for you to break some rules.

2. As you grow older, it's worth noting these concepts of cognitive age and youth doppelganging. You don't need to dress ten years younger to be attractive. Doing so may even create feelings of disharmony and insecurity (more incongruence!). Just look at Michelle Obama, Iman, Lauren Hutton, Helen Mirren, Yoko Ono, and the slew of Instagram influencers over fifty (my fave? @iconaccidental): Nothing is more modern than dressing like a grown-up.

KEEPING IT OLD-SCHOOL? TIME TO HEAL YOUR TEENAGE STYLE SCARS

Roland Barthes called wearing clothes "a profoundly social act."[6] It follows, then, that what you wear has a profound effect on your social relationships. Any middle schooler can tell you that. In fact, middle school is usually when it all begins. It's when we reach a new level of self-consciousness, and it's usually when we are first free to express our self-identity through clothes (i.e., when Mom can't tell us what to wear anymore). It's also when we suffer our first fashion fails. And so clothes become a huge emotional deal. "Artsy" tweens wear t-shirts depicting their favorite bands, while their "sporty" peers wear Under Armour or Adidas. And they all sit together at cafeteria tables grouped by their style uniforms. "On Wednesdays we wear pink," declare "The Plastics" in *Mean Girls*. Using money I saved from waiting tables, I once disobeyed my father and bought a Coach bag to fit in with the label-conscious clique at my high school. We affirm or defy our relationships with what we choose to wear. As a result, style is an ever-present factor as we pick up emotional baggage.

Adolescence is a fraught time at the crossroads of style and identity. This explains why some of our adult beliefs about clothes can be traced back to adaptive behaviors we developed during our emotionally turbulent formative years. "Girls use clothes, accessories, and fashion to define themselves, make statements about their choice of peer group, and to establish their psychological identities," writes New York City psychologist Dr. Stephanie Newman in *Psychology Today*. She describes the processes of "mirroring" and "twinning." (No, it's not just an Internet buzzword!) That's when young people dress almost exactly like their peers in order to solidify both social relationships and their own fledgling identities. A girl's clothing choices, Newman writes, can be a fast track to the in crowd or a vehicle for "opting out of her school community entirely."[7]

Now you might suppose that in the digital age, social media stars have the most influence over a young person's style identity. After all, we're always reading about how much cash the Kar-Jenners pull in for a single promotional product post. But this is not the case. Kids' *peers* are actually the most influential of all. One consumer research firm asked teens what factors they consider when choosing styles and brands. They ranked the *opinions of friends* at 45.2 percent—significantly higher than social media (35.1 percent) and celebrity styles (27.5 percent).[8] When you're young, your friends (and frenemies) hold sway over your fashion preferences and developing identity—for better or for worse. But it doesn't have to be this way for the rest of your life.

What's the takeaway for you? Whether you are parenting an image-obsessed tween or you're an adult still working through your damage from high school, I want you to know there's a legitimate psychological reason for all the intense emotion. I am here to validate you. Those years—and those peers—actually matter a lot. They tend to leave their mark.

But here's the good news about fashion and identity. It is *healthy* to change and evolve. If you are still dressing at forty the way you did at twenty, I want to know why. Could you still be dressing like your teenage "twin"? Are you denying yourself a certain color, print, or shape you're drawn to because someone once made you feel like crap when you wore it—or even when you took a style risk, period? Do you still ask yourself *Will my squad think this is cool?* before you buy or wear something? It's time to figure out what *you* like to wear—not your mom, not your daughter, not your friends. After all, one of the best perks of being a fully realized adult is dressing for your own pleasure rather than for someone else's approval.

HIDING IN PLAIN SIGHT

Our clothes tell our stories—including the tragic parts. In my practice I've seen clothes used as an emotional Band-Aid, even an unconscious cry for help. According to a 2012 study conducted by psychologist Karen Pine of the University of Hertfordshire in Britain, 57 percent of women will put on a baggy top when depressed, compared with 2 percent who select one when they feel happy. (She surveyed one hundred women to gather these figures.) Conversely, her subjects would be ten times more likely to put on a favorite dress when happy (62 percent) than when depressed (6 percent).[9] So from this we can conclude that in general, drab, oversize, or unkempt clothes can be a tell. (Remember Jim in chapter 1?) If I notice a client is consistently looking disheveled or hiding herself in her clothes, I might use that visual information as a way in. Her clothing choices may be the first clue I follow to help her identify an emotional wall she's built to insulate herself from pain.

It makes sense that people use clothes for emotional protection: This turns out to be a very effective defense mechanism! Clinical psychologist Nadene van der Linden writes about what she calls "The Grey Rock Method." It's a strategy for dealing with toxic people by basically turning yourself into a gray rock—acting emotionally flat, disengaged, unstimulating in order to repel the undesired social contact. "The idea is that you keep your head down like a grey rock and blend into the landscape," she writes.[10] It's even been suggested that we may dress in dull, neutral clothing, without makeup, accessories, or other flourishes, in order to bore the aggressor into moving on to a more exciting target. But avoiding conflict is just one reason someone might dress to disappear.

Let's listen in on a counseling session I had with a different college student client we'll call Sonal.* I chose to include her case here because she exhibits many of the behaviors I just defined in the Fashion Psychology Glossary (so I highlighted those in bold). Notice how her family impacts her self-image and style choices. Maybe, like this client, you don't love your body. Maybe your self-esteem is also so low that you feel like you don't deserve to look good in your clothes. Maybe you got lots of C's and D's in the quiz you just took, and you recognize yourself as a fashion avoider or repeat offender. If you relate, read on to learn how clothes might make her—and you—happier.

CASE STUDY: THE VANISHING GIRL

Dawnn: *Tell me about your body image, and how that affects your shopping habits.*

Sonal: *To be honest, I only really shop once in a while. I'm insecure about how thin I am. So I try to buy pants that are kind of loose so no one will see how skinny my legs are. In the past few years, I've been to visit my mom's family in India three times, and everyone there said I look sick, like I have some kind of disease. They said American doctors don't know shit. So my mom's relatives actually got me tested in India to see if maybe I have a thyroid problem.*

Dawnn: *How did that make you feel?*

Sonal: *Bad. I told my mom and she was like,* I get you tested regularly here! You're fine. You just need to gain a little weight. *I can eat anything I want, I just have a small belly. More* *recently, I ended up going to see a US doctor, and she said, based on the blood tests she took, that everything is fine. She said I'm just a little bit underweight but that that's very common.*

Dawnn: *So you're not sick?*

Sonal: *No. But [in India] they said I look really sickly. My mom's sister made fun of me for being skinny. Her daughter is curvaceous. So my aunt would say, "Why is it that my daughter is the perfect size and you're so skinny?"*

Dawnn: *That kind of comparison coming from your own family. How does that make you feel?*

Sonal: *Well, I don't know. It did give me another perspective on how I look. And I became more insecure about my clothes. My aunt said I'm so skinny, it doesn't even look like I'm wearing any clothes. She was so proud that her daughter is va-va-va-voom.*

Dawnn: *So when you buy clothes, you buy them bigger than your size? Does that make you feel more comfortable?*

Sonal: *Yes, exactly. Usually I buy long-sleeve shirts to hide my arms. I'm so skinny I avoid skinny jeans and try to buy straight pants. I wear sweats.*

Dawnn: *To hide your body?*

Sonal: *Yeah.*

Dawnn: *Here in America, especially in the modeling industry, the beauty ideal is to be thin. And you're here now. So does that have an effect on you?*

Sonal: *Okay, well, here the beauty ideal is to be thin, but most guys still like a girl with a little junk. Everyone who's considered beautiful in India has some kind of boobs or booty.*

Dawnn: *But again, here in the New York fashion world, where thin is in, you would be considered very beautiful. Do you see how our standards of beauty can shift depending on our cultures and contexts, on who is deciding what's beautiful?*

Sonal: *Yeah. But you're a female, so of course you're going to say something positive to try to make me feel better. I mean, we all try to empower each other. I have never had a guy come up to me and say, "Oh, you're so skinny and beautiful."*

Dawnn: *So if I think you're beautiful, that doesn't hold much weight. But if a guy said it . . .*

Sonal: *It would validate it.*

Dawnn: *You said you wear sweats. Do you choose stylish sweats, or dress them up with heels? Or are you just like, I don't care.*

Sonal: *I just don't care. The only time I unleash it all is when I have to dress up, like for a wedding. But that's once in a blue moon.*

Dawnn: *So when you do dress up for a special occasion and "unleash it all," as you say, you're not wearing oversize clothes, you're wearing clothes that fit you. Do you feel beautiful then?*

Sonal: *I mean, I'm all dolled up wearing makeup, so I feel like my face makes up for it.*

Dawnn: *So your face and pretty clothes compensate for your body? And when you're dressed up, it doesn't feel like it's actually you?*

Sonal: *Exactly. With formal Indian clothes, even if the sleeves are long, they're made out of net, so it still showcases how thin my arms are, unfortunately. The good thing is, you're not really allowed to wear tight clothes there, so . . .*

Dawnn: *Do you have hope you will overcome this insecurity someday?*

Sonal: *My mom told me that she was skinny like me too when she was young. She has a little bit of junk now, because she gained weight after she gave birth to me and my brother.*

Dawnn: *So your body type is hereditary. You don't have a disease. There's nothing wrong with you.*

Sonal: *That's what I told my aunt and uncle, but they were like, "Nah. We remember our sister. She was never that thin!" Once I* have kids, I'm pretty sure it'll make me feel womanly. I'm pretty sure by then I'll have a guy who will love me for who I am instead of for my body. It is possible.

Dawnn: Let's go back to the oversize clothes. Would you be willing to wear ones that are cute and trendy?

Sonal: I mean, how would I even do that?

Dawnn: That's where I come in. I'm going to research some styles that are still the oversize look, but cute.

Sonal: Wow. Okay!

Dawnn: Then, the next time we meet, I'll show you some pictures of options. My thinking is, you can definitely still cover up your figure, but maybe put a bow on it. If you're going to wear these oversize clothes, we can jazz them up. That might help with your confidence.

Sonal: Oh my God, okay!

Dawnn: I think it's about being comfortable with yourself, and that includes being comfortable with your insecurities. You can deemphasize what makes you insecure and still look good doing it. Does that make sense? How does that make you feel?

Sonal: Thank you! So much better.

Okay, guys. Lots to unpack here. There are cross-cultural issues at play (**Fashion Identification Assimilation, Fashion Situational Code Switching**) that inform Sonal's self-perception. She is also clearly buying into some romantic rescue fantasies. But primarily and most urgently, she is wrestling with body image concerns. The goal is to help her find self-acceptance, to embrace who she is, insecurities and all. It is not my intention to rob her of her protective armor — her baggy clothes — as her sense of self is currently quite delicate.

Style Rx

Thanks to the athleisure explosion, there are tons of style options available to Sonal. She can try a trendy long-sleeve sweatshirt cut in a modern silhouette, to give the illusion of a crop top. She can push up the sleeves to just below the elbows to reveal only her wrists; showing skin strategically will offset the sense that her clothes are swallowing her up. Joggers or harem-style sweats will similarly offer coverage but still feel fresh. This type of outfit ticks all the boxes: It is modest, modern, and comforting. Another option could be a boilersuit that covers her entire body, limbs included, unbuttoned to just above her navel, with a crop top underneath. Once again, she'd be strategically showing just peeks of skin at the clavicle and rib cage. Overalls with a chunky sweater underneath would create a similar vibe but leave her completely covered. As she's petite, wearing ankle boots with built-in wedges could give her a lift, physically and emotionally.

*Above all, we've got to honor Sonal's feelings of wanting to cover herself. Remember: She thinks she's unattractive. Her family members have convinced her she looks ill. Sure, we could get a glam squad to transform her—she is sample size, after all—but oversexualizing her with body-con clothes would only add to her problems from both a psychological and cultural perspective, given her community's modest style conventions. We don't want to dishonor her culture or her feelings and put her in a situation that exposes her to more scrutiny or criticism. This would risk worsening her family relationships and further damaging her self-esteem. Once again, this is why the makeover trope doesn't work, because it rarely takes into consideration cultural norms and sensitivities. If I were to push her too far, too fast, into a new look, she would say, This is not me. It would only perpetuate the inauthenticity and **incongruence** she feels when she dresses up for* *weddings. Any dramatic new look would be antithetical to her current emotional state. We would be creating misalignment, exacerbating her feelings of gloom. Instead, my plan is to encourage her initially to **Mood Illustrate** with baggy basics. Then I'll introduce small doses of funkier fashions (clothes that offer coverage but in more stylish cuts, like the boilersuit or overalls) including **Focal Accessories** to ultimately **Mood Enhance.***

Here's what I've learned in my practice: You have to allow people to feel their feelings, even wallow in them. Some people get comfortable wallowing; at least then they know what to expect. Eventually they may get tired of wallowing. Given her age, Sonal may be on the cusp of self-discovery and self-definition. My role is not to drag her kicking and screaming out of the pit where she's wallowing, but — with a bit of style advice — to help her take one toe out, then another toe. And then, lo and behold, she's blossomed.

- - - - - - - - -

A NOTE ABOUT SELF-DISCLOSURE

As you read more Case Studies throughout this book, you may notice that I occasionally share something about myself with clients. If you are familiar with Freudian analysis, in which the mental health practitioner acts as a blank slate upon which the patient projects her feelings, you may have questions about my methods. What I'm practicing is called self-disclosure.

It is a therapeutic method wherein the counselor reveals a relevant piece of information about herself to the client, in an effort to aid or enhance the therapeutic process. Often substance abuse counselors disclose stories of their own sobriety, for example. As clinical psychologist Alexis Conason explains in *Psychology Today*, those who argue against self-disclosure posit that it takes much-needed attention away from the patient. But "others believe that therapist self-disclosure could help demystify the therapeutic alliance, model disclosure for the patient, normalize their experience, and challenge negative beliefs the patient might hold about their impact on others."[11] I am in the latter camp.

Some studies—including one conducted with eating disorder patients in the UK—have shown that relevant self-disclosure can benefit patients if it is perceived as helpful. Those researchers found that the therapist's self-disclosure was associated with a stronger therapeutic alliance, greater patient self-disclosure, and reduced shame.[12] I have seen similar results in my practice. We all want to feel less alone, less embarrassed, more understood and accepted.

It is important to clarify that I think very carefully about what to disclose about myself, and even then, I do so sparingly. I also do not disclose anything that is not directly related to the issues the client brings up. I methodically consider each personal revelation, disclosing only what I believe will be helpful to the client. In a paper titled "More Than a Mirror: The Ethics of Therapist Self-Disclosure" published in the journal *Psychotherapy: Theory, Research, Practice, Training*, Zoe D. Peterson, director of the Kinsey Institute Sexual Assault Research Initiative, writes, "The ethicality of a particular self-disclosure is likely to depend on the content of the disclosure, the therapist's rationale for the disclosure, the personality traits of the client ... and the specific circumstances surrounding the disclosure."[13] I always consider these factors before self-disclosing. I believe the mirror metaphor is an apt one: I am holding up a mirror to the client, echoing and validating her experience by revealing a fragment of my own.

I find this particularly helpful when humanizing issues around fashion. Let's just pause for a second and think about the word "fashion." You hear that word and what images come to mind? Runway models? *Vogue* covers? Larger-than-life billboards starring semi-cyborgs with bleached eyebrows, buzz cuts, and shockingly expensive purses? No one we know IRL actually looks remotely like that. The way we experience Fashion (with a capital F) as a culture is inherently exclusive and alienating. It offers a very limited range of emotion. Fashion is artificial, surreal—almost like a caricature of the average person's experience. Thinking back to my modeling days, I can see that the emotional range I was taught to express was completely detached from reality: a smile for elation, a grimace for seriousness, a pout for sensuality. And that's pretty much it! I was taught to negate my own emotions so that the clothes could evoke whatever emotions the designer sought to evoke.

Fashion is inaccessible. Roped off. It can make you feel desperately left out.

Through self-disclosure, I hope to reveal humanity behind the image. When I am able to create intimacy and trust, it helps my clients open up and rid themselves of shame.

THE BOTTOM LINE
KEY TIPS AND TAKEAWAYS FROM CHAPTER 2

- **Define yourself.** Everyone has style behaviors that can be labeled, demystified, and worked on. See the Fashion Psychology Glossary on page 50.
- **What lies beneath?** Your clothing choices are rooted in emotion. Style problems (ruts, risk aversion, shopping addiction, to name a few) are outward expressions of underlying emotions. Understanding your issues is the first step toward improving your look.
- **Look back and move on.** Style identity generally forms during childhood and adolescence. Your family of origin and adolescent peers likely had a lasting impact on how you think about clothes as an adult. Examine your long-held beliefs about what you're "supposed" to wear. Bust those myths!

Chapter 3

THE SCIENCE BEHIND SHOPPING

I like my money right where I can see it — hanging in my closet.

— Carrie Bradshaw

I have a confession to make: I hate shopping. Don't get me wrong — I love clothes. But when I do buy new stuff, it's primarily online. As a highly sensitive person, I get anxiety when I walk into a store, not only because of the sensory overload but also because of the overabundance of choice (see: Decision Fatigue). Contributing to my discomfort, personally, is the prevalence of retail micro-aggressions. As a black woman, I am always attuned to the potential for verbal, behavioral, or environmental indignities — such as being followed around a store by a suspicious salesperson or, to recall recent controversies, seeing clothing aimed at a plus-size audience shown off by straight-size models online.[1]

In the summer of 2019, singer SZA tweeted that an LA-area Sephora employee called security to make sure she wasn't shoplifting. She happened to be in the store trying to shop for beauty products from Rihanna's Fenty line — a line for which she has starred in an ad campaign. In response to outrage on social media, Sephora shut down all four hundred of its stores to implement hour-long "inclusion workshops."[2] But what would have happened if SZA had been just an average girl and not a celebrity with 6.3 million Instagram followers and an amplified voice? Whether intentional or not, these incidents communicate hostility to marginalized customers. As you might imagine, these are all occupational hazards for which I've had to develop some pretty effective coping strategies.

If I *do* set foot inside a brick-and-mortar store, it's because I have already thoroughly researched and targeted something I want, and I am going into that store specifically to see, touch, or try on that item. I have to walk in with a purpose or I don't walk in at all. Some people wander into stores like H&M or Zara to browse. To me, this would be like playing with matches near an open flame. "Just looking" is detrimental to my credit card and to my mental health. So if I go into a store, it's because I already know what I want. A salesperson may say *Can I help you?* to which I always reply, *The only thing you can help me with is finding this . . .* And then I hold up my phone to show her a picture of what I've already decided I want. I'm also careful to limit the amount of time I spend in the store. I go in, see what I came for, and I leave. If there's something else that catches my eye while I'm in there, I do not buy it because I didn't come in for it. I usually buy a few new things every season to keep my look current, but preplanning my shopping expeditions is key to minimizing my stress.

It also helps that I keep my standards high. A piece has to be pretty spectacular if it's going to draw me into a physical store. You know how you'll look at a dress on Instagram or a shopping site and then, all of a sudden, ads for that dress start popping up and following you across the Internet, even while you're doing unrelated surfing? This is extremely effective marketing capitalizing on something called **the familiarity principle,** and it's one of many tactics I'll detail in this chapter. But I'm bringing it up now because I want to tell you that *of course* these tricks get to me too! I'm only human. Here's how I get around them: I screen-grab and file away any new item that calls to me. I keep all those images in a digital photo album called "Potential Purchases." This mimics the feeling I get from actually purchasing something online; it *feels* as though I've already bought the item and I am just waiting for it to arrive at my door. I have scratched the itch to own something new and quieted my impulse to shop.

Here's another useful shopping strategy: Invest in your everyday staples, the clothes you wear most often, the things most people actually see you wearing—your jeans, sweaters, tops, t-shirts, accessories, and coats—as opposed to the special occasion outfits that entice us to splurge. The upside of spending more money on and paying more attention to your everyday wardrobe is that your basic essentials probably won't fuel your fashion fantasies the same way a glittering evening gown would, so you'll be better able to distinguish between wants and needs. An individual piece's price will become easier to evaluate. You can justify spending $60 on a sweater you'll wear once a week to work. But $60 on a pair of shoes you'll wear to the only wedding you're attending this year? Feels like more of a stretch. And since you'll actually wear that sweater more often, if you do buy a new one, it'll have a stronger positive impact on how you look and feel. Let's meet a client who needed an intervention in this exact area.

CASE STUDY: ONE AND DONE

*Barbara is a fifty-something journalist originally from Scotland. She is a naturally chic silver fox with some major **Fashion Incongruence** going on. When I met with Barbara at her home, her closet revealed itself to be a high-fashion graveyard. She owned vintage silver Gucci and fuchsia Kate Spade formalwear, along with some edgy leather looks she's held on to since her twenties.*

But as a work-from-home writer, Barbara had developed an everyday look that was much more utilitarian: gray, navy, and black slacks and loose, comfy, caftan-style tops. Her bright and bold items turned out to be single-use pieces she'd purchased for family weddings or industry events. She hung on to them for emotional reasons—because a fashionable friend once told her she looked lovely in pink, for example. As we talked, she revealed that one time when she was thirteen, her peers made fun of her party dress. (See Keeping It Old-School? Time to Heal Your Teenage Style Scars in chapter 2.)

Barbara had a closet full of barely worn but costly investment items just sitting there collecting dust. "I bought them because they were beautiful, but again, I never got around to wearing them more than once or twice because I never felt they were 'me,'" she wrote after our session. "They were impulsive buys, racier and more attention-grabbing than I have ever really been comfortable with. Why do I even have this stuff?"[3]

I helped Barbara draw the connection between her teenage Mean Girls moment and her adult insecurity about party dressing, helping her become conscious of a wound that had been hurting for four decades. As a result of this single incident, "I have never trusted my own instincts when it comes to style, and I don't like to stand out from the crowd," she wrote. "I bought Gucci, for example, because it was a sought-after designer in the nineties and I saw the outfits in Vogue. I probably thought a bit of that fashionable stardust would rub off on me, but I always felt faintly ridiculous in them."

Do you recognize yourself in Barbara's story? The lesson for her and for you is to honor your own style instincts. Look for things that please you as opposed to what you think will satisfy an audience. You may make mistakes, but at least they'll be your mistakes — and you'll learn from them.

Style Rx

Simply placing more importance on (and allocating more of her money toward) her weekday clothes as opposed to her special occasion one-offs could do wonders for Barbara's confidence. If, like Barbara, you're unsure about what to wear to social events (and who isn't?), consider adopting a **special occasion uniform.** You can't go

wrong with a black tuxedo-style pantsuit worn over a silky camisole,
a solid-color jumpsuit, or an LBD. Black pointy-toe pumps, a metallic
clutch, and an eye-catching cocktail ring are fail-safe finishing
touches. Make this your go-to outfit anytime a party pops up.

– – – – – – – – – –

ARE YOU AN EMOTIONAL SHOPPER?

I read this on Instagram the other day: "Do I want bangs or do I need to talk about my feelings?" It made me laugh out loud in recognition. Often, when we feel the urge to shop or change up our look, it's an indication that something is bothering us; that there's an issue we want to ignore or escape from, an anxiety we want to snuff out, or boredom we want to shake off. I can give you strategies for how to delay pulling the trigger on your next purchase. But until you address what's going on emotionally—what void you're trying to fill with shopping—you'll be white-knuckling your way around the mall or across the Internet.

When I do brand consultations, I am often asked how retailers can make personal connections with shoppers. Once you realize brands are paying experts to learn how to connect with you emotionally, once you understand the game and the tricks they're employing to seduce you (from filling the sales floor with invigorating fragrances to recasting stores as "experiences" to maximize FOMO), you can learn to break shopping's magic spell. You guys, businesses are hiring neuroscientists and consumer psychologists to capture your attention and separate you from your money. Would it be awesome to see these experts direct more of their energies elsewhere—say, toward helping the mentally ill? Definitely. But let me remind you, fashion is a massive economic engine. It only makes sense that brands would seek input from the most brilliant minds. My goal in this chapter is to teach you how to interact with stores in the healthiest way possible. Unmasking a few marketing mysteries will make you a savvier, more strategic, and—most important—calmer consumer.

Fashion Psychology Tips

How to Resist Retail Temptations

- Know that most clothes really can be worn year-round. You don't actually *need* a new spring jacket or a fall dress. That's why God invented layering.
- Take advantage of your own impatience. Never autosave your credit card details on shopping sites; that way you'll be forced, annoyingly, to reenter them every time. Research shows that the average online shopper expects a Web page to load within two seconds, and 40 percent of shoppers will wait no more than *three* seconds before logging off.[4] Being required to pause mid-purchase to enter payment info will often stop you in your tracks.
- Reframe your relationship to retail. Shopping is not a way to celebrate a win or recover from a loss. Seek out different activities to reward yourself for a triumph or rebound after disappointment (cooking a great meal, indulging in an at-home beauty treatment, unplugging and prioritizing sleep, walking in nature, taking a day off).

Let's go back to envisioning your closet full of clothes — no doubt representing a small fortune — and that *Ugh, I have nothing to wear* feeling. One major reason for this? We shop and shop and shop but, according to the *Wall Street Journal,* wear only 20 percent of what we own. That means 80 percent of your clothes are sitting there unworn, taking up physical space in your closet and mental space in your life. "The retail industry counts on this and knows that people buy for many more reasons than actually needing something," writes the *Wall Street Journal's* Ray A. Smith.[5] Those reasons tend to be emotional.

Building and refreshing your wardrobe probably feels like a costly, never-ending process. Why is what we have never good enough? Why does fashion feel like an insatiable beast that forever needs to be fed? Well, for starters, a lot of people make a lot of money convincing you that you need new clothes almost all the time. According to economic analysts, the US apparel market is the largest in the world, pulling in $328.07 billion in 2017.[6] The average American spends over $1,800 a year on apparel and services, according to USA Today.[7] The fashion industry continues to grow nearly 5 percent annually and has shown no significant signs of slowing.[8] According to a report by Congress's Joint Economic Committee, in New York City alone, the retail market generates $15 billion in annual sales.[9] NYU's prestigious Stern School of Business recently became the first US business school to offer a fashion and luxury MBA. Why? Over the past decade, student enrollment in fashion, luxury, and retail courses has grown more than 500 percent, reports the program's director, Kim Corfman: "Fashion and luxury have seen the largest growth of all career interests."[10] Make no mistake: Those bright business students are following the money.

Our urge to shop can feel so powerful, we sometimes do it to our own financial detriment. Even during times of economic uncertainty, women still feel compelled to revamp their wardrobes every season, as Reuters reported in the midst of the 2008 recession.[11] In both boom times and lean times, the pressure—particularly on women—to buy new clothes just doesn't let up. On one hand, going to work may provide us with disposable income; on the other, it fuels the need to look fashionable. As Sheila Marikar writes in the New York Times, "Dressing for work is work, and the cost—in dollars, time, distraction—is borne disproportionately by women."[12] Factors like the wage gap (research shows white women earned seventy-seven cents for every dollar white men earned in 2017; black women earned sixty-one cents, and Latina women earned fifty-three cents) and the "pink tax" (the phenomenon whereby women are charged more than men for equivalent goods and services) also put us at an economic disadvantage.[13] No wonder you feel agitated about buying clothes!

This is a modern issue. In 1930, the average American woman owned nine outfits. Today, according to *Forbes,* she owns thirty—one for nearly every day of the month—though again, she probably only wears six of them.[14] Globally, 73 percent of women update 25 percent of their closet every three months.[15] Most of you are spending a serious chunk of your money and a hell of a lot of your precious time on clothes (and that's not even counting the cash you drop on beauty, fitness, wellness, etc.). Yet I bet in spite of decades of practice following trends and reading fashion advice, you still don't feel a confident sense of command over your clothing choices. And maddeningly, you're being presented with more choices than ever.

Like Barbara in the Case Study, "every woman has the feeling of opening up her closet and seeing the dozens of dead dresses that she's worn only once," Rent the Runway's CEO Jennifer Hyman (a Harvard Business School grad) told *The New Yorker.* She notes that 75 million American women spend at least $3,000 annually on work clothes.[16] Rent the Runway and other retail-disrupting businesses offer customers an unlimited array of new outfits to choose from. They expertly deliver the hit of dopamine, and the fantasy of the reinvented self that shopping provides— for a reduced price. It's an innovative service that's been deservedly celebrated. But whether they're bought or borrowed, acquiring new clothes (even temporarily) still costs you time, money, and energy. My question to you is: Do you really want to be working this hard on this aspect of your life?

There are distinct downsides to what Marikar calls the "never-ending cycle of outfit accumulation." Whether you passionately love fashion or merely accept it as a means to an end (looking presentable), when you shop mainstream retail, you are participating in a cash grab by big business. You're also potentially contributing to an environmental crisis, as almost three-fifths of all clothing ends up in incinerators or landfills within a year of being produced, according to the *New York Times*.[17] When you shop (and shop and shop some more), you might also be undermining your long-term financial security. Women are especially vulnerable to the emotional pull and addictive pitfalls of online shopping. According to financial psychologist Dr. Brad Klontz, compulsive buying disorder is more likely to affect women than men. "What's made it more challenging is that before [technology] you had to get dressed up and actually *go* somewhere to buy something, and now you can do it in your pajamas on the couch," he tells PureWow. "Temptation and the availability of impulse shopping has just escalated dramatically."[18] On those days when I'm feeling cynical about all of this, I think about this old quote: "Too many people spend money they haven't earned to buy things they don't want to impress people they don't like."[19] And yet, even knowing the negatives, many of us—myself included—still fall passionately in love with clothes. We love clothes, but do clothes love us back? As with any emotional affair, it's complicated.

Time to look inward. Let's sort out whether *you* think your shopping behaviors are healthy or harmful.

- How do you feel when you go shopping? Cool, calm, and collected or euphoric, anxious, and guilty?
- How often do you suffer from buyer's remorse? Some of the time, most of the time, or all of the time?
- Have you ever sworn to yourself you would stop shopping for a certain time period but failed to keep that promise?
- Do you feel like trends are moving so fast that anything you buy looks stale way too soon? Does this make you feel compelled to buy more and more new stuff?
- Do your Instagram style influencers inspire you or fuel your insecurities?

SHOPPING AND THE MIND: THIS IS YOUR BRAIN ON RETAIL

Shopping can feel like an emotional roller coaster. For some people, it offers a visceral lift, the animalistic thrill of the chase as you hunt down a new must-have/exclusive/limited edition/flash-sale-reduced item. "Only 2 left!" insist the ads as your heart races and your palms sweat. One survey featured on CNBC found that the average American consumer spends a whopping $5,400 a year on impulse buys. And clothing was one of the most common impulse purchases, second only to food.[20] Since we make many of our buying decisions so quickly, we frequently feel out of whack in the aftermath. This psychological whiplash (Anticipation! Excitement! Regret!) can seem way too intense. So why is it so hard just to opt out and stop shopping?

To understand the answer to that question, it helps to get a handle on the science used by the marketing pros who play on your emotions. Once you do, I believe *you* can control your shopping experiences and not vice versa. In her BBC article "Shopping a Sale Gives You the Same Feeling as Getting High," business journalist Alina Dizik interviews various addiction therapists, psychologists, and consumer researchers who offer evidence that shopping stimulates the brain similarly to other addictive stimulants like alcohol and drugs. Shopping and other compulsive behaviors like gambling and disordered eating catalyze similar neurological responses (dilated pupils, pleasure center activation, and emotional engagement).

But what I find most eye-opening about Dizik's article are her interviews with experts in the emerging field of *neuromarketing.* Yes, there are accomplished neuroscientists who devote their considerable expertise — even using MRIs — to mapping the consumer brain.[21] Uma R. Karmarkar is an assistant professor at Harvard Business School with PhDs in both marketing and neuroscience. In an interview featured in *Forbes,* she said: "The more desirable something is, the more significant the changes in blood flow in [a certain] part of the brain. Studies have shown activity in that brain area can predict the future popularity of a product or experience."[22]

Marketers also capitalize on the fact that human beings are, by nature, pack animals. You may be familiar with phrases like "Most visitors who share your profile choose this option" or find yourself directed toward "Recommended items other customers often buy again." This language plays into your instincts for social comparison. You buy things you believe other people who are similar to you have bought, not only because you implicitly trust their opinions, but also because you want to fit in with a group; you want to belong.[23] If you thought walking into a store or making a purchase online was a simple act of free will and that you are immune to marketing manipulation, think again.

Here's another wake-up call: Women are targeted by marketers in ways that destabilize our self-esteem. "Something is wrong with you but—great news!—you can BUY something to fix it!" You can't shop for a bra or moisturizer without confronting a campaign aimed straight at your emotional Achilles' heel. Actress-activist Jameela Jamil has called out Avon for marketing anti-cellulite cream using body-positive language. "The way this industry sells fear to (only) women about the inevitable effects of time and gravity and a slowing metabolism makes me feel sick," she tweeted. "The corrective beauty industry is booming at an all-time high, because they have ensured our self-worth is at an all-time low."[24] Despite an objective lack of need, according to a report in Quartzy, wrinkle-free millennials are the biggest consumers of anti-aging skincare. In this day and age, Serums + Sheet Masks = Self-Care whether you're twenty-two or fifty-two. "Beauty is a business that has always thrived by fostering women's insecurities," writes Quartzy's Sangeeta Singh-Kurtz. Modern marketing messages may have been modified to include buzzwords like "self-care" and "empowerment," says Singh-Kurtz. But the mission remains the same: to sell us more stuff by capitalizing on our insecurities—about wrinkles and pores, body hair, bloating, stretch marks, and cellulite. No matter how you spin it, the subtext is still shame."[25]

It's not just our skin that could (apparently) be better. It's our bodies, too. In 2018 the Victoria's Secret fashion show came under fire for its lack of inclusivity and size diversity on the runway. As Becca McCharen-Tran, designer of lingerie label Chromat, told the *New York Post,* "If that's what girls are seeing as the beauty that is celebrated, to not see yourself in that is just so limiting. I think [the Victoria's Secret show] just shapes so much of our cultural conversation about what beauty is, and who's deemed worthy of desire, and who's beautiful and who's not."[26] In reality, 68 percent of American women wear a size 14 or higher.[27] Google searches for plus-size swimwear rose by 43 percent in 2018.[28]

Smelling blood in the water, rival lingerie company ThirdLove called for a boycott of the Victoria's Secret fashion show. In an open letter published in the *New York Times* and elsewhere, ThirdLove founder Heidi Zak wrote: "It's time to stop telling women what makes them sexy—let us decide. We're done with pretending certain sizes don't exist or aren't important enough to serve. And please stop insisting that inclusivity is a trend."[29] ThirdLove's move was an expression of "the right values," to be sure. But it was also part of a razor-sharp marketing campaign. Nowadays a brand's "values" have never been more important to its bottom line. With an abundance of options, shoppers are increasingly selective, according to a 2017 report co-authored by consulting firm McKinsey & Company and industry bible *The Business of Fashion:* "More and more, they base their purchase decisions on whether a company's practices and mission aligns with their values."[30]

This all seems great. If you need a bra, it probably *is* better to buy one from a company that is moving the cultural conversation in a positive new direction, as opposed to one that makes you feel bad about yourself because you are not Gisele Bündchen. But are we entering murky moral territory when a for-profit brand touts its "values" in an effort to drive sales forever upward? I'm not slamming companies for embracing women's curves or promoting diversity in any form; it sure beats the alternative, and it's a vast improvement on precedent. But ultimately, when the motivation is to *Sell! Sell! Sell!* it behooves us to pull back the curtain and see what's behind it.

SHOPPING UNDER THE INFLUENCE: WHO CAN YOU TRUST?

With the rise of smartphones, online shopping has altered the landscape forever. Since 2016, e-commerce has accounted for more than 40 percent of US retail sales growth, according to McKinsey: 42 percent of millennials prefer shopping online and avoid stores entirely when possible.[31] Over a quarter of all apparel sales now take place online.[32] More and more consumers are visiting shopping sites via social media.[33] In a single day (Black Friday, 2018), US consumers spent $2 billion using only their phones.[34] Seventy-two percent of Instagram users report making purchasing decisions on the basis of something they saw on the site.[35] In 2017, 8,642 brick-and-mortar stores closed across the country.[36] There's no doubt about it and there's no going back: We are shopping less and less in physical spaces and more and more in virtual ones.

To stay alive, stores are being transformed into exclusive social clubs, restaurants with a side of retail, community spaces, event venues, "experiences," or colorful photo studios where you can shoot your own content—synergistically promoting both yourself and your chosen brand on Insta. In fact, some stores no longer even stock product, serving instead as way stations where customers can pick up or return items they've already purchased online. "Brand museums" or pop-up spaces created by fashion houses like Hermès, Chanel, Tiffany, and Dolce & Gabbana are offering everything from tarot card readings to wellness classes to breakfast, all to entice visitors to post about their (promotional) experiences.

Desperate times and shifting ground are forcing traditional retailers to reinvent their sales methods. Associates at Neiman Marcus pitch luxury items directly to shoppers via Instagram.[37] And OG influencers— celebrities, fashion editors, Kar-Jenners, and other tastemakers—are reportedly paid up to $1 million a post to promote products. But as a projected $2 billion a year is spent on influencer marketing, ultra-famous people aren't the only ones cashing checks.[38]

You know that friend-of-a-friend travel or parenting blogger you follow and feel a real connection with? She may be selling you stuff without saying so. "A third of brands admit to deliberately not disclosing influencer marketing as sponsored content as they believe doing so will impact consumers' trust," reports *Marketing Week*.[39] In fact, some experts are betting the most effective influencers aren't even famous at all. Brands are increasingly employing "micro-influencers" (social media stars with between 100,000 and 1 million followers) and "nano-influencers" (regular people with between one hundred and ten thousand followers).[40] Their goal is to create more "authentic" spon-con and reach more targeted audiences. It's effective. Nano-influencers are people you're already loosely connected with socially. People you could conceivably meet in real life and therefore people you are likelier to trust. Because of this, according to one industry survey, nano-influencers engage (meaning they get likes and comments from) up to 8.7 percent of their audience, whereas the engagement rate is only 1.7 percent for celebrities with more than a million followers.[41] Buyer beware.

Why do these new marketing tactics work so well? Simply raising your *awareness* of a product by getting it in front of your eyeballs and making it feel familiar makes you likelier to buy it. Often, awareness turns into action. This is due to a psychological phenomenon called the "mere-exposure effect." Also known as the familiarity principle, this explains why we prefer people or things simply because they are familiar. Notes Gillian Fournier of Psych Central: "This is interesting because it has no basis in logic. Just because we see a stranger occasionally does not make them any more trustworthy...We just feel like they are because we 'know' them."[42] And the more we see a product, especially one recommended by a social media "friend," the more familiar—and thus trustworthy—the product seems. "Familiarity has a major impact on our decision-making process, whether we realize it or not," according to data-driven market research firm CXL. "That means it has a major impact on conversions [purchases] as well."[43] Harvard-educated business guru Dr. Jeffrey Lant is famous for his theory that to penetrate a customer's consciousness, "you have to contact the [customer] a minimum of seven times within an 18-month period."[44] This finding is known in marketing circles as "the rule of seven." The next time you want to buy a new piece of clothing, ask yourself if people or brands you trust have shown it to you, and if so, how many times.

What is the point of all the data? Well, it's me raising *your* awareness. I want you to understand that even when it's clear something is an #ad, it may still be working its marketing magic on you because it is penetrating your consciousness. Your "friends" may be shilling spon-con without saying so, making a product or brand feel familiar and ultimately irresistible. I want you to know that retailers are constantly finding new ways to get product into the hands of the right people and in front of the right eyeballs: yours. Because once something slips into your consciousness, it's never been easier to click a button and buy it.

HOW TO SHOP MINDFULLY

So what's the answer to all this influence? In my experience, the best way to get off the retail therapy treadmill and break the cycle of buying, regretting, then buying some more is mindfulness. The goal is to redirect your energy, to find new outlets for your anxiety and different pleasure center triggers. This Fashion Psychologist is here to help you reframe the way you think about shopping in the first place.

So let's get brutally honest about why you want to shop right now.

- Does shopping feed a fantasy you have about yourself, about how your life is going to be once you buy that tempting item? If so, then what steps can you take to recognize and appreciate the reality of who you are and what you have right now, in this moment, in real time? How about writing out a list acknowledging what you are thankful for? **Gratitude** has been proven to help us delay gratification, thus leading to fewer impulse buys.[45] So whether you count your blessings by journaling, meditating, or scrolling through photos of loved ones, you'll be less likely to shop to fill an emotional void. Practicing gratitude "creates a sense of abundance," writes consumer psychologist Kit Yarrow, making you "less likely to subconsciously try to fill emotional holes by...accumulating more stuff."[46]

- Are you bored or lonely right now and hoping shopping will fill the void? What will **nourish your need to connect**—a superficial chat with a salesperson or a heart-to-heart with an old friend? Make the call.

- Are you anxious and craving a sense of control? What if you took the money you are about to spend on a shirt and transferred it to your savings account instead? Science tells us that **experiences** make us happier than things. Writes James Hamblin, MD, health correspondent for *The Atlantic:* "Nothing material is intrinsically valuable, except in whatever promise of happiness it carries."[47] That dress is a costume for a fantasy; it guarantees nothing. But saving for a plane ticket somewhere warm promises a change of scenery and perspective.

Once you really sit with yourself and separate your needs from your wants, you can take incremental steps to fill yourself up in ways that don't require you to buy new things. In my experience, the antidote to anxiety is action. Pick up the landline. Call a friend. Call your grandma. Go for a walk in nature. Perform an easy task and cross something off your to-do list. Watch a movie. Read a book. Try out a new recipe. Make a solid plan to volunteer. Research your next vacation. Starting small is better than sitting on your hands. These skills, much like mastering a new language or learning to dance, can be practiced and honed. Self-regulation is like a muscle that gets stronger with training. We can teach ourselves not to be triggered by sales the same way we can practice calming down in traffic or containing flashes of anger at our loved ones.

Of course, you can't avoid shopping forever. A full life means you have places to go and people to see and you want to look fresh doing it. That's a beautiful thing. But there is mindless shopping and then there is mindful shopping; the former will upset your life, and the latter will improve it. Shopping offers us "the mental vacation that comes with imagining how a product can be used, such as 'I'll turn heads in this outfit,' or 'We'll have the wildest parties with this cocktail shaker,'" writes Yarrow. But if you don't have concrete, immediate plans to wear your new look or a party locked in on the calendar, there's no real need to buy those things. Again, resist the urge to spend money on your fantasy self or your imaginary life. And if you *are* going to spend, here's a helpful guide to navigating the retail landscape.

Fashion Psychology Tips

How to Shop with Intention

Touch what you own: Anytime you want to buy something new, go and physically touch the clothes hanging in your closet. Doing this makes you aware that you already have an abundance of clothes, and that perhaps your desire to shop is about something else. If you see a cute dress online and your heart starts racing in anticipation of wearing it on your next girls' night out, get up and go through your dresses. Is there one already hanging there that you have road tested and know you feel great in? Touch it. Reflect upon the pleasant memory of the last time you wore it. Most important, check your datebook: Do you actually *have* an upcoming girls' night out scheduled? If not, admit that to yourself, and the urge to buy the dress should diminish.

Quality > quantity: Save your money and spend it on one quality classic that will last for years as opposed to multiple fast-fashion pieces that will disintegrate after a few washes. According to a study published in *Advances in Consumer Research*, shoppers experience buyer's remorse because of "a suspicion they spent too much time or effort buying something that later doesn't seem worth the time or effort."[48] Shoppers don't usually regret *splurges*. What they regret is passing up a special, unique, high-quality item *in favor of* a more "sensible," cheaper choice. They end up resenting/regretting that second-banana selection because they feel like they've settled, which leads to wearing it less or not at all.

In with the new, out with the old: Anytime you buy something new, something old has to be gotten rid of. Donate or sell any redundant items that are similar to what you've just purchased. Sites like Poshmark, thredUP, Depop, and The RealReal can help you convert your discarded duds into cash.

Demand versatility from your clothes: Try to limit your new purchases to workhorse items you can wear all year round, regardless of the season and for multiple occasions. For example: A black pleated maxi skirt that looks chic with a t-shirt in spring or a turtleneck in winter. A bustier bodysuit that looks sexy with high-waist jeans and elegant under a tuxedo suit. Wide-leg pants that can be dressed up with heels for a night out or dressed down with sneakers for a coffee run.

Nothing beats the convenience and privacy of shopping online (right, millennials?). But I have found that when clients assess an item using their physical senses, they make more informed and suitable purchases. Or because an item has failed to satisfy their senses, they feel more certain about rejecting it. Thoughtfully engaging the senses while shopping also forces you to slow down and focus, which leads to better decision making in general.

You should know that retailers use visuals, store layouts, sounds, and scents to attract your cents (sorry, couldn't help myself). Up to 20 percent of US retailers pump fragrances like coffee, freshly baked bread, or piña coladas through their stores using the A/C system. The purpose of doing this "really is to keep customers in your store, to create this welcoming environment—and it works," Mike Gatti, executive director of marketing at the National Retail Federation, tells the UK's *Independent*. Customers stay in the store longer, "it helps people feel better in their shopping, and in a lot of cases causes them to spend more money."[49] In a famous study, Chicago neurologist and psychiatrist Dr. Alan Hirsch asked a group of shoppers to look at two identical pairs of Nike sneakers in two identical-seeming rooms. One room was filled with purified air, while the other was filled with a mixed floral scent. Eighty-four percent of the subjects preferred the Nikes in the scented room and were willing to pay over ten dollars more for them than for the "unscented" sneakers.[50]

The next time you're out shopping, take note of the music pumping through the store. How is it making you feel? Anxious and amped up? Eager to buy what you're holding and hightail it out of there? Excited, hip, and spend-happy? Music is a proven sales tool too. Step into any H&M or Urban Outfitters, listen up, and you'll see—or rather hear—what I mean.

Fashion Psychology Exercise

MAKE SHOPPING A SENSORY EXPERIENCE

When we shop, we utilize our senses of sight, touch, smell, and hearing. I designed this method for parents shopping with children who have sensory processing challenges, but it can truly benefit everyone.

Sight: When you first walk in, glance around the store. Are there certain colors, fabrics, or textures that instantly attract you? Take note of those, and then proceed, ignoring any items that do not meet those specifications. This will quickly help you narrow down your options.

Touch: When considering trying on an item of clothing, touch the fabric by placing it between your fingers. Does it feel scratchy, low-quality, or cheap? If you like the texture enough to try it on, consider not only how it looks but also how it *feels* on your body. Does it squeeze you too tight? Does it create the dreaded "muffin top"? Is there an itchy tag or seam? Is the material irritating your skin? An item may technically "fit," but if it makes you feel uncomfortable, you will never, ever wear it. (Ask anyone with a pile of untouched mohair sweaters in her closet!)

Smell: At the risk of seeming wacky, take a subtle sniff of the item you're considering. A rented item may possess a lingering fragrance or body odor, turning you off no matter how gorgeous it looks. A new item may smell synthetic, emitting the scent of the manufacturing facility where it was made. Certain fabrics like organic cottons smell "clean" after washing, but polyester is known for trapping and retaining malodorous bacteria. You may not consciously realize it, but you might be avoiding wearing certain items that offend your olfactory senses, even when they're flattering AF.

Hearing: Assess the sounds the item makes. Does a skirt swish when you walk? Envision yourself speed-walking down the hallways of your office. Do the pants make a scratchy sound as your thighs rub together? Will the click-clack of those heels in your marble lobby make you feel self-conscious?

Really take a moment to observe and honor your responses to these sensory stimuli. If an item fails to elicit a pleasing reaction from even one or two of your senses in the store, do not buy it. Try to separate your feelings about the clothes in your hand from the music in your ears and the smell in the air. Once you do, if the urge to buy diminishes, move on. Are you actually super-excited about the jacket you're holding, or are you just anxious to make a purchase so you can feel a sense of accomplishment and get out of the noisy store (or away from that visually overstimulating website)? Given all the effort and expertise aimed at getting you to open your wallet, walking away with nothing is an accomplishment in its own right.

THE BOTTOM LINE
KEY TIPS AND TAKEAWAYS FROM CHAPTER 3

- Take the stressing out of party dressing. Adopt a **special occasion uniform** to wear anytime an event pops up.
- **Elevate your everyday outfits.** Invest in versatile, seasonless staples (t-shirts, cardigans, a faux leather moto jacket). What you wear most often will have the strongest impact on your style and emotions.
- **Death to browsing.** Avoid walking into a store or visiting a site unless you have a specific item or upcoming party or meeting in mind. If the event is not in your calendar, don't shop for it.
- **Use your senses.** Touch what you already own. It will restore your sense of abundance and remind you that you don't really *need* anything new. Never buy anything that doesn't look, feel, sound, *and* smell amazing.
- **Beware the familiarity principle.** You may buy coffee from the same friendly food truck guy every single morning. But that doesn't mean you would take him home with you. The same goes for clothes: Just because you've seen an item many, many times (on your social media feed, perhaps?), that does not mean you need — or even necessarily *want* — it in your closet.
- Documenting **gratitude,** planning for **experiences,** and nurturing **relationships** can all replace the urge to shop.

Chapter 4

A DIFFERENT WAY TO GET DRESSED

I wear my sort of clothes to save me the trouble of deciding which
clothes to wear.

—Katharine Hepburn

If you are hoping to refresh your look and reduce your stress level, now
is the time to roll up your sleeves. I have four important goals in this
chapter. I want to help you...

1. Learn why having a signature style (or personal brand or fashion
   uniform) could be right for you. Then figure out what yours looks
   like.
2. Become convinced that repeating outfits is not only okay—it can
   be the key to sanity and style.
3. Create a well-edited Capsule Wardrobe and look better with fewer
   clothes.
4. Break out of a rut if your current uniform is holding you back.

What's the first clue in solving the mystery of what to wear? Knowing
who you are. Personally, I tend to look at tempting new trends or potential outfits through the lens of *Me or Not Me?* I have a pretty clear sense of
my signature style. I call it Minimalist Glam. I love clean silhouettes in
bold colors, prints, and fabrics. I have never met a leopard-print, hot-pink,

or sparkly item I didn't want to take home. But I balance those out with crisp classics like oxford shirts and slim-fit pants. I'm also obsessed with high heels. (For me, sneakers are for the gym or for running from a dog.) Since I know my style so well, I'm more easily able to avoid looks that don't suit my vibe. If I were to diagnose my Fashion Psychology behaviors using the concepts introduced in chapter 2, I'd say I'm all about **Focal Accessories** and **Mood-Based Dressing.**

So I know what I like, but of course I still make mistakes! You know that trend of wearing satin pajamas out in public but dressing them up with fancy accessories like heels and jewelry? Oh, I went there. I wore pajamas outside my apartment and felt ridiculous. I had to come home in the middle of the day to change. That look was officially not me. But a leopard cape? Hell, yeah, that's me. As far as I'm concerned, leopard is a neutral; it goes with everything. When I wear animal prints, I feel elegant, fierce, sleek—almost like I'm embodying the characteristics of the animal itself. I move faster. And capes are an easy way to add drama to a monochromatic foundation (all-black tank top + leggings + heels + leopard cape = amazing). Fuchsia power suit? Me x 3. It's figure-flattering, mood-brightening, and unexpected. Bring it on. Trendy Dad Sneakers? Hard pass. I just don't feel as confident when I'm flat-footed. When I'm up on my tippy toes in heels, I feel balletic, poised, and graceful.

Now *your* style might be the opposite of mine. You may love flowy linen neutrals and flat sandals or athleisure and hype-beast kicks. But no matter what you're into, having a clearly defined style makes it easier to sidestep any clothes that are likely to make you uncomfortable. It's a saving grace when you shop.

I also shamelessly repeat my outfits. I dip in and out of uniform dressing depending on what is going on in my life. Whenever I travel, I have a go-to airport uniform. It's a black sweater, black skinny trousers, and black high heels. I find it helps me blend in no matter what country I'm in, no matter how casual or formal the setting, whether the local style customs are modest or anything goes. This uniform seriously reduces my travel stress. Lately I have been deluged with professional obligations, and I have spent a lot of time working from home. So I have already worn the same all-black leggings and cardigan combo for several days this week. I am so taxed emotionally, I do not want to expend any extra energy selecting an outfit. Instead, I've opted to focus my mental resources elsewhere — on my professional productivity.

I'm hardly the first person to embrace this approach. Apple founder Steve Jobs, in his trademark black turtleneck and jeans, was the original poster child for Repetitious Wardrobe Complex. His look became synonymous with his brand and offered a new model for what Silicon Valley visionaries could wear. (His turtleneck was so strongly associated with tech innovation it was cunningly mimicked by the now scandalized Theranos founder Elizabeth Holmes.) According to his biographer Walter Isaacson, Jobs "came to like the idea of having a uniform for himself, because of both its daily convenience ... and its ability to convey a signature style."[1] President Obama also saw the advantage of wearing the same thing over and over while in the Oval Office. "You'll see I wear only gray or blue suits," he once told *Vanity Fair*. "I'm trying to pare down decisions. I don't want to make decisions about what I'm eating or wearing. Because I have too many other decisions to make."[2] During a public Q&A, Facebook founder Mark Zuckerberg echoed this explanation for his unchanging daily uniform: "I really want to clear my life to make it so that I have to make as few decisions as possible about anything except how to best serve this community."[3] Dr. Dre reportedly wears Nike Air Force 1s every day for the same reason — to minimize distraction and maximize productivity.[4]

But it's not just men who have mastered style uniforms. In fact, when women do it, there is often an art to the practice we can all be inspired by. Gayle King, Kate Middleton, Mary-Kate and Ashley Olsen, Elizabeth Warren, Angelina Jolie, and Victoria Beckham (to name a few) are all faithful to instantly recognizable visual aesthetics. So what are the advantages of committing to one look (or to one specific range of similar looks)?

For one thing, it's good for your brand. For another, it's great for your brain.

We may think picking out our clothes is no big deal, but when we're mindful about it, it actually requires a lot from us. It is estimated that the average adult makes roughly 35,000 decisions per day, and research shows that our cognitive capacities get depleted with each one.[5] Bypassing the decision about what to wear reduces your chances of burnout by taking something significant off your plate. Experts tell us we have limited bandwidth for willpower or self-control—that our ability to make clearheaded, satisfying choices is a finite resource. Think of your mental energy and emotional reserves almost like a battery that runs down, or a tank of gas that gets used up over time. Having a uniform is simply good fuel efficiency. "The most successful people...conserve willpower by developing effective habits and routines in school and at work so that they reduce the amount of stress in their lives," writes John Tierney, co-author of *Willpower: Rediscovering the Greatest Human Strength,* in an article for the *New York Times.*[6] Having a consistent fashion uniform is the definition of a stress-reducing habit or routine.

If you are shopping or getting dressed without any sort of guideline or system in place, you are far likelier to become overwhelmed. When you walk into a store, open up a shopping site, or confront your overstuffed closet, your heart rate may increase with anticipation and excitement. But soon your emotions veer between extremes. You initially feel like you want to buy the whole damn store (euphoria), but within minutes, you want to run screaming from it (Decision Fatigue). You may try on ten different outfits, then, when nothing lives up to your ideals, feel crushed. There are distinct psychological processes at play during these scenarios. "Having too many options causes a sort of paralysis in the decision-making process, which leads to avoidance behavior—i.e., choosing to do nothing at all," writes consumer behavior analyst Dr. Liraz Margalit in *Psychology Today.* "In the instances when a choice *is* made under these conditions, it is usually accompanied by frustration."[7] This explains why, after finally throwing together a look because you have run out of time and you must leave for work, you walk out the door dissatisfied. It's the same with buyer's remorse. You were forced to override your impulse toward avoidance, and therefore the purchase you did make just doesn't feel right.

So what's the solution to all this angst? FEWER OPTIONS.

Psychologically speaking, when you are faced with fewer choices, you are likelier to believe you've chosen correctly. The inverse is also true: When you have too many options, you would rather *avoid* selecting something to wear because it is less likely to be the right choice. It's simple math or probability, Margalit explains. If you have two choices, you have a 50 percent chance of picking the "right" one. If you have ten choices, you have only a 10 percent chance of picking the "right" one.

So how do you get to fewer options? By editing your closet down to just the items you genuinely love. But starting can be daunting. How do you know that—after getting rid of a big pile of your clothes representing money, memories, and time—you'll be happy with what's left? That's where I come in. I'm going to help you figure out what you love to wear by helping you identify your ideal look. Then you're going to keep—and *actually wear*—all the items from your closet that fit within that framework. These are the building blocks of your style uniform: a remixable rotation of killer pieces you can turn to anytime you wish to remove uncertainty from your routine. Not only will this lead to calmer mornings, but it will also present a cohesive message about who you are to others, which in turn promotes personal power. An incoherent sense of style muddies your messaging and dilutes your personal brand. As Vera Wang told the *Harvard Business Review:* "Fashionable is what's new. But you have to move within your own space...If you're going to jump from a turquoise bikini with feathers to a Savile Row tweed suit to a ball gown with flowers all over it to being 90 percent see-through, then you can never build a brand, because who are you?"[8]

A closet featuring only the effortless essentials you love—a limited number of key items that can be mixed and matched in myriad ways to create a variety of outfits—is also called a Capsule Wardrobe. (Learn how to build one on page 120.) I've got one and I'm happier for it. Not only do I know who I am and what my signature style looks like, but I also know exactly what I own. When I look at my closet or even think about its contents from afar, I know precisely what's in there for me to work with, minimizing my anxiety. There are no forgotten items hiding in piles, shoved in corners, or (gasp!) sitting in unopened shipping boxes from emotion-fueled late-night online shopping sprees. To me, there is nothing worse than discovering something I spent money on but forgot to wear. My biggest motivator? I don't like to feel stressed about my clothes. I have too much going on already.

And here's the very best thing about having a limited quantity of clothes to begin with. When certain items are at the dry cleaner or in the laundry hamper, I am forced to work with what's left—i.e., I have even *fewer* options. This has challenged me to get creative and inspired me to put together some of my most successful looks yet, in terms of both how I felt wearing them and how others reacted to me when I did. Cutting down my closet's contents has left me no choice but to maximize the potential of every item I own, resulting in some of my most exciting outfits ever.

I'll give you an example. Recently I was invited to a fashion show and gala at FIT—the most prestigious and glamorous event of the year for the fashion school. I was thinking of calling one of my favorite designers and asking to borrow a dress but instead decided to try to work with what I already owned. As luck would have it, my go-to party dress was dirty, and, being a minimalist, I didn't have a slew of suitable backups. On the day of the event, I assessed my mood. I felt like Beyoncé! I was really feeling myself. I decided to illustrate that mood and go for a fashion-forward look. So I got inventive. I paired a leopard-print blouse from Express that I typically wear to work with a purple floral ball gown skirt by Akira that I had originally intended to wear (boho-style) with a white t-shirt on weekends. My leopard-print heels (by Aldo) and my metallic clutch (from a neighborhood boutique) finished off the look. The whole outfit cost less than $300, head to toe. Let me tell you, the scene at this party was intimidating. There was a red carpet, a crowd of photographers, executives from brands like Tommy Hilfiger; people were wearing red-bottom shoes, you guys. But guess what? Not only did I feel like I fit in, I felt like I stood out (in a good way!). My unexpected mix of prints really popped, and the dramatic length of the skirt made the whole look super eye-catching. I felt incredible! And compliments from my fellow guests, as well as the photographers, enhanced this feeling. One attendee even asked me, "Are you *sure* you're a professor? You really look like you belong in this industry!"

Here's what I reaffirmed that night. You do not need an excessive amount of clothing. The goal is to own one or two of the same type of item, max. Think of it this way: If you have five pairs of black pants, you'll probably end up wearing only one or two of them regularly. But if you have only *one* pair of black pants, and those are in the laundry pile, you will have no choice but to move on and find something else to wear. This is how you force yourself to break out of style ruts. Now, this doesn't mean that when your go-to black pants are dirty, you go out and buy something new. It means you take a second look at a different option you already own. You may surprise yourself—like I did—and find you love wearing a casual top with your formal skirt. But you never would have tried that fresh new combo if you had four extra pairs of black pants to fall back on.

HOW TO FIGURE OUT WHAT YOU LIKE TO WEAR

To get the most out of your clothes, it helps to have a Rolodex of outfit options. I encourage clients to put together a digital photo album or "catalog" of their favorite looks. This catalog will be available for you to scroll through and pick from when you wake up in the morning and assess your mood. No more starting from zero every day.

This is a time-honored industry trick. Professional stylists take Polaroids of outfit options on photo shoots, or pop them up on pegboards in a client's closet. If you're ever backstage at a fashion show, you'll see a poster board of photos showing each model's head-to-toe look displayed in the order in which they will come down the runway. The idea here is similar, but it involves deeper self-reflection, because it brings your emotions into the mix. Keeping a personalized outfit catalog will be your secret styling weapon when that "nothing to wear" feeling hits.

There are many ways to execute this plan: I love taking a selfie every time I feel fabulous in my outfit, then filing it away in a photo album on my phone. But you can also grab a pen and journal or use your phone's Notes app and jot down a brief description of exactly what you're wearing anytime your look is working. No matter how you document this information, you will want to keep a list/file of solid outfit options for future reference. You can even organize them by work looks, party looks, weekend looks, etc.

To help you get started, I have a little homework assignment. I call it "Next Time/Last Time." Over the next few weeks, document the answers to these questions and begin to formally recognize the looks that make you feel your best. The goal? Revealing—and remembering—your most winning clothing combinations.

Fashion Psychology Exercise

NEXT TIME/LAST TIME

- When was the **last time** you dressed up for a special occasion and really slayed?
- The **next time** you get a wonderful compliment on what you're wearing, or on your presence in general, document exactly what you have on, top to bottom, including accessories. Write down what the person said and how the compliment made you feel.
- When was the **last time** you felt your best in an everyday situation (at work, hanging with your kids, running errands, grabbing coffee)? What exactly were you wearing? How did that outfit make you feel? How productive were you that day?

- The **next time** you want to feel cozy and comfortable, write down what's on your mind and exactly which clothes you reach for to soothe yourself.

- When was the **last time** you bought a new item that you *didn't* regret? Maybe it was an investment purchase you've worn a million times, or perhaps it was a basic item that elevated your everyday style. What made it work so well? Why did it deliver? Was it a certain color, fit, or fabric? Did it have a certain neckline, shape, or hem length?

- The **next time** you are required to look polished and professional, write down what you decide to wear and why. What emotions and reactions are you hoping to elicit with your look? Later, when you get home and change, reflect on what about your outfit worked for you or why it didn't.

THAT'S *SO* ON-BRAND: THE BENEFITS OF HAVING A STYLE UNIFORM

Picture a razor-sharp bob-and-bangs haircut and oversize sunglasses. Who do you think of immediately? *Vogue*'s Anna Wintour, of course. Next, envision a tracksuit, slicked-back bun, big hoop earrings, and high-heel boots. Who does that look conjure? Raise your hand if you said J.Lo! Next up: a gray bomber jacket, bodysuit, and bike shorts tucked into over-the-knee stiletto boots. It's Yeezy-era Kim Kardashian. If I described an elegant woman in a buttery leather pencil skirt, silk button-down, and suede pointy-toe pumps, that would be oh-so on-brand for Meghan Markle. Certain public figures are so adept at sustaining a signature style, they have crossed over from celebrity to icon. And, naturally, icons have their own iconography. These women have successfully created personal brands—trademark looks that seem to express their very essence.

Let's study them for a second. We notice that their style is consistent, yet not boxed in or boring. Jennifer Aniston almost exclusively wears black dresses on the red carpet, but each one is a little bit different in terms of fabric and design. Your goal is to pare down your clothing options while still leaving room for creativity and experimentation, along with the occasional infusion of a new and refreshing item. Your signature style is a blueprint and a road map, not an ironclad contract. Now, at this very moment you may be looking at your closet and seeing a mishmash of totally unrelated items. Floral summer dresses here, a black velvet blazer there, a what-were-you-thinking turquoise satin mullet dress you wore once to a wedding, and a pile of gray sweaters jump out. None go together, and none seem like "you." Do not lose hope! You *can* find the diamonds in all that rough. Before you decide what to keep and what to cull, take this quiz to home in on a look that feels truest to you.

How to Identify Your Signature Style

1) Pick a style icon.
   A) Meghan Markle (elegant, luxe, glamorous)
   B) Jennifer Aniston (minimalist, classic, relaxed)
   C) Willow Smith (modern, edgy, experimental)
2) Pick a word/phrase.
   A) Chic
   B) Chill
   C) Cutting-edge
3) Pick a dream vacation destination.
   A) Paris
   B) Hawaii
   C) Tokyo

4) Pick a shoe.

   A) D'Orsay ballet flats

   B) Platform espadrilles

   C) Velvet Doc Martens

5) Pick a favorite clothing color.

   A) Cream

   B) Black

   C) Neon pink

If you got...

Mostly A's: You gravitate toward **Elegant, Timeless** styles. Brands like Cuyana, Everlane, Misha Nonoo, and Amour Vert won't steer you wrong. Think long lean lines with high-waist trousers, silky button-downs, linen oxford shirts, a classic trench. Trend-proof, effortless essentials. Ask yourself: What would Victoria Beckham wear? Invest in wardrobe staples you wear all the time like soft tees and cashmere sweaters. Jewelry = gold, dainty, and stackable. Don't shy away from faux croc or animal prints—in small doses. Breton stripes, always. Avoid razzle-dazzle embellishments like sequins or studs.

What this look says about you: You're the grown-up in the room. You are polished, refined, wise, and you believe less is more. You have impeccable taste. You are not trying too hard to impress anyone because you already know how impressive you are.

Mostly B's: You're all about Zen comfort with a **Relaxed Bohemian** vibe. You like California cool clothes that are simple and tread lightly instead of making a statement. Look to brands like & Other Stories, Nation LTD, Madewell, Jenni Kayne, and Mott & Bow for soft t-shirts, fisherman sweaters, relaxed denim, and leather slide mules. Stick to quieter color schemes like beige, gray, black, and white, then accent your look with accessories that vibe natural (turquoise jewelry, muslin infinity scarves, straw fedoras).

What this look says about you: You are creative, worldly, and self-aware. You don't take yourself too seriously, but you also don't play games when it comes to your health or the environment. You are comfortable in your skin, so why the hell would you be anything less than comfortable in your clothes? You are serious about curating a beautiful life full of many passions, and you're not afraid to roll up your sleeves and work hard to get it.

Mostly C's: You're **Fashion Forward** and you know it, so go ahead and show it. If you're young and work in a creative industry, feel free to push the envelope with your look. Just make sure your clothes will last more than a season. Look for items that manage to be cutting-edge yet perennially classic, all at the same time: Leather motorcycle jackets (try them over slip dresses or with satin skirts). Knit beanies. Patent-leather ankle boots. You will always find what thrills you at Zara, H&M, Mango, RIXO, Reformation, and Urban Outfitters. But beware of moment-driven trends like bike shorts and stone-washed denim miniskirts. Just because you're cool enough to wear something doesn't always mean you should.

What this look says about you: You are social and plugged in, with your finger on the pulse. You are fierce and fearless. You are not a sheep. You lead with your creativity and confidence. You are cool but you aren't cold. You are aware of the moment in all its beautiful complexity and ready to stand up for causes that matter. You are also ready to live it up and party at a moment's notice. Your motto? Work hard, play hard, and pics or it didn't happen.

RETHINKING REPETITION

When you commit to a style uniform, you are vowing to wear the same types of clothes repeatedly. This can be challenging, given the social media pressure to post a new #OOTD...well...daily. But is coming up with a new look every single morning good for you or anyone else? In chapter 3 we discussed marketing gimmicks. An especially hot topic is the practice known as "greenwashing." This happens when — against the backdrop of climate change — fashion lines present themselves as "sustainable" when in fact the issues are much more complex. Hey, it's a beautiful thing when designers commit to ethical manufacturing and employment practices. According to industry documentary *The True Cost,* 85 percent of poorly paid workers pumping out fast fashion in countries like India and Bangladesh are women.[9] And it's fantastic when brands use less toxic materials; another devastating documentary, *RiverBlue,* exposes how noxious chemicals from textile factories and tanneries are being dumped directly into waterways in clothing production hubs in India, China, and elsewhere. These environmental atrocities are implicated in "cancer villages" and children losing their sense of smell. More than 8 percent of global greenhouse gas emissions are produced by the apparel and footwear industries, according to the *New York Times.*[10] It's not a good look.

To be clear, I'm not against shopping. But I *am* against buying stuff only because you are bored or sad. If you think about it, even the most eco-friendly brands contribute to a glut of apparel clogging our closets at best, and the landfill or incinerator at worst. According to *The Atlantic,* the average American buys sixty-six garments a year. And each of us also throws away nearly eighty pounds of clothes and textiles annually.[11] The public was shocked in 2018 when Burberry admitted to burning 28.6 million pounds of clothing and cosmetics (worth about $37 million) to "preserve brand value" by preventing those items from being sold at a discount. (They've since vowed to cease and desist.)[12] As popular fashion influencer Bryanboy tweeted: "I'm gonna jump off a bridge head first if I hear about yet another 'sustainable' clothing line. There's nothing sustainable about creating something new en masse. Just stop. Please. You wanna know what's sustainable? Wearing your old damn clothes, that's what. Bye."[13]

Wearing stuff you already own — and hopping off the fast-fashion trend treadmill—not only has a positive impact on the world at large; it can vastly improve your life. The key is *liking* what you already own enough to re-wear it. Maybe that means identifying colors, cuts, prints, and fabrics that make you feel your best, like we did in the Next Time/ Last Time exercise. Perhaps it means remixing items in unexpected new ways. (Here's an idea: You know that paper-thin concert tee you wear to bed? Wear it with your pencil skirt and heels instead of with jeans and sneakers.) It definitely means editing out ALL the stuff that makes you feel "meh." And it means having the confidence to show up to a party or the office in something your friends and colleagues have seen you wear before—many times before.

REPEATS AT WORK

I'll pause here for a second. As much as I'm an advocate, I want to get real with you about the repercussions of repeating your outfits in a profes-sional context. As we've just established, successful people minimize their stress by eliminating Decision Fatigue, and for men that may literally mean wearing a slight variation on the same exact thing every single day. But can you imagine if a woman in your workplace did that? Being able to regularly repeat nearly identical outfits must be acknowledged as a privi-lege. It is far trickier for women and people of color to wear the same daily look, or to adopt the hoodie-heavy laissez-faire uniform of a Silicon Valley wunderkind. Recently, when Goldman Sachs officially relaxed its corpo-rate dress code, NBC News reached out to me for a reaction and commen-tary. Here's what I told them: If a woman or a minority working at Goldman Sachs (or in some other similarly high-stakes corporate environ-ment) were to show up at the office or to a client meeting wearing jeans, a t-shirt, and gray Nikes (Mark Zuckerberg's fashion uniform)—or even in a non-European hairstyle—she would likely be met with unspoken bias and her career might suffer for it. If she were to wear that look every single day without deviation, she would most certainly be seen as eccentric or quirky at best. The expectation for some professionals is just completely different. So the relaxing of dress codes and the new acceptance of outfit repeats may not really benefit everyone, since not everyone is truly held to the same standard, no matter what the updated employee handbook says.

Looking great at work matters because — to be blunt — it tells people how smart and capable you are, which has a direct effect on how much you get promoted and paid. Competence. Power. Intelligence. Character. Sociability. I am not merely listing the attributes any employer would want in a new hire or rising star. These are the precise qualities our clothes convey, according to research by fashion scholar Mary Lynn Damhorst. She looked at 109 studies about clothing and social perception conducted over the course of forty years and published her findings in a paper called "In Search of a Common Thread: Classification of Information Communicated through Dress."[14] Our clothes, she concluded, telegraph our ability to get the job done. People determine our aptitude first by looking at what we are wearing — before we ever utter a word. A different study also published in the *Clothing and Textiles Research Journal* found that, in a classroom setting, teachers and students both assumed that female students who (for the purpose of the experiment) wore shorts and t-shirts were *of lower intelligence and scholastic ability* than their peers who were asked by researchers to dress in suits.[15] So you see, looking polished and professional at work is not just a choice; it's a necessity. One way to do it without depleting your paycheck or emotional reservoir is to create a well-edited closet.

To change your approach to getting dressed, you have to change the way you think. Many of us have internalized the biases I just mentioned. We worry that repeating our outfits makes us look weak, uncreative, unhygienic, or lazy. Reporting on fashion in the workplace, Thrive Global revealed that "49 percent of women have felt self-conscious about repeating outfits at work." By contrast, wrote founder Arianna Huffington, repeats are "a great way to begin to close the style gap, affording women the same freedom (in the form of time and money and thought) that men have in putting together their outfits for the day."[16] Tiffany Haddish famously wore the same $4,000 Alexander McQueen gown to host *SNL*... and to present at the Oscars...and throughout her *Girls Trip* red carpet tour...and more recently to sit down with David Letterman. As she declared in her *SNL* monologue, "I feel like I should be able to wear what I want, when I want, however many times as I want, as long as I Febrezed it."[17] Kate Middleton and Meghan Markle make headlines every time they "recycle" a dress, because seeing a celebrity in the same outfit twice is downright groundbreaking. It didn't used to be this way and it doesn't need to stay this way. Princess Diana repeated her looks, you guys. Keira Knightley wore her own damn wedding dress on the red carpet. Twice. If royalty (Hollywood and otherwise) can push back against this ridiculous stigma around repeats, then so can we.

RITUAL OR RUT?

Now, I don't need to tell you that human beings are complex creatures. Up to this point I've been praising repetition to the rafters. And in general, I do believe it's a key ingredient for a less anxious life. But there are some cases when repeating your looks doesn't reduce worries—it's a symptom of them. I'd like to draw the distinction between healthy repetition and harmful style ruts. To help do so, I'll introduce you to two clients who represent both sides of this coin.

For the past year or so I've been working with Lauren, a *Cosmopolitan* fashion editor in her twenties, who noticed she owned well over a dozen striped shirts.[18] She wondered if her Repetitious Wardrobe Complex was something she should worry about or strive to change. After talking, we discovered it was the opposite: Stripes are a hallmark of her personal brand. Let's listen in to understand how we parsed the distinction between comfort item and style-stifling crutch.

CASE STUDY: NEVER CHANGING HER STRIPES

Dawnn: *When did you begin to notice your closet was full of striped shirts?*

Lauren: *I first noticed in middle school that it was a signature pattern I kept going back to. But I definitely wore striped clothes even earlier, like when I was a [little] kid. Lately, even my mom has started making comments that I need to stop buying striped clothes, because every time I see something with stripes, I don't know what it is, I just need to buy it. Even though I know I already have so many other striped shirts in my closet.*

Dawnn: *When you wear something that is not striped, like a solid color, how do you feel?*

Lauren: *Well, earlier today I was wearing a plain white sweater. But I definitely feel at my most comfortable — I just like my outfit better — when I am wearing stripes as opposed to not wearing them. I'm drawn to them. I can wear them with more things, and they add some extra color to my outfit.*

Dawnn: *Since you've been gravitating toward this print since childhood, and it's something you continually go back to, it seems like stripes hold some type of comfort for you. They're almost like a security blanket or a home base when you're playing tag; you can always return to them for safety. No matter what is going awry or if things are hectic in your world, stripes are ordered and stable. They don't fluctuate. They're always available in stores. They're never going to go out of style. I suspect all of this is unconscious. Most people are not aware that they look to familiar patterns or styles for comfort and security.*

Lauren: *Definitely. I would say that is pretty spot-on.*

Dawnn: *When we are not feeling confident, it's usually because our sense of security is shaken, right? Stripes are what grounds you, what centers you; they bring you back to who you are. Whether* you're in sixth grade, a grown-up editor . . . Whatever your role is — as a daughter, as a student, as a professional — stripes are your foundation, your security. They represent essentially who you are. Now you're in the fashion world, where you actually have access to a plethora of clothing, but you still go back to this pattern, which is interesting, right? My impression is that someone who likes stripes may be good at multitasking, and may have a lot going on in her life. She's someone who wears many hats, plays many roles, and is good at balancing it all. What stripes do is create some order if you are feeling overwhelmed, even if you are someone who works well under pressure.

Lauren: *That definitely makes sense. But am I not being inventive with outfits if I keep going back to the same pattern? Even if it's something comfortable for me and makes me feel my best, is it perceived as a weakness if I keep relying on the same pattern over and over again? Honestly, I have so many striped things that I haven't even shared with you. I have striped shirts packed away for the summer, more stripes in a suitcase under my bed. It's a lot.*

Dawnn: *Look, it's only a problem if you can never, ever, ever wear anything but stripes. You're actually using this pattern to empower yourself. I'm not going to advise you to do away with something that gives you confidence. That would be crazy. That would be like telling a guy not to wear a business suit to a job interview. Taking away something that makes you feel secure is not going to make you feel better. You look great in stripes! Now that you know what they do for you psychologically, I would actually encourage you to turn to them when they can be helpful. Say you're stressed out or you had a terrible day. I would say, "Go home and wear those stripes! Just put 'em on." There's nothing wrong with finding comfort in our clothing. It's like when you were a child and you had your favorite teddy bear or blankie.*

Well, as adults, we're not allowed to have teddy bears and blankies; we can't carry those things to work. But what do we have? Our clothing. Stripes offer security for you. Use that.

As a Fashion Psychologist, I do not see it as my role to tell Lauren, "Oh my God, you should not wear stripes anymore because your mom says you wear too many. And look, you're wearing them five days a week." That's the makeover ideology from decades ago, when experts would put people in front of a 360-degree mirror and berate them, then the glam squad comes in and voilà, they walk out and don't even recognize themselves. As I told Lauren, my job is to get to the root of why you wear what you wear. And then, if you want to introduce some new patterns, go for it. But my first goal was to empower her, and to highlight how stripes are working for her. I did, however, give Lauren some homework.

Style Rx

I asked Lauren, going forward for the rest of the week following our session, to assess how she feels when she wears stripes versus how she feels when she doesn't, to draw some comparisons. I advised her to ask herself in the morning, before her feet hit the floor, Am I going to wear stripes today because I'm in this particular mood? Or, Am I not going to wear stripes today because I'm in this particular mood? Once she gets a clearer understanding of when she needs her stripes most, she can identify other days when she might feel emboldened to branch out.

- - - - - - - - -

To paraphrase Lauren's question, is having a Repetitious Wardrobe Complex a good thing or a bad thing? Is wearing the same thing over and over solving a problem or creating one? Are your wardrobe choices consistent or compulsive, disciplined or disordered? "Paralysis in the decision-making process" (as Dr. Margalit put it) due to too many clothing choices may lead you to reach for the same tired old outfits over and over and over again. This is different from having a signature style or fashion uniform because it is a passive, defeated decision, not an active, empowered one.

As with any other habitual behavior, a lot comes down to how repetitious clothing choices are impacting your life. Are you able to stop wearing the same look repeatedly? Do you wear it every single day? Or is it merely a go-to that you lean on for a sense of security as needed? Are your looks a variation on a theme? Lauren has striped tops in many different styles and cuts, from polo shirts to bodysuits, and pairs them with a variety of bottoms, keeping her rotation looking fresh. Repetition is problematic only when it impedes your happiness, productivity, relationships, growth, or well-being. If wearing a tightly edited, remixable collection of clothes makes you happy, gives you confidence and control, cuts down on stress, and increases feelings of ease and efficiency, then uniform dressing is working for you. If, however, you are so entrenched in your routine that it stops you from doing things you want or need to do, then that's a sign your uniform could be an impediment. Let's meet the second "repeat offender" who struggled along these lines.

CASE STUDY: THE GRADUATE

A few years back, I worked with a Brooklyn-based magazine editor in his thirties.[19] He came to me for help revamping his office wardrobe after noticing that—in spite of his sizable clothing collection—he wore khaki pants with a light-blue or pale-yellow button-down shirt every single day without fail, and regardless of the season. He felt boring and unstylish compared to his colleagues. He genuinely wanted to make a change but couldn't seem to let go of his self-imposed uniform. His goal, he said, was to "examine ways that I can break this repetition complex that still feel comfortable." After talking further, we discovered that his workweek rut stemmed from his childhood. He attended a Catholic school for twelve years, where he was required to wear a daily uniform of khakis and a light-colored button-down. Understanding the WHY behind his clothing choices helped him feel more open to considering change. After we worked together, he was able to loosen his grip on his uniform.

Style Rx

I suggested he start small. The first thing we did was go through his closet and find an understated watch with a very subtle red detail. I encouraged him to put it on. In introducing this tiny pop of color, my mission was to gently prove to him that he was capable of wearing something different. I took great care not to shock his system. Adding the watch only slightly changed his usual look, and the difference was nearly imperceptible to outside observers. A bright clothing item or drastically different cut would have pushed him too far out of his comfort zone, creating undue anxiety and self-doubt. The watch turned out to be enough to make him feel like he was out of his rut. To this day he still wears the same uniform. The work we did together was more of a soul-searching exercise. Introducing that watch showed him that he was capable of disrupting his pattern, if he so desired. He did not need to publicize his effort or walk into the office a new man. He proved something to himself — that he was not a prisoner of his khakis; that his uniform was a choice but not a requirement.

- - - - - - - - -

I'm really into self-affirmation, mindfulness, and meditation. I believe in rituals. They are one of the best anxiety-busters around, and they have been for millennia (see: religion). Repeated, ritualistic behaviors like my morning check-in, or your nightly skincare regimen, or a child's bedtime routine "buffer against uncertainty by evoking a sense of personal control and orderliness," writes psychologist and neuroscientist Dr. Nick Hobson in *Psychology Today*. Rituals create calm because they "trick the brain into thinking that it's experiencing the pleasant state of predictability and stability." The more regularly we perform our rituals, the more powerful they become. And it doesn't take long: Research shows new habits may take root in as little as four days.[20]

For those who benefit from Repetitious Wardrobe Complex, there is freedom to be found in uniform dressing. If you often stand in front of your closet wishing a Hollywood stylist would just magically appear and tell you what to wear, you may love having a style system. But what does it feel like when repetition goes wrong? If the thought of wearing anything new or outside your comfort zone fills you with dread, that could be cause for concern. If you hesitate to attend a formal event such as a wedding or your spouse's office holiday party because it would require you to dress up or modify your look, that's a red flag. If you have been wearing the same clothes or styles over and over for years and feel locked in, if you fear something bad will happen if you change, that's unhealthy. If you ignore shifting fashion norms entirely or otherwise disassociate from your physical self, then Repetitious Wardrobe Complex may be veering into disordered territory and should be addressed with a competent, experienced mental health professional.[21]

Those who are hurt by Repetitious Wardrobe Complex tend to see clothes as an inescapable burden; their role in your life takes on exaggerated significance. Redundant clothing and decision avoidance can be — but are certainly not necessarily — symptoms of obsessive-compulsive disorder. In general, people with Repetitious Wardrobe Complex gravitate toward certain pieces of clothing because those items feel safe and familiar. This becomes a negative only if you feel stuck in a rut, like your clothes are holding you back from living life to the fullest. Remember: It's only something *good* that bears repeating.

CURATION SENSATION: THE ART OF DOING MORE WITH LESS

As Vivienne Westwood has said, "Buy less, choose well, make it last. Quality not quantity."[22] Having a style uniform doesn't make you boring. It makes you iconic. Coco Chanel had a uniform. So do Janelle Monáe, Reese Witherspoon, Erykah Badu, Tilda Swinton, and Kate Moss. Think of fashion designers like Carolina Herrera in her trademark white button-down and ball gown skirts, or Alexander Wang in his black t-shirt and leather pants. Uniforms work for those tastemakers, and yet they never look stale. Not surprisingly, designers who latch on to the idea of paring down our wardrobes and streamlining our lives are finding more commercial success than ever before. When Eileen Fisher, who famously created a "system" of clothes built on eight key pieces, first moved to New York, she was overwhelmed by trying to look the part of a fashion designer. "I was struggling to put myself together," she told the *New York Times*. "I felt clothes were too complicated, especially women's clothes, always changing. I just needed to look good, and I needed to not think too much about it."[23]

Looking good without thinking too much about it. That, my friend, is living the dream. In 2013, a young corporate executive named Sarah LaFleur felt a frustration similar to Fisher's. So she partnered with the former head designer of Zac Posen and created a line of expertly tailored mix-and-match boardroom basics. She based her brand, MM.LaFleur, on the notion that "for some women, buying clothes is just not a priority for one reason or another, but it doesn't mean that they don't care about good style or looking elegant." She was onto something. MM.LaFleur grew a whopping 600 percent from 2014 to 2015.[24] Clothing line Cuyana also skyrocketed from obscurity to household name with the tagline "Fewer, better things." And the red-hot line AYR stands for All Year Round. Its philosophy? "We design season-less apparel for everyday life." What have all these blockbuster brands capitalized on? *Less is more.*

As the poet Rumi reportedly wrote, "Life is a balance of holding on and letting go." This is a profound truth—and seriously great advice for editing your closet. Picture an uncluttered clothing rack showcasing just the following: a crisp white button-down, a striped boatneck top, a soft neutral turtleneck, a long cardigan, a skinny leopard belt, an LBD, a dark pair of jeans, a pair of flattering black trousers, a blazer, a trench coat, and a winter jacket of your choice (puffer, teddy bear, wool swing coat, etc.), chic flats, fierce heels, classic leather boots. Full stop.

There are two reasons this image seems so soothing:

1. Everything goes with everything else. All elements can be mixed and remixed in appealing ways. For example:
   o Cardigan + leopard belt at waist + black trousers + heels
   o White button-down tucked into black trousers + trench + ballet flats
2. Its finite possibilities. Having fewer clothes but loving the ones you do have is the key to calm. Less choice = less stress.

HOW TO DO AN EXPERT CLOSET EDIT

Fashion Psychology Tip

Cristóbal Balenciaga once said, "Elegance is elimination."[25] To dress well, **it's not about what you buy; it's about what you get rid of.**

Elimination diets are super-popular nowadays. The idea is you cut out any and all foods with the potential to upset or inflame your system. Then you slowly add foods back in, so you can instantly recognize and remove the culprits that make you feel terrible. Well, the methodology here is strikingly similar.

Step 1: If it's not a hell yes, it's a no. Ruthlessly edit out any clothes that don't fit, are falling apart, or make you uncomfortable in *any* way.

Maybe that sweater is itchy. Maybe that skirt gives you muffin top. Maybe you never got around to replacing that blouse's missing button. There's a reason you aren't wearing these things. They make you feel less than your best. Dump them like toxic friends. No mercy.

Step 2: Last chance any items you're on the fence about. You know that famous pearl of wisdom that says, *If you haven't worn it in a year, get rid of it?* Instead, I give myself one final week to wear my benched items, just to see if I can remix them in a fresh way. If, once their week is up, they still fail to inspire, they're officially expired.

Step 3: Notice any themes emerging? Once you do a rigorous elimination, you will be left only with pieces you truly love — clothes you feel great in, that are comfortable, that befit your present lifestyle — not your idealized past, not your fantasy future when you lose ten pounds. I have a hunch most of those clothes will share a common aesthetic.

Step 4: Hang similar items together to identify redundancies. This way you can see what you need to shop for — if anything. You knew you were nuts for striped tops. Did you realize you owned eight? Maybe you can't resist a high-waist trouser. Which is obvious from the six pairs you have hanging there. Or you never met a floral print you didn't fall for. That explains why your closet looks like the botanical gardens. Use all of this to inform — or cancel — your next shopping trip.

Fashion Psychology Tip

HOW TO BUILD A CAPSULE WARDROBE

The clothes you are left with after you edit out all the noise will be the building blocks of your "brand." But don't panic if, at the end of the editing process, you are faced with a problem. You may end up with way too many tops and hardly any pants. You may have kept all of your drop-dead-gorgeous formal dresses but have nothing left to wear on the weekends. If you find yourself in this situation, you may need to (temporarily) rescue *a few* items from the reject pile while you save money to fill in the holes. Or you may decide to revive those castoffs by mixing them with unexpected elements. If you do shop for a few updated items, remember: You are not dressing a new you. You are dressing you now.

The typical definition of a Capsule Wardrobe hinges on having a set number of items (I've seen the number thirty-six mentioned online) in a limited color palette so that everything goes together. To this I say, Oh hell no. You do not need to get that formulaic. But I do believe in the basic principle of creating lots of outfits out of only a few key pieces.

For me, building a successful Capsule Wardrobe means satisfying three basic requirements:

- **Versatile pieces:** As I mentioned, I'm a big fan of layering. I make sure I have pieces that can be worn on their own *as well as* under/ over each other. As long as a piece flatters me and expresses my personality, I don't pay much attention to seasonality, since I can always add a camisole underneath or outerwear for warmth.

- **Low numbers:** Personal style is subjective. The majority of my items pop, and then I have a smaller supply of all-black foundational basics (leggings, t-shirts, etc.). You may prefer a quieter color palette and subtler prints than I do. But no matter what you like, you simply don't need to be drowning in clothes. It really is a numbers game. The goal is to own *no more than two* of the same type of individual item. Bear in mind that a long-sleeve black t-shirt is different from a short-sleeve black t-shirt. But unless they are a cornerstone of your uniform, you probably don't need multiples of each.

- **Fulfill each category:** The specific styles, cuts, fabrics, colors, and silhouettes you want to own depend on you: your body type, your professional dress code, your favorite icons, your preferences. It's the *categories* that are universal. Everyone needs **foundation elements** (tops and bottoms), **outerwear** (sweaters, jackets, coats), **special occasion clothes** (dresses, skirts), and **accessories** (shoes, jewelry, belts, hats, etc.).

Consider your lifestyle. Someone who works from home may not need a ball gown skirt. Someone who works with kids may not need a huge selection of sexy party dresses and may prefer to invest in jeans. I love straight-leg trousers. You may love palazzo pants or high-waist flares. My number one goal for you is to redefine what it means to have "enough." To bring this idea to life, let's open up the doors to my closet so you can see exactly what—and how little—I actually own.

INSIDE MY CLOSET I HAVE...

Category 1: Foundation Elements

5 pairs of black leggings. They can be dressed up or down, worn as pajamas or workout gear. (Versatility.)

5 black t-shirts: 2 sleeveless, 2 short-sleeve, 1 long-sleeve. (Low numbers.)

1 black turtleneck. (Low numbers, versatility as it can be dressed up or down.)

3 pairs of skinny-fit straight-leg trousers in white, orange, and blue. Mine are by Massimo Dutti. (Seasonless and versatile.)

5 button-down blouses in various prints and colors: 1 leopard print, 1 pale orange to match the orange pants, 1 turquoise to match the blue pants, 1 white to match the white pants, and 1 hot pink. When I do the color-blocking trend, I pair the pink blouse with my orange trousers. (Seasonless and versatile.)

2 matching outfits: One is a floral-print blouse with matching pants by
Ann Taylor. The other is a Versace-inspired paisley print in primary colors. All four of these elements (2 tops, 2 pairs of pants) can
be worn separately or together. For a recent TV appearance, I put
a white cape over the paisley outfit and accessorized with caramel-
colored heels and a matching handbag. (Seasonless and versatile.)

1 pair of jeans. (Low numbers.)

Category 2: Special Occasion Clothes

1 floor-length ball gown skirt. Can be worn with a casual t-shirt or
dressed up with a formal top and heels. (Low numbers, seasonless
and versatile.)

5 body-con date-night dresses in various colors and fabrics. I love
architectural necklines or off-the-shoulder styles. I'll sometimes
tuck a minidress into pants so that only the bodice shows, treating it like a bodysuit. Layering alert! (Versatile.)

1 colorful sparkly floor-length gown with a tie-front bodice from
Zara. I might wear it with a long-sleeve tee over it, to create the
illusion of a separate maxi skirt. (Layering, versatility.) It is fancy
enough for a formal affair if worn with heels, but with a floppy
straw hat, it works as a casual summer dress. (More versatility
and seasonlessness.)

Category 3: Outerwear

2 dramatic capes: 1 white, 1 leopard. (Low numbers, layering.)

1 black poncho sweater to transition between seasons, to wear for
comfort. (Versatility, layering.)

1 black-and-gold brocade robe. It adds elegance to an all-black foundation of leggings and a t-shirt. (Layering.)

1 denim jacket to wear on its own or to pair with jeans for the
denim-on-denim "Canadian tuxedo" look. (Versatility, low
numbers.)

Category 4: Accessories

- 1 pair of black block-heel sandals for warm weather or formal evenings
- 3 pairs of pumps: 1 black, 1 gold, 1 caramel
- 3 funky pairs: leopard-print heels, strappy sandals with pom-pom embellishments, 1 pair of rhinestone heels for weddings. All by Aldo.

I also own a small collection of delicate jewelry, belts, investment handbags, and the aforementioned floppy straw hat.

Here's one final tip that may make you feel less frightened to live with less: Once you've edited your wardrobe down to the MVPs, you can jazz up your looks with attention-grabbing extras—jewelry, hats, handbags, belts, shoes—to your heart's content. Like adding spice to a dish, a little dash of bold fashion goes a long way. A study in the *Journal of Consumer Research* calls this "The Red Sneakers Effect."[26] In the study, observers responded positively to individuals who only *slightly* challenged the status quo with their style. When someone's outfit featured a small flourish, like a tuxedo with a red bow tie instead of a black one, or Converse sneakers with formal attire or in a professional setting, that individual was perceived as more competent and higher status than someone who dressed exactly as expected. "The results suggest that people judge these slight deviations from the norm as positive," reports *Scientific American,* "because they suggest that the individual is powerful enough to risk the social costs of such behaviors."[27] Translation? Be just a little bit extra.

THE BOTTOM LINE

KEY TIPS AND TAKEAWAYS FROM CHAPTER 4

- Keep a digital file or **"catalog" of selfies** documenting every outfit you love. Pick your day-to-day looks from this pre-planned collection, according to the mood you find yourself in.

- **Identify your signature style.** Find an icon to emulate, whether it's a celeb, vintage photos of your mom in the '70s, or a social media influencer, then edit your closet accordingly. Let go of items that fall outside of this framework.

- **Spot the common thread.** Hang the same types of clothes together in your closet (white button-downs, black pants, floral dresses—all together now). Notice any redundancies? Resell or donate excess items. Then notice: What do your favorite clothes have in common? Spend a week wearing only what you *absolutely love* and see if themes emerge. Notice what colors, cuts, prints, and fabrics make you feel amazing.

- **Less is more.** Aim to own no more than two of the same type of item. (Do you really need *five* pairs of black pants?)

- **Style, slay, repeat.** If you are reluctant to repeat your looks, think about the gendered and societal forces fueling that fear. Remember: People are more likely to notice you for looking fashionable than for wearing the same thing twice!

- When building a Capsule Wardrobe, **keep your numbers low and versatility high.** Look for seasonless pieces that can be remixed and layered. As long as you fulfill the four key wardrobe categories (basics, formalwear, outerwear, and accessories), you'll be good to go.

Chapter 5

MOOD MATTERS

Fashion has to reflect who you are, what you feel at the moment, and where you're going.

—*Pharrell Williams*

Clothes are a mood-altering substance. Your clothes affect your mental state, for better and for worse. Look down at what you have on today. Does what you are wearing reflect the way you truly felt when you woke up this morning? Or were you thinking of a big presentation you had to give, a person you were hoping to impress, a comment someone once made about your appearance? Perhaps you gave zero thought at all to your outfit. You just threw something on to get it over and done with, because what you *really* wanted to do this morning was crawl back into bed. Let me ask it this way: How has your look served you so far today? Was your dress digging into you at your desk? Were you dying to rip it off the second you got home? Did you feel boring and basic in your go-to gray sweater? Or sunny and optimistic in your yellow dress? Has your outfit helped you today? Or has it hurt or held you back in some way?

I believe in styling from the inside out because what we wear on our outsides has a real effect on our insides. Research can explain this. In her blockbuster book about the mind-body connection, *Presence*, Harvard social psychologist Amy Cuddy includes a chapter called "The Body Shapes the Mind (So Starfish Up!)." In it she writes, "The way we carry ourselves from moment to moment blazes the trail our lives take." After conducting groundbreaking research on body language, Cuddy explains how power posing—expanding the body, standing tall, with hands on hips, feet spread apart, taking up maximum physical space—can actually convince us we *are* powerful. In one study, Cuddy and her colleagues asked participants to hold power poses for a minute. The researchers tested their subjects' saliva both before and after they posed. And by looking at the hormones associated with confidence (testosterone) and stress (cortisol), they discovered that this simple act of power posing actually increased the former and reduced the latter. These researchers proved that if your body acts out a story, your mind will believe it.[1] If a power pose can achieve this, then why not a power suit?

Believing that you are taking good care of yourself by dressing nicely (however it is that you define "nicely") can actually help you feel good about yourself. We see these concepts proliferating within pop culture every day in the self-care movement. Self-care is a booming business and a social media phenomenon not because we all *need* to have glittery sheet masks for our booties or to soak in $50 bath salts at the end of a hard day. Self-care sells because we feel better when we *believe* we are taking good care of ourselves. Simple as that. Dressing up is self-care. Placebo medicine, power posing, double-cleansing K-beauty skincare regimes, quartz-crystal-infused water bottles, bullet journaling, and scented candles—all of these props and practices have parallels to the Mood-Based Dressing concepts I'll outline in this chapter. Experts have proved the body shapes the mind. Put on a clean, crisp shirt and you will feel clean and crisp. You are worthy. Dress like it and you're likelier to believe it.

Here's another example of how this idea plays out in society. Managers at Swiss bank UBS caught a lot of flak a decade ago when they sent their employees a forty-four-page dress code manifesto instructing them in everything from acceptable grooming habits (no black nail polish, no strong perfume) to appropriate jewelry (earrings only). This employee style handbook included the lines "A flawless appearance can bring inner peace and a sense of security" and "Adopting impeccable behavior extends to impeccable presentation." Also, "The garment is a critical form of non-verbal communication."[2] I'm not nearly that restrictive (I love me a bangle bracelet and a big cocktail ring), but I have to admit those boss bankers made some strong points. There is plenty of evidence to support the notion that our outer appearance plays a part in determining our self-perception and performance. And that, my friends, is precisely why it's so important to pay serious attention to what we wear.

Outfits set expectations, especially for women. It's been suggested that we have stronger reactions than men to what we put on our bodies because we internalize so many messages about how we are "supposed" to look. In a famous study published in the *Journal of Personality and Social Psychology*, a group of women were asked to try on swimsuits and then take a math test. A different group of women were asked to try on *sweaters* and then take the math test. The group that had tried on the swimsuits performed much more poorly on the test than the sweater-clad group. The title of the study? "That Swimsuit Becomes You: Sex Differences in Self-Objectification, Restrained Eating, and Math Performance." The authors, including noted psychologist and researcher Jean M. Twenge, concluded that because American women are socialized to internalize outside perspectives on their physical appearance, they then self-objectify. This, they theorize, "consume[s] attentional resources, which is mani-fested in diminished mental performance."[3] It's pretty clear that anyone who is *not* burdened by these cultural beauty standards would have the advantage of optimal, undistracted mental performance. The researchers also asked different groups of men to try on swimsuits or sweaters, then take the math test. Guess what? The swimsuit effect diminished mental performance *for women only*. This confirms what you already know: Obsessing negatively about your looks and internalizing culturally driven body shame literally depletes your intellectual resources.

What would happen if you applied those resources elsewhere, like at work, or with your family, or toward improving your health or learning a new skill? As sociologist and women's studies professor Dr. Gail Dines is widely reported to have said, "If tomorrow, women woke up and decided they really liked their bodies, just think how many industries would go out of business."[4] Hyper-critical focus on your perceived physical flaws comes with a real cost—psychological and professional. It steals your attention, your emotional and intellectual reserves. This study is so important because it confirms two things:

1. Our clothes impact how we feel about ourselves, which has a very real effect on our performance.
2. Style offers a way to take advantage of this, flip it, and reverse it. If you know you need to perform well, wear something that helps you do it.

I love this quote from Oprah: "You get in life what you have the courage to ask for."[5] What if we translate that to clothes? You get in life what you have the courage to dress for. Whatever you wear, your mood will sink or rise to match it. You'll get the kind of day you have the courage to dress for. If you don't feel you deserve to shine, and you present yourself accordingly, the world is far less likely to treat you like the badass/boss b——/glamazon/(insert power moniker here) you are. Why? Because YOU won't feel you deserve the very best treatment and thus you won't demand it from the world. What you wear can elevate your mood or bring you down, comfort or discomfit you. It's your call. It's not about spending tons of money to look amazing. It's about wearing whatever the hell makes you feel that way.

Mood-based Fashion Psychology says dress your best, and the rest will follow. Taking your emotional pulse before you approach your closet, thoughtfully selecting your look from a smaller batch of pre-edited options, shopping intentionally (not mindlessly or frantically or to fill an emotional void), caring for your garments so they are freshly cleaned, wearing something that's even slightly more special than what's called for or expected—these are all ways to send yourself the message that you deserve to be treated well. The better you believe you look, the better you will feel.

In this chapter I'm going to show you how your clothes influence your mood, and how to use them to inspire a good one. But first, to bring to life the mind-body connection or, more specifically, the clothing-psyche connection, I want to introduce you to a client. She is a perfect example of someone whose clothes are telling her story. Style is a symptom of her problems—but it is also an integral part of the solution. Her outfits are deeply connected to her outlook, and she's on the cusp of transforming both. Let's meet her.

Amber* is struggling with her self-image. She is in her mid-thirties and works from home, which means she is alone much of the time. Having gained a lot of weight in the past decade, she's now in the process of reclaiming her health.

CASE STUDY: THE COVER-UP

Dawnn: *Let's talk about your body image journey. How did you used to dress, how do you dress now, and how are you feeling about yourself?*

Amber: *Well, about six months ago I started doing the keto diet, so I've been dropping weight kind of drastically. I really can't say I ever had a particular style. Most of the clothes I choose are to cover up my stomach. I don't have an hourglass shape. I have more of a "boyfriend body." That's what I heard Tyra Banks call it on her show. I have slim hips, and my stomach comes out around the same size as my hips. So even with the weight loss, I'm a little nervous about what to wear.*

Dawnn: *What kinds of clothes do you feel flatter your midsection?*

Amber: *I have gotten comfortable with wearing big t-shirts. I love fall, because I'm able to layer. I'm a leggings, tank top, and* cardigan girl. Leggings have become my best friend. So if you look in my closet and find twenty pairs of black leggings, don't be alarmed. That's just what I've been wearing because of the weight I gained these past few years. But leggings lie to you and make you think you're still a certain size because they don't hurt when you're putting them on.

Dawnn: *As opposed to jeans? Because if you've gained weight, you can physically feel it because it hurts to button jeans up?*

Amber: *Yes, exactly. I gave up all my jeans. After I got past a size twelve, I decided jeans were uncomfortable because they wouldn't stretch when I was eating. I am an emotional eater. I'm working through that. The leggings don't do anything for my shape. They're just comfortable. I would say my style is comfort.*

Dawnn: *So your go-to uniform is leggings, a tank top, and a cardigan. This helps you feel less self-conscious because you're able to cover up with layers?*

Amber: *Yes. When I wear that type of outfit I do feel less self-conscious. Especially compared with how I feel in the summertime, because you can't really hide. This past summer, I fell into a depression because I stopped wanting to go places. I didn't want anyone to see me. Especially if I go out and see people from high school and they're expecting to see the chick they knew back then. I just never wanted to be that girl. Like, "Oh, she's a has-been." I didn't want to look funny to them. It made me feel bad. So I've stayed in the house a lot because of that.*

Dawnn: *It sounds like this is affecting your ability to socialize. Do you feel isolated?*

Amber: *I DO feel isolated. That's crazy.*

Dawnn: *Why do you say that's crazy?*

Amber: *Because you caught that. I never really put that word to the way I feel. I definitely feel isolated. Thankfully, a lot of my* confidence is coming back through my weight loss. I've lost about twenty pounds so far. I'm hopeful that my confidence could come back, and I'll be able to crawl back out of this hole I put myself in with food and comfort clothes.

Dawnn: *What do you wear during the summer when you can't wear your go-to uniform?*

Amber: *I wear yoga pants. They're not exactly leggings; they're lighter. I'll wear those with t-shirts, tennis shoes, or sandals. I always look like I'm going to work out when in actuality I haven't seen the inside of a gym in forever.*

Dawnn: *It sounds like you have an athleisure look. Does wearing athletic attire motivate you to want to work out or eat healthier?*

Amber: *No, because it's not the cute athletic gear. I go to places like Target or Walmart and just pick out a pair of black yoga pants. They're easy. You can re-wear them a lot. But that's not what I really want. When I am comfortable with the way my body looks in clothes or when I can fit into a pair of jeans comfortably, I don't want to just be in the athleisure category. I want to be able to look good. I want to be able to wear high-waist pencil skirts without a kangaroo pouch hanging over the top.*

Dawnn: *You are making really impressive strides with the keto diet. Do you plan to continue? What's your ultimate goal?*

Amber: *My ultimate goal is to lose sixty pounds. I want to get back down to one fifty. I have a way to go, but that's when I want to be done with the athletic clothing.*

Dawnn: *What will you wear then?*

Amber: *Summer dresses used to be a go-to for me. I never considered myself very stylish, but I like summer dresses because I don't have to put anything together.*

Dawnn: *Right. They're effortless. But they also don't allow you to hide yourself.*

Amber: *Yes.*

Dawnn: *I want to offer you some advice. Do not beat yourself up if you have a cheat day or if you fall off the wagon with your diet. You are human. You said you are an emotional eater. I think you need to address your emotions before the rest falls into place. I wonder if because you are isolating yourself, you're experiencing more negative emotions that you are then trying to soothe with food . . . Could your isolation be triggering your emotional eating?*

Amber: *It's definitely possible. It is harder when I'm alone and not talking to anyone to stay accountable or strict about my diet.*

Dawnn: *I would encourage you to watch out for these periods of isolation. When you feel isolated, are there friends you can call who know what you look like now and accept you as you are? Make every effort to hang out with those friends. Your emotional eating leads you to comfort dress, but the isolation is at the root of everything. I would encourage you to wear whatever makes you comfortable until you feel ready to pull those summer dresses back out.*

Amber: *I get that completely.*

So what exactly is going on with Amber? Right out of the gate I observed she is **Mood Illustrating** with her comfort clothes, but unfortunately, the mood she's perpetuating is sub-optimal. She's also experiencing **Fashion Incongruence.** She's wearing workout clothes but not working out. She is in her thirties but is focused on an idealized past (her high school self) and a fantasy future (how she'll dress when she loses weight). She is choosing to stay home alone rather than risk being judged, furthering depressive feelings that trigger her emotional eating and lock her in to her yoga pants (**Repetitious Wardrobe Complex**).

On the positive side, Amber is currently taking decisive action to meet her weight loss goals (the keto diet). And she already owns the clothes she plans to wear once those goals are realized. If she said something like "I can't wait to go out and buy pencil skirts and summer dresses once I lose the weight . . ." but was taking zero action to achieve those goals, there would be other issues to address.

Style Rx

Given her weight loss, Amber's body is still changing. Rather than advise her to wear different clothes immediately, I suggested she first work on healing the most urgent emotional problem *that is within her power to address*: her social isolation. That, coupled with her continued health progress, will likely improve her confidence and her mood, leading her to illustrate it with a wider, more stylish variety of clothing. I would also encourage her not to get so hung up on the number on the scale. Her summer dresses beckon as a motivator, but I am willing to bet that as soon as she starts to surround herself with more accepting friends and continues to take better care of herself physically, she'll find the confidence to wear those dresses regardless of how much weight she actually loses.

What's the lesson? I've spoken from my own personal post-assault experience about putting on great clothes to elevate my mood, and feeling better (at least in the short term) as a result. But you still need to do the emotional heavy lifting. Dressing better alone is not going to bring about lasting change. You'll need to reckon with your emotions eventually in order to make your style evolution stick.

- - - - - - - - -

IT ALL STARTS WITH YOU

As you read on, I want you to keep this fundamental idea at the forefront of your mind: You have to dress for internal factors *before* you ever consider external ones. What do I mean by external forces? Social media trends; the endless deluge of new seasonal clothing collections or "exclusive drops" hitting stores; the expectations of your friends, family, and colleagues; the approval of some type of looming authority figure like a boss; an event's dress code; etc. (See chapter 8, "Are You Dressing for Yourself or for Someone Else?") All of those things matter. But they matter *less* than how your clothes make you feel. You can dress to *reflect* how you feel when you wake up in the morning or dress to *change* the way you feel, or to make yourself feel better, as long as you dress for yourself *first*. If it's freezing cold outside and you want to wear lime green, wear it. Being "overdressed" (too fancy) or "underdressed" (too casual) is less dangerous than misalignment between your mental state and your clothing choices. The worst thing you can do is force yourself to wear something that is at odds with how you're feeling. These ideas form the foundation of Mood-Based Dressing.

I know I sound like a broken record, guys, but I can't emphasize enough the value of an early morning check-in to assess your mood. We are deeply emotional creatures. But in my experience, most of us don't acknowledge our feelings until they reach a boiling point of anger or debilitating melancholy. Like an ice cube that keeps bobbing up to the top of a water glass, even though we tend to push down hard things, they keep fighting to float to the surface. Rather than suppressing your feelings morning after morning, what if you made acknowledging them a daily habit, like brushing your teeth? Don't wait until you're about to have a panic attack before you become aware of your mood. Take a good hard look at how you feel (or how you *want* to feel) and then dress accordingly.

When I wake up on rainy days, I tend to feel melancholy. There are days when I decide to roll with that feeling, when it feels right to stay in that zone — to keep myself calm, neutral, and relaxed. When I feel a bit fragile or down, I often don't want to wear clothes that rock the boat. But there are other days when I actually *do* want to modify my mental state, to feel a bit more chipper, so on those days, I look for bright or perhaps sequined clothes to boost my mood. Noticing this behavior led me to break down my Mood-Based Dressing theory into the two key categories I introduced in chapter 1: Mood Illustration Dress and Mood Enhancement Dress.

> **Mood Illustration Dress** means dressing to match your mood, to maintain your equilibrium, to not push yourself, to stay even-keeled, to perpetuate your current emotional state.
>
> **Mood Enhancement Dress** means dressing to change your mood for the better.

At first this can seem a little tricky to apply in real life. Stay with me. Mood Illustration Dress does not necessarily mean pulling on cozy sweats. You could be feeling like a supermodel and want to illustrate that with an envelope-pushing look, like I did with my leopard and floral formalwear at the FIT gala I described in chapter 4. If you are feeling bold and powerful, then wearing a bold and powerful outfit is illustrating that mood. If I'm feeling hot before a date, I'll put on a red minidress and gold heels. You can dress to draw attention to yourself and still be Mood Illustrating.

Mood Enhancement Dress simply means dressing to feel better. You may be feeling totally overstimulated, frenetic, and stressed out after a long day at work or with your kids. (Or hell, you may wake up feeling that way!) In this case you could choose to *enhance* your mood with those cozy sweats. Enhancing your mood *can* mean dressing to calm yourself down. As long as you are dressing to feel better, and not to stay the same, you are Mood Enhancing. I practice this all the time in my personal life. I suffer from anxiety. When I go to therapy, I cocoon myself in black leggings and a long sweater so soft it might as well be a snuggly blanket. When I'm feeling anxious at home, I reach for a silk kimono or an oversize fleece men's robe. I notice that when I wear one, my anxiety decreases, my appetite improves, and I'm calmer. My robes offer comfort. Mood Enhancement simply means taking your mood from bad to better. That doesn't necessarily mean from sweats to high fashion. Think of it this way: Your mood is the symptom and your clothes are the remedy.

Now, you may worry that dressing to change your mood will breed feelings of incongruence or inauthenticity. I'll delve much deeper into that in chapter 8. But for now I'll say this: Dressing to Mood Enhance does not create incongruence because it's an active choice you are making to change the way you look and feel for the better. We suffer from incongruence when we dress for external factors—to fit in, to avoid ostracism, to please others—and negate our own needs.

When I discussed these theories on NPR, my interviewer asked me an important follow-up question: If the goal is to dress according to your mood when you wake up in the morning, is it then a mistake to lay out your clothes the night before? After all, you don't know how you are going to feel when you wake up. Here's my answer: You most definitely *should* plan your outfits in advance—but plan several options. You must allow for flexibility.

Taking your emotional temperature before you get dressed in the morning is the only surefire way to know whether you would benefit from maintaining or elevating your mood. But staying present can coexist with preparation. I definitely advocate troubleshooting problems in advance. Here's a tip for that.

Fashion Psychology Tip

PREPARE TO SLAY

Preselect two outfit options at night for the next day. Style one that is simpler and more low-key and another that is more colorful, accessorized, textured, or fashion forward. This reduces the likelihood of Decision Fatigue (too many options) while still preserving the opportunity to dress according to mood.

You can dress for your emotional well-being and still be practical. Michelle Obama spoke on the *2 Dope Queens* podcast about the necessity of wardrobe prep. Any given day could find the former FLOTUS meeting with a dignitary, running around with schoolchildren, or doing push-ups on international TV: "So much of fashion was not just *Ooh does it look cute?* but *Am I hugging somebody?*... So you have to think about, *What is your hair doing? Are you sweating?*... *Does the jacket allow you to do push-ups?*... There's a whole other life to black hair, black wardrobe in the public eye."[6] Imagine you are getting ready to go on a job interview, to an office party, or on a first date. In the days before the event, think carefully about how you want to feel in your skin, what your goals are for any social interactions, what types of reactions you hope to elicit from others. Maybe you're thinking... *Comfort is key. I don't want to have to suck it in all morning. I cannot deal with shapewear and still think clearly.* Or *I want to feel glamorous and sexy as hell, all eyes on me.* Or *I want to communicate competence and sophistication.* Ask yourself: Will this outfit generate the types of compliments I hope to receive? Will I spend the entire evening worrying about my cleavage spilling out or my skirt riding up? Will I flop-sweat through this silk shirt? Thinking ahead can be the difference between cool confidence and fashion calamity.

MOOD ILLUSTRATION: DRESSING TO MAINTAIN YOUR EQUILIBRIUM

Some days you don't want to break the mold. And that's okay! I am here to officially give you permission to wear what feels good. Not glamorous or sexy or edgy. Just plain old good enough. Have you ever had a day when you just *know* something is wrong with your outfit? You're unhappy with what you're wearing, and this discomfort morphs into feelings of insecurity. There simply are times when it's better to wear clothes that *match* your mood as opposed to modifying it. If you wake up feeling blah, give yourself a break by wearing a comfortable, easy outfit that will feel relaxed and soothing. (One-piece black jumpsuits, cozy sweaters, figure-flattering high-rise jeans, and classic flats are all great, stylish options.) There's no need to add further worry to your day by forcing yourself into something new, constricting, or overly formal. A tried-and-true outfit you know you can count on, like my all-black airport uniform described in chapter 4, will soothe and relax you. And you can still be totally stylish! This type of Mood Illustration Dress all but guarantees internal-external congruence.

Similarly, if you are feeling confident and energized, ready to conquer the world, don't you dare bring yourself down with boring clothes! If you're in a great mood, illustrate it! You can maintain those upbeat feelings with a glitzy or funky outfit. (See "How to Take a Style Risk" on page 145.) That's Mood Illustration too. As long as you dress the way you feel, you'll own it. I think "Fake it till you make it" is misguided advice. Instead, I'd go with this pearl of wisdom from Dolly Parton: "Find out who you are and do it on purpose."[7]

As I write this, I am practicing Mood Illustration Dress. When I woke up this morning, I was feeling feminine and laid back. I knew I had a day of writing ahead, so I wanted to tap into my spiritual, creative side. I selected my colorful maxi dress. It's freezing outside (the words "Polar Vortex" keep popping up on my news feed), and I have zero intention of going out. But even though I won't be seen by another soul, I'm still dressing the way I feel because I want to maintain my goddess vibes. Dressing this way may not be typical, but it sure does make me feel good.

Lady Gaga also demonstrated Mood Illustration Dressing at *Elle's* 2018 Women in Hollywood gala. That evening, she told her audience that after trying on gown after gown after gown, couture corsets, beaded fabrics, the finest silks, and the most luxurious feathers, she felt sick to her stomach—and desperately sad. At the height of the #MeToo movement, when it seemed like every hour a new public figure was coming forward to name the perpetrator of her sexual assault, Gaga publicly wrestled with the possibility of naming the entertainment industry figure who raped her years ago. (As of this book's publication, she still has not named him publicly.) Then, as she said in her speech, she spotted in the corner of her dressing room a voluminous gray menswear suit by Marc Jacobs, and she began to cry. Here's what she told the crowd (emphasis mine): "In this suit, *I felt like me today*. In this suit, *I felt the truth of who I am well up in my gut*. And then wondering what I wanted to say tonight became very clear to me . . . As a woman who was conditioned at a very young age to listen to what men told me to do, I decided today I wanted to take the power back. Today I wear the pants."[8] On that night, Gaga didn't use clothes to heighten her emotions or alter her mood; she dressed to reveal them. She wasn't performing artifice; she was seeking authenticity.

MOOD ENHANCEMENT DRESS: DRESSING TO LIFT YOURSELF UP

Recently, on her Instagram stories, Congresswoman Alexandria Ocasio-Cortez declared that changing into matching loungewear at the end of a long workday is "the key to productivity." In addition to having a distinct work uniform, she believes that having a pre-set "lounge uniform" conditions the mind to switch from work mode into relaxation mode and combats the chronic stress of the constantly plugged-in professional: "Putting on a pajama set is different from sweats and a t-shirt. It's a tactile and visual signal that you are in 'off' mode," she told her followers. "Plus the conscious decision to put it on helps you switch modes . . . TRUST ME I used to think matching pajamas were corny but they seriously were a game changer."[9] Can I get a hallelujah? Besides crystallizing the benefits of uniform dressing (see chapter 4), AOC's off-duty loungewear is quintessential Mood Enhancement Dressing. The congresswoman wishes to relax, to unwind, to feel better, so she is dressing to ensure that she does. She's aware of how she wants to feel, so she dresses to get herself there. It really is that simple.

Mood Enhancement Dressing simply means selecting clothes that increase your happiness, raise your spirits, and make you feel better, stronger, safer, or more empowered. Much in the same way you cue up a specific playlist to evoke the mood you want to feel, you can dress to cheer yourself up when you're feeling low, energize yourself when you're sluggish, or boost your confidence in anticipation of an important task.

The catch is, this works only if what you put on feels *authentic*. Mood Enhancement Dress isn't simply dressing fancy when you're obligated to. It's using clothes to shift your perspective as needed. A great example would be wearing happy colors to help offset seasonal depression—to literally brighten your outlook. If you're having a tough time emotionally, you might consider dressing not for the way you currently feel but for the way you *want* to feel. (You might enhance your mood with a metallic jacket or shimmering accessories.) If you try this in baby steps by wearing more avant-garde outerwear or small sparkly accessories, you are less likely to feel like a fraud.

Your outfit can help you break out of a mood pattern. Clothes can shift your inner paradigm. I sometimes call this lesson "How to Sasha Fierce–ify your life." That's because no one does Mood Enhancement better than Beyoncé. Although she's long since tapped into a wellspring of realness (see: *Lemonade,* Beychella), back in the day, the admittedly shy star relied on an alter ego named Sasha Fierce to...well...bring the fierceness. This other persona enabled Beyoncé to wild out onstage. Sasha Fierce was fearless. She moved differently from Beyoncé. She sounded different. She certainly dressed different. Sasha Fierce exists only onstage, Beyoncé told Oprah during a TV sit-down: "When you put on the wig and put on the clothes, you walk different...I feel like we all kind of have that thing that takes over." Beyoncé would begin to embody Sasha Fierce moments before she hit the stage, and clothes were necessary to summon her: "Usually when I hear the chords, when I put on my stilettos...Then Sasha Fierce appears, and my posture and the way I speak and everything is different."[10]

Notice how high heels play an integral role in shifting (or enhancing) Beyoncé's mood. Model and green beauty entrepreneur Josie Maran also uses Mood Enhancement Dressing in professional situations. When she appears on QVC to sell her mega-successful organic beauty line, she wears tight, colorful Bebe bandage dresses and high heels that "put me into this personality and character," she once told The Cut. Her TV outfit allows her to "zip up into this other character, this vibrant, fun, charismatic, energetic personality. And I have big hair. I have a philosophy that says big hair equals big sales."[11]

Of course, these are extreme examples. For you and me, Mood Enhancement Dressing doesn't require putting on something skintight or sequined. You don't have to become a costumed character to feel happier. (You also don't want to let your look get too far out of sync with your authentic self.) A little bit goes a long way. Put it this way: Mood Enhancement Dress is like coffee. One cup and you're energized and enlivened. Three cups and you're a shaky mess. It's really that straightforward: Mood Enhancement Dressing simply means wearing whatever lifts you up in the moment. Next time you want to feel better, put on something "special," whether it's a lacy bralette beneath your blazer that no one else will see, or a studded bucket bag to brunch. It's not the price or in-your-face-ness of the look that matters; its effect on you is everything.

CASE STUDY: YOU CAN'T LIE DOWN IN AN LBD

I am currently working with a client named Patricia.* Patricia is in her early fifties and recently lost her job at a nonprofit after-school program working with at-risk youth. This job, which she held for decades, had been a great fit for her. She excelled at it. And she was so invested in her work that over the years, it became a big part of her identity. Then there were budget cuts, and she was downsized and let go. Since she had been working with kids, Patricia's day-to-day uniform was leggings and sweaters with sneakers or flats. Now she's home, unemployed, and still wearing the same clothes she associates with her former job—a reminder of all she's lost. Understandably, wearing these clothes is exacerbating her sense of sadness and failure, and she is becoming depressed. "I'm in my next stage of life," she said during a recent phone call. "All my kids are in college. I'm at home. I'm supposed to still be working. I just have no clue what to do with myself." Thankfully Patricia is not under financial pressure. But she is suffering an identity crisis. She confessed that without her rigorous work schedule, she has begun sleeping all day.

Style Rx

In this chapter's first Case Study, I encouraged Amber to do the emotional work first, before she turned to clothes to modify her mood. For Patricia, because of her sudden job loss, I felt the case was more of an emergency. I could sit there and encourage her to job hunt all day, but because her despondence centered on her unemployment, I worried this was a task she might avoid. I decided to take a different approach, using clothes as a way in. I advised her to dress to Mood Enhance—immediately.

As an exercise, I asked Patricia to wear her favorite daytime dress and the chicest heels she owns, even if she has no plans to leave the house. I told her, "I want you to feel like a woman again, to feel like a human being again, to remember the physical sensations of confidence. Once you are dressed up, see if you can work up the energy to go to a café with your laptop for an hour and take the first steps toward polishing your résumé. Put out one feeler, send one email to someone in your professional network. This will be a process," I told her. "But you should put your old work clothes aside for the time being. You're not going to sleep all day in a little black dress. You cannot lie down in earrings and pumps. If you put on a white button-down shirt, gray slacks, and *black kitten sling-back heels and grab a nice handbag, you're more likely to be on the computer, drinking your coffee, trying to be productive. You'll have a reason to go to that WeWork space or to Starbucks to look for jobs online."*

What's the lesson? Mood Illustrating may not be useful when the mood you're perpetuating is melancholy. Dressing to match her emotions would only compound Patricia's deteriorating self-esteem, but Mood Enhancement Dressing just might improve it.

- - - - - - - - -

RISKY BUSINESS

I'm a big believer in exposure therapy. This is when a therapist creates a controlled, safe environment wherein she gradually exposes the patient to the things (objects, activities, situations) she fears and avoids. The purpose is to prove to the patient that the consequences she fears are unlikely to occur, and to show her what she is capable of, ultimately improving her quality of life. One example is asking someone who fears public speaking to give a speech in front of a friendly prepared audience. This helps the patient confront and overcome her anxiety.[12]

When we apply this to style, it means wearing something you find exciting, even if it makes you a little nervous. You might prove to yourself that nothing terrible will happen (you will not be laughed at or stared at) if you wear lavender, or sequins, or a skirt. I recently wore a gilded bronze minidress and brown high-heel sandals with leather tassels on the toes. Definitely a riskier look for me — but I toned it down and tied it all together with a creamy brown leather satchel bag. I tried something new, pulled it off, expanded my horizons, and enhanced my mood. I felt fabulous. I can trace this drive to overcome my fears back to my childhood. At my dad's house on the weekends, we would have large family dinners where my brothers and I would be expected to contribute thoughtfully to discussions on current events and politics. After dinner, at random, my father would ask me to sing a cappella in front of my entire family. His goal, I later understood, was to improve my performances and quell my stage fright. This really did help prepare me to speak in front of large audiences today. Taking a fashion risk is similar. You just have to do it, and the more you do it, the more accustomed you get to confronting and conquering your fear. Then comes the confidence. And taking small style risks goes hand in hand with Mood Enhancing. I recently read this incredible quote by singular designer Rei Kawakubo of Comme des Garçons: "You need to occasionally wear something strong, and that can feel strange. It makes you aware of your existence . . . When you put on clothes that are fighting against something [conventional], you can feel your courage grow. Clothing can set you free."[13]

Here are some tips to bring on the bravery.

Fashion Psychology Tips

HOW TO TAKE A STYLE RISK

1. Small things often

Psychologist and relationship guru Dr. John Gottman has a famous motto: "Small things often."[14] His theory is that if you do little nice things for your partner frequently, it will have a stronger cumulative positive effect on your relationship than performing grand dramatic romantic gestures once in a blue moon. This applies to your style as well. Rather than reveal your most glamorous self once a year for that special occasion (remember Sonal in chapter 2 who "unleashed it all" once in a while for weddings?), try to add a touch of glamour to your everyday outfits. Accessories are the safest, simplest way to try new things. Think leopard-print, faux snakeskin, or croc-embossed booties, a pastel leather fanny pack (or "belt bag"), big bold statement earrings, a leather midi skirt paired with a white t-shirt and Adidas Stan Smith sneakers. You might even try tying a high ponytail with a black velvet ribbon and leaving the rest of your outfit super-simple. Classic.

2. Road test your new look on the weekend

Pick a weekend when you have low-key, low-stakes plans. Maybe you're having dinner with your parents or going on a movie date with a girlfriend. That would be the time to bust out those snakeskin booties (leaving the rest of your outfit jeans-and-white-tee neutral) and see if you feel self-conscious.

3. Neutralize bold prints

If you're going to try an animal print, try it in a small, subtle pattern rather than big glitzy spots. A classic navy summer dress with restrained small white polka dots is a safer bet than a white dress with huge black Dalmatian spots. A delicate or abstract floral will feel easier to pull off than bright, oversize buds. When working a plaid blazer, go for a gray houndstooth as opposed to a big black-and-white checkerboard pattern. Quiet graphics still speak volumes.

4. Pick a colorful "hero"

For reasons I'll cover in the next chapter, certain colors stimulate stronger emotional reactions than others. If you have a closet full of black, white, gray, and cream, it can't hurt to branch out, I promise. Opt for pretty pastels in interesting cuts (a lavender sweater with exaggerated shoulders, a long robin's-egg-blue belted blazer, pale-pink palazzo pants). And select one colorful outfit element to start. Think of this as your "hero" item—the star of the show. Keep the rest of your outfit denim or monochrome.

5. Try statement outerwear

A neon puffer coat, a blue faux fur bomber, a leopard overcoat, a gorgeous silk trench. (Even if the color is neutral, the unexpected texture will stand out.) Once again, wear monochrome or jeans and a t-shirt underneath. The beauty of this tip is, if you're uncomfortable with the bold coat, you can always take it off!

FASHION'S HEALING POWER

Fashion critic Robin Givhan was once asked in an interview, "Does fashion have the capacity to influence our mood and emotions?" Her answer? "Absolutely!" She noted that when women need a "pick-me-up," they often look for new shoes or a new lipstick. "It's a manifestation of the fact that people feel better about themselves if they feel they look good."[15] Organizations like Dress for Success and Smart Works (a Meghan Markle–supported UK nonprofit) are so effective because they harness the power of clothes to change perception as we endeavor to show our best selves. These charities provide a key service to millions of disadvantaged women, giving them professional attire and personal shopping assistance. They are so helpful because they *know* looking good can literally change your life.

Dressing well has historically been a potent upper in dark times. UK newspaper columnist Hannah Betts once described shopping for gorgeous clothes as a way to comfort both herself and her mother while the latter was dying of cancer. Recalling how she would show her mother new purchases to admire, she describes how the clothes signified "cheer, undiminished selfdom, and the promise of some different future; it was as much about joy as it was armor." In the same column, Betts points out that after World War II, when victims of the Holocaust were freed from concentration camps, "observers noticed that the mood became more optimistic not with the arrival of food, but lipstick... Only via ornament was a sense of humanity restored."[16]

Being of Jamaican heritage, I have done a deep dive into the mores and meanings of Carnival, the annual Eastertime bacchanal that sees various Caribbean islands electrified by colorful costumes, dancing in the streets, parties, and parades. Carnival has traditionally been a chance to throw off the trappings of slavery; to celebrate—and thus reclaim—the collective body.[17] Caribbean slaves were brutally mistreated. Clothing was used as a tool to reinforce their "inferior" social status, as slaves were forced to literally dress in rags that exposed the ravages and scars of their abuse. They were disrobed, and therefore robbed of their humanity. Attire was also used to distinguish between master and slave, owner and property. Slaves seeking freedom through escape understood clothing was a way to assume agency—not only to look free but also to feel free. Colonization brought embroideries, silks, lace, and cotton to the Caribbean, which translated into the colorful, ornate costumes still worn during Carnival today. Over time, Carnival continued as a way for the descendants of slaves to tend to their bodies, restoring their dignity. Dressing up for Carnival has since been elevated to an art form. Just google Rihanna's annual eye-popping getups in Barbados for evidence. This is not least because donning an elaborate costume involves venerating the body—a daring, defiant act and a colorful countermeasure to the mistreatment the enslaved body endured for so long.

My instinct to dress to the nines in the aftermath of my sexual assault. Women battling grave illness seeking solace and selfhood through beautiful things. The opportunity for delightful dress-up that Carnival confers upon the progeny of the enslaved. All of these acts of reclamation share something with the Japanese art of *kintsugi*. *Kintsugi* is the ancient method of repairing broken pottery with gold, silver, or platinum, illuminating the cracks or fractures in the porcelain with precious metals. This practice dates back to the fifteenth century and, according to historians, celebrates each artifact's unique history by emphasizing where it has been broken, damaged, and scarred, rather than hiding or disguising these marks. *Kintsugi* makes the repaired piece even more beautiful, as it takes on a new, altered form and is given a second life.[18] My hope is that we all may become more beautiful and unique as we heal ourselves. Wearing interesting, exciting clothes is a way of highlighting—not hiding—who we are: Stronger for having been broken. Shining in gold, platinum, and silver.

THE BOTTOM LINE

KEY TIPS AND TAKEAWAYS FROM CHAPTER 5

- **First things first.** Your emotions should be the *first* thing you consider when deciding what to wear. Before trends, dress codes, or the opinions of others.

- **Clothes are a mood-altering substance.** We internalize our outfit's messages. Whether you reach for comforting cotton basics or an energizing cocktail dress, clothes can help take your mood from bad to better.

- **If you're depressed, dress your best.** It's harder to lie down in an LBD, earrings, and heels.

- **Be prepared but present.** Plan out two potential looks the night before an important event or meeting. In the morning, assess your mood, then select the look that best matches or modifies it, as desired.

- **Take bold baby steps.** To take a style risk, start small: Try an unexpected accessory, colorful outerwear, a delicate print or pattern. Road test the look on the weekend, in front of a friendly audience.

Chapter 6

COLORS IN CONTEXT

Can't we just stop pretending that anything is ever going to be the new black?

—*Nora and Delia Ephron*, Love, Loss, and What I Wore

Several years ago I gave a talk at the Kyiv Security Forum in Ukraine. The panel I was on focused on the ways people's subconscious affects how they dress. The moderator, BBC journalist David Eades, joked that he'd given no thought whatsoever to his ensemble that day. But as I explained to him, and to the audience, the bright-red tie he wore actually did communicate a sense of competence, power, and leadership to those around him. Whether he was aware of it or not, he chose that tie for a reason. Meghan Markle—supposedly chafing against the monarchy's stringent style rules—broke royal protocol when she wore black nail polish at the 2018 British Fashion Awards. (Her Majesty Queen Elizabeth exclusively wears a pale pink Essie polish called "Ballet Slippers.") "Mannnn, Meghan Markle DGAF!" tweeted one fan, as reported by *Glamour*. "Black nail polish too? I STAN A GORGEOUS REBEL!"[1] That's a strong reaction for something as subtle as nail polish. And it's a testament to the power of color.

COLOR AS COMMUNICATION

Everyone prefers certain colors over others, and individual preferences can speak volumes about someone's personality and attitude. How do we explain all of this? And how can we use this information to our advantage when we get dressed, to best actualize our intentions? For starters, wouldn't it be great if we could all scroll through some sort of clothing color decoder? Couldn't we all use a handy guide to tell us which hues are best for important life events like job interviews or mother-in-law meet-ups or first dates? Well, that's exactly what this chapter will provide. I've got your colors covered!

In the pages that follow, I analyze every color in the fashion rainbow and explain the feelings and reactions each tends to inspire. We'll go through them all, color by color, and I'll advise you on when it's ideal to wear certain shades, offering real-life styling tips that anyone can execute. My hope is that after reading this chapter, you will no longer shy away from color. Instead you will begin to see—and use—it as an essential instrument in your style toolbox.

But first, in general, it helps to understand that color is unmatched when it comes to impacting perception through clothes. Take red, for example. I'll be blunt, you guys: Red is sexy AF. Did you know that simply looking at the color is a proven aphrodisiac?[2] That's just one example of a power color in action. I've taught courses on Color Psychology and have extensively studied the relationship between a wide spectrum of shades, mood, and behavior. Let's take a look at a Case Study that highlights some of these dynamics.

CASE STUDY: A SHOCK OF COLOR

- -

About a year ago, I met with a young man named Andrew.* He came to me because he was heartbroken, having recently been dumped by his boyfriend. It was also a time of transition for him, as he was about to leave college and begin life as an independent adult. He'd been distracted and depressed about the progressive demise of his relationship, and his grades had been dropping all throughout the second semester of his senior year. He felt like he had lost all motivation and joie de vivre. The timing wasn't great. He had several interviews lined up for entry-level positions in the fashion industry, as he hoped to start working right away after graduation. He was in a funk. He felt foggy and unable to prepare for these important meetings. Andrew and I barely had any time to sit down and talk through the specifics of his breakup. The first time he approached me to talk, he had an important interview for a paid internship scheduled for the very next morning.

Style Rx

Time was of the essence, so I decided to focus on fashion right away, even before we could delve more deeply into Andrew's emotions and background. I said, Okay, what's the fastest way we can lift your mood now so you can go out and kill it on this interview? We quickly settled on an eye-catching interview outfit: a neon-yellow button-down and gray trousers. This look was not outside the realm of propriety, since the company where Andrew was applying encouraged self-expression. The neon, I theorized, would shock his system and revitalize him, almost like a defibrillator in an emergency room. My prescription was "Laugh now, cry later." I strongly encouraged Andrew to come back and see me the following week, telling him, "The only way this is not problematic is because we will cry later." About a week after his interview (which went well—he reported feeling more confident, and he got the internship!), we ultimately did sit down and address his feelings. But we'd shocked his system with color first because he needed a burst of energy to face a daunting situation.

When Andrew saw himself in neon, it encouraged him to adjust his mood to the color and become more optimistic. The rainbow and bright colors in general have cultural meaning within the LGBTQIA+ community. They communicate pride and resilience. In that particular moment, in order to cope with his stress, Andrew needed to compartmentalize his heartbreak. But I insisted he come back to see me because if he had used clothing only to suppress, mask, or push down his emotions, they almost certainly would have popped up later through some negative or self-harming behavior. (Andrew told me he was prone to seeking out one-night stands when he was feeling upset, or if something had threatened his self-esteem.) I believe the neon brightness of his shirt helped lift Andrew's gloom temporarily and redirected his attention out of a dark abyss. But his clothes were a Band-Aid, not a permanent solution to his problems.

What's the lesson? A standout color can lift your spirits and help you stand out from the competition. You might try a hot-pink bodysuit with white pants or an orange cross-body bag over a camel coat. There's no need to wear Day-Glo head to toe. But I highly recommend considering color if you need to break out of a funk and get noticed.

COLOR AND CRIME

We are confronted with colors all the time, but our subconscious interpretations of them can lead to some shady behavior. (See what I did there?) Therefore it's important to remember that our associations with certain colors are based only partially on fact. The rest is pure projection. Here's an example: Since ancient times, black has been associated with mystery and death.[3] We sleep in darkness. Sorcerers practice black magic or the dark arts. The Grim Reaper wears a long black robe. So does the killer from *Scream*. The color itself has long been painted with a sinister brush. And this may bleed into real life. Between 2000 and 2010, more than one hundred people connected with serious crimes in New York City wore navy-blue or black Yankees apparel, either at the time of the crimes or during their arrest or arraignment. "No other sports team comes close," writes Manny Fernandez in the *New York Times*. Some criminologists and consumer psychologists have attributed this phenomenon to the hat's association with gangsta rappers or even Jay-Z, he reports.[4] I wonder if the garments' dark color also plays a role. Of the ten team hats worn most frequently by street gangs, half are black, gray and black, navy blue, or dark green. These are not shiny happy colors.[5] They don't communicate the rainbow-bright optimism of a Taylor Swift video. The other five are red. This is also noteworthy. Red, of course, has sexual and romantic connotations, but red is also associated with danger, warning, blood, and flashing sirens. Red is stimulating. Red spurs action. Red means war.

In my Color Psychology class at FIT, students and I discussed the fact that Trayvon Martin was wearing a dark-gray hoodie the night he was killed. In fact, one of the officers investigating the seventeen-year-old's tragic shooting suggested he was profiled not because of his skin color but because of his clothing.[6] According to documents from the case, homicide detective Christopher Serino "believes that when [self-appointed neighborhood watchman George] Zimmerman saw Martin in a hoody, Zimmerman took it upon himself to view Martin as acting suspicious."[7] In the media storm that followed, Geraldo Rivera declared, "The hoodie is as much responsible for Trayvon Martin's death as George Zimmerman was." Gangs in the Florida neighborhood where Zimmerman lived and where Martin was visiting his father reportedly wore hoodies.[8] But Martin, it turned out, was just an unarmed high school student walking home from a convenience store where he had gone to buy Skittles.

After his death, in a sign of solidarity and a clarion call for justice, lawmakers, NBA players, and mothers who have buried children under similar circumstances donned hoodies in tribute. My students and I explored whether Zimmerman's negative assumptions about Martin could have been influenced by the color of Martin's skin *in combination* with the color of his sweatshirt. We questioned whether the two things ever stood a chance of being evaluated separately. We debated whether the latter even mattered at all.

Here's the question we were circling: Does dark clothing signal aggression and danger? (We know it signifies death.) According to a study out of Cornell, published in the *Journal of Personality and Social Psychology,* professional athletes who wore black jerseys appeared to play more aggressively than their counterparts in white jerseys. How do we know this? NHL and NFL records from the period of study indicated that teams wearing black uniforms ranked near the top of their leagues in penalties. Simply switching from non-black to black uniforms resulted in "an immediate increase in penalties" according to the study's authors.[9] But the reason for this (if you'll forgive the pun) isn't exactly black and white. The researchers found that donning black caused the players to behave more aggressively. But they also found that the color created bias on the part of the referees evaluating them. It seems that once the players put on black, the officials in positions of power interpreted their actions as more aggressive and thus doled out more punishment.

What we're dealing with here is a power imbalance. Whether the players were inspired to behave more aggressively when they donned black *is* a question worth examining. But the players should not bear all the responsibility for the change in dynamic. We must acknowledge the subjective interpretations on the part of the refs, who are, after all, human beings with inherent biases. I believe people are prejudiced against the color black. Culturally, historically, we are taught to interpret anything black as bad, negative, or demonic, whereas white is pure and angelic. The perceiver needs to be aware of this. An ambitious player in white may be seen as assertive (a positive attribute), while a player in black behaving in the same way may be perceived as aggressive (a negative). The distinction has real-life consequences.

Black, of course, also signifies mourning and depression (a black day, the black dog). But to legions of New Yorkers, Audrey Hepburn enthusiasts, and minimalist fashion fans, it's simply the coolest color around. So when you wear it, will you be perceived as goth or glamorous? Macabre or metropolitan? How do you know if the color you are wearing is sending the message you intended, both to yourself and to others? Let's meet a client who needed clarity on her own color choices.

CASE STUDY: GOOD GRIEF

A few years back, I worked with a client named Marion* who always wore black and dark-gray clothing. She came to me for help breaking out of this color rut as she was feeling bored by her uniform. But as we went through her closet, she was resistant to the idea of letting go of her familiar dark-colored sweaters. I could sense that whenever I brought up the idea of donating them, it upset her emotionally. Once we started talking more deeply about her life, she and I both realized that her intense attachment to dark colors began about a decade earlier, soon after her husband had died. I pointed out to her that black is associated with grief. To my surprise (and to hers), she had never consciously made that connection before.

*I explained to her the concept of **Emotional Contact Time**, meaning the period of time we need to spend feeling connected to an issue before the intensity of the feeling passes. I wondered if she needed more Emotional Contact Time to connect with her bereavement. I encouraged her to understand that grief does not operate on a timeline of our choosing, and that we are not obligated to "get over" our feelings once a given period of time — say, a year — has passed.*

Style Rx

I encouraged Marion to talk about her grief, to reminisce about the man she called "my one true love," and, yes, to wear her dark clothes. When you acknowledge your emotions, you are able to move through them. Dressing in dark colors was a way of feeling her feelings. Once Marion embraced these realizations, she became more open to the idea of healing and moving forward with her life, and gradually started to incorporate more color into her wardrobe. Since Marion still felt unable to part with her dark garments, I suggested introducing pops of color through accessories. And she did so willingly. Adding small doses of color to her sea of black helped her envision the next chapter of her life.

– – – – – – – – –

COLOR AND CULTURE

Ready for an eye-opener? Men and women literally see things differently. Men are less able to perceive color differences than women. (It's due to neuron differences in the visual cortexes of our brains.)[10] Up to 8 percent of northern European men are color-blind to red and green, while only .5 percent of northern European women are.[11] That's the biological piece. But color associations are also cultural and historical. Many of our emotional connections with color — feeling blue, blacking out, being green with envy — go back centuries. Traditions that feel incontrovertible, however, such as brides wearing white wedding dresses, can in fact be traced back to specific historical moments or movements. In this case, Queen Victoria's ivory lace wedding gown in 1840. Before Victoria, brides wore bright colors like red. White had been reserved for mourning (and in some Eastern cultures, this is still true).[12] Wearing such an easily blemished fabric demonstrated twenty-year-old Victoria's wealth, in that she could afford to have it cleaned.[13]

All of these examples illuminate how, though our modern, Western color associations seem set in stone, they are in fact merely trends and traditions. As noted by Valerie Steele, director of the Museum at FIT, color is a social construct. In 2018 she curated an entire exhibition on pink fashion and quoted color historian Michel Pastoureau. "It is society that 'makes' color, defines it, gives it meaning," he said. "Color has no objective meaning. Color is what we make of it."[14]

Knowing all this, it makes sense that different societies assign colors distinct and sometimes divergent meanings. Different culture, different code. Here's an example: Researchers looked into the color terminology of children from the Himba tribe in northern Namibia and compared it to that of English children the same age. As it turned out, the colors that English children would differentiate as red, orange, or pink are categorized by one all-encompassing word in Himba: *serandu*. Himba children also use one word, *zoozu,* to describe the variety of shades that English speakers would call dark blue, dark green, dark brown, deep purple, dark red, or black.[15] In America, orange is worn by prisoners. In Southeast Asia, it's worn by monks. Western fashionistas generally believe black and white are sleek and sophisticated while colorful prints and patterns are . . . something else. Global. Tribal. Ethnic. Other. But if you ask me, that's a pretty dull way to look at the world.

Color also has gender associations — a fact that parents-to-be embrace the minute they throw their pink or blue gender-reveal party pics up on the 'gram. But dividing the sexes along these color lines is also a total invention. Until the twentieth century, Western babies often wore white. At one point, blue was for girls and pink was for boys. Here's a passage from a June 1918 issue of a trade magazine for baby clothes called *Earnshaw's Infants' Department:* "The generally accepted rule is pink for the boys, and blue for the girls. The reason is that pink, being a more decided and stronger color, is more suitable for the boy, while blue, which is more delicate and dainty, is prettier for the girl."[16] We now consider the inverse to be true, thanks to mass marketing trends that took off after World War II and solidified in the 1980s.

In fashion, there are roughly ten basic color categories, similar to the ROY G BIV spectrum we're taught as schoolkids: red, orange, yellow, green, blue, purple, pink, brown, black, and white. (For those who are curious, I'd argue that popular composite colors like gray, turquoise, and coral elicit similar emotional reactions to their base colors: black-white, blue-green, and red-orange, respectively.)

In the pages that follow, I analyze every color in the fashion rainbow to help you understand the messages it sends. I'll advise you on which colors to select to complement your moods and achieve your objectives. Choosing what color to wear is a more nuanced, emotional, and meaningful decision than we often realize. But color can be a powerful ally. I encourage you to be bold. Splash out. Yes, it takes confidence to call attention to yourself—and that's exactly what certain colors do. But if you're up for it, wearing color is a fashion risk with a huge payoff. With your deeper understanding of what each color symbolizes, what it sets off in you and others, you'll have yet another powerful weapon in your style arsenal, and a more informed perspective from which to approach your closet.

RED

Red is hot. Red is equal parts romance and danger, fire and fury. Just think of *The Scarlet Letter*. The oppressive red robes of *The Handmaid's Tale*. Racy, lacy lingerie. Red roses. One study showed that women who wore red to bars were approached more by men than women in any other color. In another study, men chose to sit *closer* to a woman wearing a red t-shirt than to one wearing blue.[17] Yet another study found that men tend to leave *higher tips* for waitresses wearing red tops than for those wearing t-shirts in other colors.[18] (T-shirt color had no effect on how women tipped their servers.) Simply carrying a red laptop or standing in front of a red background results in women being rated (again, by men) as more sexually attractive than those carrying silver, black, or blue computers or standing in front of non-scarlet scrims.[19]

Through a combination of social conditioning and biological factors, it seems many Western men connect red with sexuality, fertility, and/or romance. Culturally, we see this playing out with red-light districts, red lipstick, red heart emojis, "La Vie en Rose," Valentine's Day, and the red XXX indicating pornography. Red is festive and takes center stage at the holidays. Urban legend even says drivers of red cars receive the most speeding tickets (though proof of this is scarce). Red gets hearts racing (literally). In the West, because of its association with our life force — blood — red symbolizes passion, vigor, excitement, energy, courage, and action. Its relationship to good health and vitality (rosy cheeks) explains why red talismans and stones like garnets and rubies have historically been worn to ward off sickness and disease.[20] In Japan, it is still believed that red has the power to repel evil.[21] In fact, in many Eastern cultures, red is a marker of prosperity, good fortune, and joy. In India, brides wear red, and a red-orange powder called *sindoor* is applied to the part of their hair during the wedding ceremony to signify they are now married.[22]

Simultaneously, red represents clashes or conflict, as when blood is spilled (many national flags contain red), anger (red-faced, meaning a hot temper), and danger (STOP!). Merely *seeing* the color can increase our metabolic and respiration rates and cause adrenaline to surge.[23] We equate red with life-or-death dangers — red sends up a flare — so when we see it, we go into fight-or-flight mode, resulting in these physiological responses. Red is both an invitation (love's first blush, a playing child's flushed face) and a warning (red flag), a signifier of rage (seeing red). Red is intense. Red is not shy. It is not subtle. So how and when should you deploy its firepower?

When to Wear Red

When it comes to fashion, the power of red can be tricky to wield. Wearing it may give you more than you bargained for and less of what you actually desire. So let's consider how to use it most effectively. Many of us have been taught that red telegraphs strength and power, but, given how it's been eroticized, especially for women, it might not send the ideal signals in a work situation. It *is* a power color, but I would say proceed with caution when wearing it in a professional setting. A body-con red dress may be overkill on a job interview, or interpreted as too attention-seeking in a corporate context. In fact, in competitive scenarios such as written exams or sporting events, its mere visual presence can lead to declines in performance, according to research from the University of Rochester. (Might want to ditch that red backpack, kids!) And speaking of competitive scenarios, we know that red enhances women's perceived attractiveness to the opposite sex, but women may also judge other women wearing red as threatening or lascivious.[24] A small dose of red like a retro statement earring or a red accent on a silk scarf or shoe can provide a dash of boldness without taking you into the danger zone. On the personal side, if you are hoping to capture the attention of a love interest, or are headed to a party or a bar seeking to make a romantic connection, you will not go unnoticed in red.

ORANGE

Burnt orange and marigold have recently been a huge runway trend. In the West, we associate this bright hue with freshness, fun, humor, sunshine, and of course sweet, juicy Florida oranges. In Eastern cultures, orange symbolizes happiness and spirituality. In Thailand, Cambodia, and Sri Lanka, Buddhist monks wear orange robes, simply because of the plant-based dyes available to them in the region.[25] Nevertheless, the image of monks swathed in orange—and the color's association with wisdom, sacrifice, and sanctity—is indelible. Orange also has some less than holy connotations. It is synonymous with plastic junk, prison uniforms, and cheap labor (see: *Orange Is the New Black*). When combined with black, the color instantly conjures Halloween. No other color is quite so divisive. Orange straddles the line between tasteful and tacky.

When to Wear Orange

Though hard scientific evidence is still being sought, it's been suggested we may feel alert when we see orange and calm when we see blue, because these are the colors we associate with the natural cycles of day and night. In my styling experience, orange *can* do wonders for vitality. Think of it as vitamin C for your wardrobe. If you're feeling unmotivated and don't want to exercise, wearing orange can be an instant, effervescent energy boost. You can't help but feel alive in orange. I love the way a citrus swimsuit pops against chocolate skin. An orange puffer jacket over creamy winter whites is Creamsicle chic. A coral or marigold off-the-shoulder sweater looks amazing with high-rise jeans in lighter washes. Dip a toe in with preppy orange leather loafers and keep the rest of your look monochrome neutrals. On a practical level, given its high-visibility contrast in natural environments (think astronauts in their launch suits, air traffic control vests, safety cones), it's an ideal color for outdoor fitness fans.

YELLOW

In many cultures, this cheerful hue symbolizes happiness, joy, and hope. Starting with the Qing dynasty (in the mid-1600s) in China, yellow became the color of emperors and was reserved for the royal family.[26] In modern times it is associated with being fresh, crisp, and clean. Just think of a bowl of lemons in a pristine white marble kitchen. Lemon Pledge. The innocent optimism of Big Bird. An impish Harajuku girl wearing a Pikachu backpack. But yellow also has less sunny connotations. It is associated with cowardice, caution, and crime scene tape. It is the signature shade of hazmat suits and the skull-and-crossbones warning labels on toxic containers. The antiheros wear yellow rubber suits to cook meth in *Breaking Bad*. Recently in France, yellow vests (required by law to be donned by anyone involved in a traffic accident) were worn by masses of protesters demanding everything from lower fuel prices to the resignation of President Emmanuel Macron. With its working-class connotations (think construction workers in their yellow vests), the *New York Times'* Vanessa Friedman called it "one of the most effective protest garments in history." The shade dominated the photos of the protests taken from the air and, as Friedman pointed out, was "impossible to miss even on the small screens of social media . . . It is widely understood as a distress signal."[27]

When to Wear Yellow

With its Don't-Worry-Be-Happy smiley face emoji vibes, yellow can imbue its wearer with an aura of cheerfulness and approachability. If you are facing a stressful social situation like meeting your future in-laws for the first time or moving to a new city and looking to make friends, wearing a hint of yellow can convey a sense of likability. But a word to the wise: A little yellow goes a long way; you do not need to wear it head to toe in order to reap its rewards. A soft buttercup sweater pairs beautifully with denim. A neon-yellow sneaker adds a modern kick to a '90s slip dress over a baby tee. A mustard cocktail dress with glinting gold sandals will be a total conversation starter. Yellow is my go-to color for Mood Enhancement. It's just really hard to feel pissed off in yellow! If you're working with children as a teacher, or if you are a parent on a playdate, you can't go wrong wearing this happy hue. Try a chunky yellow turtleneck with white skinny jeans. Good day, sunshine.

GREEN

Green is that rare color that means virtually the same thing across the globe. Thanks to its associations with the natural world, it signifies spring, fertility, hope, rebirth, and regeneration. In the West, it is the signature color of good luck and eco-consciousness. Even the word "green" is shorthand for environmentally friendly products and practices. Of course, "green" can also mean innocent, naive, and inexperienced. The Emerald City in *The Wizard of Oz*, where Dorothy seeks a sort of divine guidance, is a heavenly utopia that may trace its inspiration back to astrology, where green is the color of celestial wisdom.[28] In Chinese culture, jadeite, which is often a brilliant green color, is the most valuable and precious of materials (akin to gold in the West). Because of its apparent indestructability, it has historically been used as a symbol of wealth, power, and status.[29] When viewed in a less positive light, green is the color of envy and avarice. Jealousy = the green-eyed monster. In any case, green still covers a lot of common ground. Whether we're talking prosperity or greed, money makes the world go round.

When to Wear Green

In my opinion, green means *go* whether you're driving or dressing. I can't think of many real-life scenarios in which wearing emerald, dark evergreen, or khaki is in bad taste. Lately, stars like Lizzo, Zendaya, and Sarah Paulson have made memorable red carpet splashes in lime. Green plays beautifully with other shades. If you want to try the color-blocking trend, go for a camo-green boilersuit and a turquoise trench draped over your shoulders. A deep forest-green satin slip dress would be perfect for any party—especially under a structured white blazer. Once again, red isn't the only power color in town. Green can send a less threatening message of strength and prestige. If you are giving a presentation or dealing with any form of social phobia, you might be inclined to reach for black because it's generally flattering, a safe bet, and unlikely to ruffle feathers. Green, however, symbolizes stability and trust and may even subconsciously inspire an association with income (and maybe, just maybe, a job candidate's ability to generate it). Try a green pencil skirt with a white buttondown and caramel-colored suede heels the next time you need to dress to impress. Green not only conjures elegance and sophistication—wearing it may also help you (*cough*) get lucky. I recently invited London-based clairvoyant and Reiki master Sacha Moon to guest-lecture in my Color Psychology class. She explained that people wear, and even eat, certain colors to align with their chakras (aka the centers of spiritual power in the human body, according to ancient Indian texts). Each chakra is believed to be a certain color, and each corresponds to specific organs as well as to emotional, psychological, and spiritual areas of your life. The heart chakra is green.[30] So, the belief goes, if you wear or even eat that color, you are focusing energy on that particular chakra and cultivating that part of your life. Therefore, if you have a broken heart, you could wear green, meditate with green stones, or eat green foods to heal you or bring you love. So eat those veggies, kids! Grain of salt optional.

BLUE

In the West, blue has traditionally been associated with peace, calm, serenity, tranquility, and reflection like the ocean or the sky. A study in the journal *Evidence-Based Complementary and Alternative Medicine* suggested exposure to blue light actually lowers our heart rate and reduces our stress level.[31] According to a survey by UK company Travelodge, people who sleep in blue bedrooms clock almost *two more hours* of shut-eye a night than those snoozing in brown or purple quarters.[32] And most fascinatingly, blue streetlights installed in Glasgow, Scotland, as well as at railway station platforms in Japan, were found to reduce the incidence of crime and suicide, according to Psych Central, perhaps because of the color's association with police presence.[33] Blue is also shorthand for reliability ("true blue"), trust, and authority (think Marine uniforms, the Citibank logo). Navy blue is a conservative, corporate color—elegant, classic, and strong. Brighter blues have romantic overtones. Brides wear something blue; the Hope Diamond is a deep blue, as was *Titanic*'s "Heart of the Ocean." Ditto Kate Middleton's sapphire engagement ring, passed down from Princess Diana. Of course, blue is also deeply symbolic of melancholy. We say "feeling blue," a "blue mood," or the "baby blues" to indicate states of depression (see also: Picasso's Blue Period). Indeed, something about its heavenly vibe puts blue in the realm of the metaphysical. In Hinduism, it is associated with immortality and with the god Vishnu, who is blue.[34] Today's popular blue "evil eye" amulets, worn to ward off negativity or envy, trace their origins back to ancient Egypt.[35]

When to Wear Blue

Anytime you are seeking calm or wish to convey a sense of authority and command, go blue. If you are being perceived by those around you as acting somehow out of control, wearing dark blue could be a way to show you really do have a handle on things. Blue is reportedly the color most preferred by men.[36] So if you find yourself needing to impress a mostly male audience (like, say, in the boardroom or during any kind of application process), wearing this conservative, traditional hue—for instance, a navy suit with a sharp-shouldered jacket and trousers—could help you appear trustworthy and competent. If you yourself are feeling frazzled, look to the serenity of blue to soothe and center you. Blue should be your go-to when you need to be taken seriously. But it doesn't have to be stuffy: cornflower and cobalt have been trending the past few years as a safe way to add color pops to your wardrobe, whether via snakeskin ankle boots, skinny leather belts, or croc-embossed bucket bags. Blue looks fabulous with metallics, black, or white. A classic navy-and-white-stripe top is a neutral (J.Crew makes great ones); wear one to tone down a slinky animal-print midi skirt or to take the S&M sting out of black leather culottes. Add a little bling, and you're good to go.

PURPLE

Rarely found in nature, historically difficult and expensive to produce, purple has long been the calling card of kings and queens, once designated only for ancient 1 percenters. Roman citizens were forbidden, under penalty of death, to wear the color reserved for their emperor. Alexander the Great and other ancient royals wore robes soaked in Tyrian purple dye, which could be made only by crushing the shells of rare and valuable sea snails (#CantMakeThisStuffUp). In the Byzantine Empire, rulers wore flowing purple robes and signed their pronouncements in purple ink.[37] Queen Elizabeth I forbade by law anyone but close members of her family from wearing the arresting hue.[38] Today, purple remains associated with high rank and valor. (Think of the military's Purple Heart.) It also has mystical, magical, spiritual, supernatural associations, which may explain its link to creative inspiration. After all these centuries, it retains its associations with royalty, wealth, ambition, and fame. It is believed to be mentally stimulating, inspiring creativity and even musicality. Just ask any Prince fan.

When to Wear Purple

Of all the colors in the fashion canon, purple has the most flamboyant personality. Purple is the Tiffany Haddish of colors: *She ready!* If you are embarking on a creative project, want to feel luxurious, or wish to tap into your spiritual side, purple could pave the way. Try lavender jeans with a pastel-pink sweater, a soft purple beanie with an all-gray outfit, or a purple suede bag to enliven monochrome looks. I once worked with a musician who wanted to feel a sense of euphoria and get his creative juices flowing during the songwriting process, without turning to mind-altering substances, as he had in the past. I advised him to paint the walls of his studio purple. And guess what? It really did seem to help! (He finished his album on time, in any case.) Speaking of royalty, purple is the color of the crown chakra, which governs the mind. So in theory, wearing purple could make you feel closer to God, or your higher power. Prince was so committed to his signature hue he once painted his West Hollywood rental home in purple stripes—and was sued for his trouble.[39] But there's no denying he made music, mystery, magic, and royalty his personal brand.

PINK

Pink is both a preppy favorite (think Lilly Pulitzer and country-club-pink polo shirts) and a subversive wink. Both Janelle Monáe's "PYNK" and Aerosmith's "Pink" are songs about female reproductive organs; see also the pink pussyhats of the Women's March. Pink sends a potent message — but context is everything. Traditionally, pink telegraphs innocence and femininity. It is delicate, nonthreatening, "girlish." In Switzerland, prison cells have been painted pink in an effort to calm inmates. This is also the approach taken by the University of Iowa, which painted the locker room for visiting teams pink, in hopes of putting athletic opponents in a "passive mood."[40] For a spate of recent public appearances, famous wives seemed to be taking a page out of Jackie Kennedy's pink pillbox playbook and, through their cotton-candy-sweet attire, positioning themselves as what one fashion critic called "power-adjacent." In this cascade of media moments, Melania Trump, Queen Rania of Jordan, Meghan Markle, and other prominent women wore pale pink, seemingly to signal conformity, to tone themselves down in order to let their men — the ones with real authority — shine. Viewed as affirming patriarchal power structures, their shade of choice was dubbed by Isabel Jones of *InStyle* "passenger-seat pink."[41] And yet, if we look back a few centuries, pink used to be a power color! As the Museum at FIT's Valerie Steele points out in her exhibition *Pink: The History of a Punk, Pretty, Powerful Color,* from men's suiting to interior design, "pink was a new and highly fashionable unisex color in 18th-century Europe — in contrast to the 19th and 20th centuries when pink was coded as a 'feminine' color." In Japan and India — and lately in Hollywood — it is regularly worn by both men and women.[42]

When to Wear Pink

We are now in an era I like to call post-millennial pink. Pink is the new black. It has been stripped of its sugary sweetness, its hyper-feminized subtext, and it is back with a vengeance. Pink is now officially gender-neutral. It is non-binary. It's no longer chained to pretty, pretty princess, My Little Pony, or Barbie. In 2019 Cardi B wore a pink suit and matching pink stilettos to criminal court. We have reclaimed its power and redefined its meaning. In terms of how to style it, pink functions the same way any other neutral would. Wear it head to toe. Go bold or go home. Try a hot-pink trench coat or a pale pastel cape, color-block an icy-pink silk suit with a coral tufted leather handbag, or conjure J.Lo/ Rihanna/Kendall Jenner and wear an explosive fuchsia tulle evening dress. Men should absolutely feel empowered to wear pink, regardless of their sexual orientation. I love a guy in a pink linen suit for a warm weather wedding.

BLACK

Black is a mystery. If it is so strongly associated with danger, death, and mourning, why are we so compelled to wear it? Here it is, the signature shade of Dracula, witches, the plague (aka Black Death), bad luck (black cats), and unintended unconsciousness (a blackout). And yet black is so synonymous with elegance and sophistication, nearly the entire population of New York City has pledged its allegiance. Our attraction to black may come down to two things that are catnip to shoppers, and primarily to women: luxury and flattery. We have internalized the idea that black is slimming and therefore makes us appear more attractive. To quote Coco Chanel, "Black has it all."[43] Black gives us confidence. It deflects unwanted attention. It gives the impression of being serious, strong, and in control. Devoid of any frippery or frivolity, it is the ultimate power color and offers a fast pass to any who want to reclaim their own. Black says, *I got this*. It also says, *Don't mess with me*. "But above all," as designer Yohji Yamamoto once told the *New York Times*, "black says this: 'I don't bother you — don't bother me!'"[44]

When to Wear Black

When we think about wearing black (the LBD, the black t-shirt and jeans), we assume it is fail-safe and foolproof. But this is flawed reasoning. (And for what it's worth, Anna Wintour hates all-black.)[45] Sometimes wearing black can overpower and obscure you rather than highlight your strengths with its simplicity. Yes, black can mask your size or weight, but it can also cover up your personality and spirit. It is easy—perhaps too easy—to hide behind black. In life, you don't always want to get washed away. If you're going to a networking event or to a party where you want to be acknowledged, or at least not fade into the background, black may not help your cause. There are, however, ways to take advantage of the security black provides: Consider a subtle, dark floral print that's just different enough to say, *Hey! Heads up. I got your attention.* Play with texture. Try a black suede sleeveless top with jeans or a threadbare gray tee with a black leather skirt, a black silk trouser with a cropped white sweater, or a black leather biker jacket worn over a slinky slip dress. There's no law that says black has to be basic.

WHITE

White is the color of purity and virtue, of innocence and sterility, of angels and hospitals, of peace-bearing doves. White is virginal, untouched, fresh as the driven snow. And that is precisely why it can be so transgressive, so primed for subversion. Sometimes white imagery can chill us to the bone: Think of Klansmen's robes or "men in white coats" coming to take away the mentally ill. White can also send a beautifully uplifting message. Suffragettes of the early 1900s wore white. Hillary Clinton paid tribute to them when she became the first woman presidential nominee of a major party. The Democratic women of Congress followed her lead and regularly donned white as a group when addressed by President Trump. "We wear white to unite against any attempts by the Trump administration to roll back the incredible progress women have made in the last century, and we will continue to support the advancement of all women," Democratic lawmaker Lois Frankel of Florida said in a 2017 statement. "We will not go back."[46] Waving the white flag of surrender? Hardly. Though we've long since abandoned the idea of a virginal bride, white remains the most popular color for wedding gowns. Even if brides don't say yes to the *dress* (see: Bianca Jagger's Le Smoking jacket or Solange's caped bridal jumpsuit), they still tend to wear white. In red carpet history, Björk's swan dress, Celine Dion's backward suit, and Gwyneth Paltrow's Tom Ford 2012 Oscars cape were white-hot fashion moments. When a woman wears white, there's no chance she'll be missed, and no mistaking she has something to say.

When to Wear White

Even though we may not be wearing white in protest, it can still be a great way to make a statement. If you're in a style rut, wearing white can reset your look. Wearing a white t-shirt with jeans offers a fresh start. White can provide a sense of rebirth, a clean slate, a blank canvas for Focal Accessories. Yes, you can wear white after Labor Day, in the winter, day or night. White offers an opportunity to flip the script. Playing with the idea of virginal purity can be seriously sexy. A white eyelet sundress with a flouncy skirt and espadrilles is a timeless summer look that shows skin in a way that isn't obvious or vulgar. White is elegant like nothing else. My go-to black-tie look is an homage to designer Carolina Herrera, whose uniform is a crisp white button-down and a long ball gown skirt. Herrera once said, "I love white shirts because they feel like a security blanket. You can wear them with anything. It's the person and the way that they wear it that makes it different."[47] When I go to a gala or a fancy affair, I like to wear a crisp white button-down with a glitzy metallic floor-length skirt. The look is balanced and harmonious—all business on top and a party on the bottom. It's my way of getting glamorous while honoring the dress code and retaining my sense of dignity and control.

BROWN

In the Chinese horoscope, brown symbolizes earth.[48] This association is shared by the Western world. Brown conveys practicality, grounding, comfort, stability, reliability — a sense of being rooted. In fashion, brown takes on the properties of its texture. Brown satin and velvet are rich, chocolaty, and luxurious. Brown canvas is utilitarian and military cool. Brown leather is soft and creamy. Beiges, caramels, and coffees are classic neutrals. A camel coat or tan trench is an avatar of chic (see: *Casablanca*). According to online fashion bible *Who What Wear*, brown "is actually now one of the most forward colors you can wear."[49] Just look at the S/S 19 runways for proof. Kim Kardashian and Kanye West (see: Yeezy season 2 and SKIMS shapewear) have built entire brands based on flesh tones, reinvigorating "boring" colors by wearing them in unexpected materials (latex, sweats), cuts (asymmetrical bike shorts and bralettes), or combinations (head-to-toe taupe).

When to Wear Brown

If you want to appear warm, wholesome, and approachable, brown is your friend (like a beloved teddy bear coat). Brown is for earth mothers. I've joked with my students that if a love interest is taking you home to meet his or her mother, wear a brown dress instead of a black one; you'll seem much more stable and reliable! If life feels like it is moving at too fast a clip and you want to slow things down and self-soothe, wearing brown can help you feel centered and grounded. I recently counseled a friend who was working toward a college degree while also holding down a full-time job. She felt flighty, frenetic, and disassociated from her body as she raced from class to work and then back home to study. She was so fried, she sat with me and cried. She felt like she was operating on autopilot while running on empty. I advised her to wear brown to help her feel more present, more rooted in reality. Brown is earthy, but it can also be heavenly. Mix tones and textures for an effect that's totally sumptuous:

Wear a copper silk slip dress with chocolate croc-embossed sandals and an oversize fluffy caramel cardigan, or a russet-brown velvet suit with glittering black strappy heels. We are talking hot cocoa.

THE BOTTOM LINE

KEY TIPS AND TAKEAWAYS FROM CHAPTER 6

- **Color me happy.** Color inspires emotional reactions. Certain colors seem to elicit physical responses (red speeds up heart rates; blue is calming), while others have strong cultural associations (purple is for royalty; green is for money). Think about the feelings you want to convey and inspire when selecting your clothing colors.

- **Rut alert.** If you are wearing the same colors over and over and feel boxed in or bored, look for the emotional reasons behind your choices. Are you dressing in dark colors to mourn a loss, afraid of getting catcalled in red? Reconsider your motivations when it comes to color.

- **A little dab will do.** To incorporate more color into your wardrobe, start with accessories. A colorful bag or shoes will pop against a monochrome (all-gray, camel, or black) outfit.

- **Lighten up.** Pastels like pale pink, lavender, buttercup yellow, or robin's-egg blue are a less intimidating way to add color pops to an outfit.

Chapter 7

POWER ACCESSORIES

Our crown has already been bought and paid for. All we have to do is wear it.

—*James Baldwin*

Is anybody reading this a Cardi B fan? If so, you might remember when she famously lost her beloved purple blankie—presumably a childhood treasure—posted a hilarious, cuss-filled rant about it on social media, and, as usual, set the Internet on fire. She later found the blankie in a closet, but not before her followers gave it its own Instagram account.

Unfortunately, most of us are not Cardi B. It is not socially acceptable for us as adults to walk around with blankies, pacifiers, or teddy bears for comfort. We *can,* however, replace those childhood attachment objects with what I call **Focal Accessories.** A Focal Accessory is any item that makes you feel calm, connected, or confident. It's an item that may be worn regularly, religiously or with reverence, and has a powerful personal meaning to you. Maybe it's your grandmother's wedding ring, your engagement ring, a scarf knitted by a favorite aunt, or a pair of leather gloves passed down by your mother. Perhaps you almost never take it off, or you wear it on only the most special occasions. You would feel terrible if it were lost or damaged. Perhaps you feel naked without it. We often say these objects have sentimental value, but it's more than that: They have power. They do not passively sit in a drawer gathering dust. When we wear them every day (or recall the memory of a loved one having done so), we come to consider them as a part of our body or, to paraphrase William James, an extension of the self. They are a piece of us, or connected to someone we love(d). They embody our legacy. And thus their ability to bring up emotion is very, very real.

CASE STUDY: CLOSE TO HIS HEART

A Chinese student I know recently explained to me why he always wears a necklace given to him by his grandparents, and why he never, ever takes it off, even when he showers. He said it feels like a part of him. And in light of its proximity to his head and heart, it gives him the sense that his grandparents are with him, influencing his thoughts and emotions. They had gifted this amulet to him for his twelfth birthday. When he moved from China to the United States to attend college, he left his parents and grandparents behind. The necklace helps him feel grounded and connected to his faraway family. Wearing it is also a way to show reverence to his elders —filial duty being an important cultural value in China. He said taking off his necklace would feel like the end of the world. Even imagining losing it triggers anxiety. If he were to remove the necklace, he would feel like his family is no longer close to him, like he's doing something wrong, betraying his roots, and that, as a result, he would suffer bad luck or some sort of grave consequence. That's how much psychological meaning he has instilled into this one delicate accessory.

Focal Accessories are not unique to Eastern cultures. In the Western world, we ascribe meaning to wedding bands, family heirlooms, friendship bracelets, a rabbit's foot, or evil eye amulets (like the one Naomi Campbell seems to wear around her neck 24/7/365). These totems have a lot of positive potential, psychologically. When Kim Kardashian West went to the Oval Office to discuss prison reform with President Trump, she used an accessory to calm her nerves: a watch that once belonged to Jacqueline Kennedy Onassis that she had purchased at auction. "It gave me some power," Kardashian West told *Vogue*. "Let's get in there and get this done!"[1] If my clients are suffering from anxiety, I often advocate wearing a meaningful accessory. They can be potent panaceas.

If this idea appeals to you but you don't own a family heirloom or any jewelry you love enough to wear every day, don't worry! A Focal Accessory can be anything: a hat, a handbag, a pair of glasses, a scarf, a belt, or a business card case. As long as you assign it symbolic value, it can help you conjure up composure and confidence when you need it most. The more you wear or use it, the more impactful it becomes, because it's the ritual, the repeated behavior, the active commitment to making it a part of your life that strengthens its effect.

Look around: Perhaps something that was gifted or passed down by someone you love could fill this role. If not, then *you* can introduce new Focal Accessories and endow them with meaning yourself. Giving yourself a special present (it doesn't need to be expensive), whether it's to mark a birthday or a career milestone, or is simply an emblem of hard-won self-acceptance, is an act of empowerment. These objects can create a sense of internal well-being, which will in turn help you to project outer poise.

We all know Elizabeth Taylor loved her some jewelry. Her dazzling collection sold at auction for a total of $116 million. But, her longtime assistant told the *New York Post*'s Page Six Style, those pieces were "more than just jewelry to her. It was so much about the sentimental value, the memory of it. When she would travel, she bought jewelry as a souvenir—she liked to commemorate things."[2] I so relate to Liz, and not just because I can't resist a diva in diamonds. Whenever I'm giving a presentation, or out on a first date, I always wear heavy bracelets. I talk with my hands, and feeling the weight on my wrists seems to ground me. Lately I've been wearing the same bracelets almost every day—a delicate vintage beaded one and another art deco–inspired piece featuring Swarovski crystals. They have become an essential part of my public-speaking uniform. The few times I've done a media appearance or taught a class without them, I've felt nervous and flighty, like a gust of wind could just blow me over. And indeed, therapists tell us that one strategy for getting through a panic attack is to focus on your body, to be aware of your breath, to notice physical sensations. You might try to zero in on the way your legs feel when you're sitting in a chair, or the particular smoothness of the pen in your hand. Once you realize that you cannot actually float away, it helps you steady yourself. Isn't it interesting that such a little item can make such a big difference in how you feel? In this chapter I'll explain why that is. But first, how to decide which accessories to wear when you want to feel a certain way.

Fashion Psychology Tip

How to Accessorize Your Emotions

Michael Kors once said, "I've always thought of accessories as the exclamation point of a woman's outfit."[3] The question is, what are you telling yourself with your outfit, and how do you hope to emphasize it? Here's a simple formula to help you figure that out: If you're feeling X, wear Y. Let's break it down.

If you're feeling . . .

Overwhelmed, try sunglasses.

Throw on a pair of shades, a red lip, a monochrome outfit, and voilà: instant glamour. No one needs to know if you've been up all night stressing (or sobbing). There may be days when you are feeling introverted and want to honor that, but still need to get to work and face the sensory overload of life in public. Sunglasses offer a socially acceptable and stylish way to put up a protective shield without offending anyone.

Exhausted, try a scarf.

In cold weather, nothing provides cozy security like a soft knit, linen, or cashmere infinity scarf. In warmer weather, I love a vintage silk scarf. They are versatile enough to function as a head wrap, a shawl, or a Parisian chic neckerchief. Scarves are basically blankets for your face. They're *hygge* on the go.

Lonely, try a family heirloom.

Whether it's your mom's necklace, a boyfriend's watch, or your father's ring worn on a delicate chain, jewelry that once belonged to loved ones can feel infused with their spirit. It's amazing how you can feel encircled by love and connected to something larger than yourself simply by putting on a family heirloom. Wearing something old and bestowed reminds you that others have come before you, that someone loved you enough to bequeath you something of value, and that this too—whatever you're dealing with—shall pass.

Down on yourself, try high heels.

There's a country music saying that goes "The higher the hair, the closer to God." That's how I feel about heels. You cannot feel unsexy in an over-the-knee stiletto boot. But the reality is, because of the way heels alter our physicality (making our backsides protrude and our feet appear smaller, causing our hips to sway when we walk), any high heel will make women more attractive to most heterosexual males. One French study published in the *Archives of Sexual Behavior* found that the height of a woman's heel correlated directly to men's willingness to answer survey questions when she approached them on the street, retrieve a glove when she dropped it, and approach her in a bar (which they did twice as quickly as when she wore flats).[4] For many women, the key to feeling sexy is feeling desired; heels speed up this process. They're also the ultimate impractical extra, which may (subconsciously) appeal to some. When we wear heels, we are unable to walk long distances, necessitating the luxury of paying for a car service or a cab. Heels are for desk jobs in carpeted offices, not for manual labor. They are often a signifier of class. As designer Sonia Rykiel once asked, "How can you live the high life if you do not wear the high heels?"[5]

Out of control, try a belt.

If you were to wear a dress with a skinny belt, or a blazer with a tie-front waist, you would be concentrating energy above your navel, the area known in spiritual circles as your solar plexus chakra. This chakra is said to be linked to self-esteem, willpower, pleasure, and personal responsibility. According to one chakra anatomy site, if this chakra is out of balance, you may be experiencing a dip in confidence, control issues, or stress-induced emotional outbursts.[6] If you are treating yourself or others poorly, seeking solace in unhealthy foods or substances, if you have a goal you can't seem to accomplish or a habit you can't seem to break, it might help to bring attention to this area.

Disorganized, try a small handbag.

In the play *Love, Loss, and What I Wore* by Nora and Delia Ephron, there is a scene called "I Hate My Purse." It details all of the ways some women "fail" to meet the obligations of a "demanding and difficult accessory" (namely, to keep it organized and to match it to our outfits). "This is for those of you who understand, in short, that your purse is, in some absolutely horrible way, you," the Ephron sisters wrote.[7] Both Marie Kondo and happiness expert Gretchen Rubin tell us: Organize your outer physical space to bring inner calm. Let's apply this to purses. Consider switching to a small envelope bag, a circle cross-body bag, a modern fanny pack, or a transparent PVC style. (Staud, Need Supply, and Mansur Gavriel all make killer ones; so does Zara.) Necessity is the mother of invention. If you no longer have a huge tote to fill with junk that you are never forced to clean out, you will have no choice but to pare down your possessions. Go tiny or go home.

See-through handbags allow no secrets. I promise I am not trying to torture you; I am trying to lighten your load. I've seen too many older ladies with lopsided shoulders from years of tote-bag abuse. Consider downloading purchasing apps or carrying cash instead of credit cards. (You'll be less inclined to spend this way; your bank account will thank you.) Limit yourself to a slim wallet or billfold, a single lip product, sunglasses, keys, and your phone. That's it. Forgo hand sanitizer and wash your hands in public restrooms. Try water fountains instead of lugging around a steel canteen. Every problem has a solution. Being a Sherpa isn't one of them. And it certainly isn't *fashion.*

TO HAVE AND TO HOLD: THE POWER OF COMFORT OBJECTS

If someone wears an accessory every day, if we see it in every photo of them over the course of years and years, we come to think of it (subconsciously) as a part of them. This explains why royal watchers rejoice when they see Kate Middleton wearing Princess Diana's engagement ring (the implication being that Diana is embracing Kate from the afterlife). It's why Lady Gaga paid over $100,000 for Michael Jackson's crystal glove.[8] It's why the image (tweeted by Yoko Ono) of John Lennon's blood-spattered glasses, worn on the day he was killed, is so very shattering. Liz Taylor was so synonymous with diamonds, her perfume White Diamonds remains one of the most popular celebrity fragrances of all time.[9] Jennifer Lopez declared her identity in *opposition* to her jewelry, telling us not to be fooled by the rocks that she's got, because she's still Jenny from the Block.

For some celebrities, accessories stand in for adjectives. Layer on some rubber bangle bracelets and rosaries and voilà: you are '80s Madonna (rebellious). Grace Kelly will be forever linked to her namesake Hermès handbag (classic). Jackie O had her oversize sunglasses (glamorous); Lisa

Bonet has her tiny ones (bohemian). Carrie Bradshaw had her Manolos (fashionista). Diane Keaton has her bowler hats (quirky). A little object can say quite a lot about a person.

Accessories also tell us our own stories. They speak to us. Touch your wedding band, if you wear one. It will probably take you back to the day you got married. Your grandmother's earrings bind you to her across space and time, perhaps even beyond death. They say, You are connected, protected; you were loved since before you were born. Your high heels may make you feel feminine, sexy, change the way you walk, and convey your socioeconomic status all at once. Those heels may tell you that you are valuable, that you are a badass boss b——. You may truly believe your rabbit's foot brings you luck or your evil eye blocks other people's envy. Or perhaps your religious pendant reminds you of your higher purpose, your community, or the values you were raised to uphold. Indeed our "lucky charms"—our accessories—take on power because we believe they can be imbued with it. No other fashion item works quite the same way.

It's harder to imagine someone having "lucky socks" (though they certainly could) or feeling an emotional bond with your grandma's... work pants. Starting in childhood, toddlers form intense attachments to irreplaceable objects, but those objects are not always objectively desirable. A chewed-up, slobbery doll may be regarded as the most precious item in the world by the kid it belongs to. (Just ask any parent who's lost one in the back of a cab.) This kind of magical thinking starts early, and actually never ends. An item is only as valuable as we perceive it to be. The good news is, that means you can decide that any item is valuable. You can buy yourself a Focal Accessory—a cocktail ring, a cuff bracelet, a scarf—and by wearing it regularly, form an attachment to it. You can come to believe it will bring you peace, prosperity, or protection.

CASE STUDY: ROCKING THE HOUSE

I recently worked with a first-time mom named Eliana who was in her thirties. Professionally, she is an opera singer and musician. But when we met, she was staying home almost all the time taking care of her new baby. Her issues—loss of identity, going stir-crazy, social isolation, relying on what she called "stretchy, flowy, and drool-safe clothing"—were common to many new parents. But they were exacerbated by the fact that her work rarely required her to leave the house, except for occasional evening performances. When we met, Eliana would make statements like "I feel like a slob. I don't even need to get dressed. My baby is throwing up on me. I don't feel sexy. I don't feel vibrant. I don't feel cute. My husband comes home and I look like sh——; I'm wearing the same clothes I wore yesterday." Her burning question? "How do I get back to me?"

My answer to Eliana was more of a reality check: You don't. As I explained to her, You're still the old you, but you are also the new you; we need to merge the two, and we can use accessories to do it. The idea, I told her, is not to do a magical transformation where you leave the old you behind and suddenly you're a new person. You need to evolve, and so does your style.

Style Rx

Eliana loved jewelry, so I suggested she wear some Focal Accessories: beaded belts with gold coin details, funky rings and bracelets—items that would make her feel connected to her old, pre-mom identity but that were safe enough to be worn around the baby. (He would tug on her earrings, so those were out.) She opted to continue to wear soft stretchy leggings for practical purposes, so I suggested she pair them with some of her favorite vibrant pre-baby tops and chic flats to make herself feel more put together. We composed various outfits following this formula, creating neutral backgrounds for her accessories to pop. I didn't put her in something totally different and push her beyond her comfort zone; nor did I ask her to dress up to stay home. Rather, the idea was to show her that she still had a closet full of options that suited her evolving lifestyle. The look we carved out for her was still practical but a bit more polished—thanks primarily to jewelry and belts. Both her style and her outlook soon improved.

– – – – – – – – –

LUXURY, LABELS, AND LOGOS: POWER TO THE PEOPLE?

I want to take a second to talk about the role accessories play in pop culture in general, and in hip-hop culture specifically. Designer logos and labels are like the hieroglyphs of luxury. And nowhere are they more visible than on handbags, luggage, shoes, sunglasses, and jewelry. Just take a second to think about these globally recognizable status symbols: Louis Vuitton's crisscross LV logo, Chanel's double C's, Versace's Medusa head. These iconic images instantly communicate the wearer's taste for the finer things, and signal that she has the bank account to afford them. In "Bodak Yellow," Cardi B declares her dominance by rapping about her red-bottom (as in Christian Louboutin) shoes. Diamonds were once a girl's best friend. Now they're a rapper's. Ice, grillz, frosting, drip, drip. Jay-Z declares his love for Beyoncé by calling her the hottest chick in the game, but it's the fact that she wears his *chain* that cements their status as a power couple.

Accessories are a defining element of hip-hop culture because of what they represent (money, swagger, ascendance). For two-plus decades now, they've been used to indicate an escape from urban poverty. Name-dropping Dolce & Gabbana and Prada, draping yourself in diamonds, showed the world you were catapulting yourself out of the hood, by any means necessary. Remember the term "ghetto fabulous"? Bling or drip offers incontrovertible evidence that you have arrived.

The power of accessories is that accessories signal power. From rappers to *Real Housewives*, people get a buzz from wearing a blatant luxury logo. A few Christmas seasons ago, Kris Jenner famously showed off a $15,000 logo-laden Goyard suitcase monogrammed with the words "RICH AS F———," taking logomania to a new level.[10] So, psychologically speaking, what do these famous people get from posing and posturing with expensive sparkly objects? Basically the same thing humans have gotten from them since ancient times: Accessories communicate status, wealth, and power. The world's oldest crown — believed to be from 4500–3600 BC and buried with a prominent member of Copper Age society — was discovered not long ago in Israel.[11] Egyptian queen Nefertiti was among the earliest accessories trendsetters. Her iconic look (kohl eyeliner and dramatic headdress) was so influential, Rihanna paid homage to it on the November 2017 cover of *Vogue Arabia*.[12] From empresses to popes to queens to Disney princesses, crowns, scepters, and glass slippers say all the public needs to know about who's on top.

When a sneakerhead sleeps on the sidewalk all night outside a Foot Locker to pay $220 for a rare pair of Nikes, what's motivating that mission? If we go back to my theory of Mood Enhancement Dress, it's easy to see how wearing designer logos slots right in. Wearing a Chanel bag tells you that you are worthy of luxury, that you are part of an elite club. Owning one makes you important. This association with luxury through accessories may even bring you actual (if temporary) joy. You may also feel a sense of community, as you connect with other sneakerheads who recognize your Nike LeBron 14's. None of these psychological benefits should be discounted (ahem).

And luxury labels work *fast*. In a series of experiments by Dutch researchers published in the journal *Evolution and Human Behavior*, people wearing obvious designer logos received preferential treatment in social situations. They were met with more cooperation when they asked random strangers to answer survey questions. They received more job recommendations at higher suggested salaries. They even collected more money than their counterparts in plain clothes when soliciting donations for charity. "People react to designer labels as signals of underlying quality," said the researchers. "Only the best can afford them."[13] Yes, the instant we see a designer logo, our brains interpret it as shorthand for a high-quality person. Even though we know this assumption may be wrong.

As with Gollum and his obsession with the Ring, it can be perilous to seek self-esteem through shiny little objects. If wearing an expensive accessory makes you feel like a poser, if there is incongruence between what the item represents (I'm rich! I'm fancy! I'm fabulous!) and who you feel you truly are, if buying it is well beyond your budget and strains your bank account, then the logo will feel more like a stamp of foolishness. Luxury accessories are not a substitute for self-worth.

Often when people wear items that loudly telegraph their status to others, it's to compensate for insecurity or to restore diminished personal power. One study in the *Journal of Consumer Research* found that our level of materialism (aka the reliance on stuff to make you happy) is highest in middle school, when self-esteem is at its lowest. When teens were given positive feedback from their peers, their sense of self-worth improved and their desire for material goods decreased.[14] Does your logo-stamped bag scream, "I feel powerless so I'm overcompensating with this obviously expensive item"? In a different study, co-authored by Northwestern's Adam Galinsky of "Enclothed Cognition" fame, individuals were asked to recall a time when they felt powerless. Right afterward, those people were much more inclined to purchase luxury items like silk ties and fur coats, and to spend more money on those items. They did not demonstrate the same drive to buy everyday items like minivans or dryers. "Spending beyond one's means to purchase status-related items is . . . a costly coping strategy for dealing with psychological threats such as feeling powerless," write Galinsky and his colleague Derek D. Rucker. And not surprisingly, minorities like blacks and Hispanics are found to spend *more of their money* on status symbols (conspicuous consumption) than whites.[15] In other words, the thirst for luxury accessories is strongest for those who face systemic powerlessness. Christian Jarrett, writing for *The Psychologist*, published by the British Psychological Society, sums it up: "How much we see our things as an extension of ourselves may depend in part in how confident we feel about who we are."[16]

So what's the antidote to all this materialism, this urge to gain status through stuff? It's finding other ways to build yourself up, to establish your worth—through fitness, sports, volunteering, seeking community, work, whatever floats your boat. Bling will not cure your blues. That's wisdom I'm going to reflect on the next time a bag that costs more than my rent starts calling my name. And the next time one calls to you, ask yourself: Am I feeling powerless? Why? And is there something self-affirming and cost-free I can do about it?

ACCESSORIES AND POLITICS: FROM PUSSYHATS TO PURSE CHARMS

Sometimes it really is the smallest objects that make the most noise. Need proof that accessories can truly pack a punch, politically? Two words: MAGA hat. When fashion hits the headlines these days, it seems to inevitably be about accessories. In 2017 Nike unveiled its Pro Hijab. Some heralded it as a mainstream step toward inclusivity. Others accused the brand of promoting women's oppression. Months later, Missoni sent pussyhats marching down the runway. Miuccia Prada once told the *Wall Street Journal:* "What you wear is how you present yourself to the world, especially today, when human contacts are so quick. Fashion is instant language."[17] Anyone who has been reading this book up to this point knows I absolutely agree with that statement. If Prada produced a t-shirt with the slogan "Fashion Is Instant Language" on it, I would have bought it and worn it to class. And yet, in the ultimate betrayal, it was Prada that committed one of the most painfully racist fashion blunders of the past decade by designing and releasing an offensive accessory. During the 2018 holiday season, the company unveiled a $550 handbag charm that bore an uncanny resemblance to Golliwog dolls and Little Black Sambo. "Fashion companies aren't just selling gadgets," wrote Robin Givhan in the *Washington Post,* reporting on the controversy after Prada apologized, pulled the charms from stores, and convened a diversity and inclusion advisory council. "They are selling personal identity, intimate fantasies, and even self-esteem. They are treading in sensitive territory."[18]

A TIP OF THE HAT: ACCESSORIES, CULTURE, AND COMMUNITY

In her essay "What the Black Church Taught Me about Lipstick," author Stacia Brown writes about an expression she often heard growing up: "You don't look like what you've been through."[19] In other words, life may have been rough on you, but you'd never know it to look at you. For Brown, who grew up poor, lipstick was an accessible means of Mood Enhancement. The magic of lipstick is, no matter what troubles the world has dropped at your door, you still have the ability to smooth some on and put your best face forward. I loved her essay.

For me, hats hold the power. Well, actually, it's not just hats. Head wraps, wigs, and hairstyles also play a huge role in black culture and in my personal history. In fact, when I contemplate the various ways I cover my head and why, it leads me to thoughts about feminism and community, identity and intimacy. These days, the headlines pummel us over and over with heartbreaking stories of insensitivity and ignorance related to black hair, such as when a black teenager named Andrew Johnson was made to cut off his dreadlocks in order to participate in a New Jersey high school wrestling match. (He opted to allow a referee to cut off his locks rather than forfeit the match, which he won.)[20] Or when a retail employee at a Denver Ross Dress for Less store was told by two white managers to cover up her Bantu knots. This was allowed to happen despite the fact that the employee handbook mandated nothing about hairstyles, and Bantu knots have been worn by white celebrities like Gwen Stefani and Reese Witherspoon without incident.[21]

In the black community, what we wear to cover our hair is interwoven with identity. And this is true for me personally. Covering my natural hair with accessories like hats, scarves, or printed head wraps is much more than a fashion statement. It's a declaration of independence. When black women of a certain age go to church, they wear elaborate hats. There's a codified system going on here. Church hats are a way to show respect for yourself, for your community, for God. Historically, this trend started as a way for women who worked as domestic servants during the week to shed their dreary maid uniforms and peacock in their full plumage on Sundays. Even if these women had a terrible week, even if their lives are falling apart, they will still dress to the nines and go to church on Sunday (Mood Enhancement 101). It is understood by our community that the hats work in a sort of diametric opposition to these ladies' life experience: the more hell they've been through, the more flamboyant the hats. We're talking beaded, feathered, bejeweled, bedazzled headwear. They wear their hats with pride, rain or shine, in extreme heat, and often over wigs, but you will never see them sweat. (The fans help.) I've always admired how, in order to keep the hats from falling off their heads, they display incredible poise and posture. Even when they testify, shout *hallelujah!*, and praise dance, the hats never move. According to North Carolina marketing professor Deirdre T. Guion Peoples, this particular way of carrying oneself is called "hattitude."[22]

As a kid, I used to love going to church just to look at the hats. Like British little girls riveted by the fascinators at society weddings, I would marvel at the beautiful parade. I've never worn one of these hats myself, however. As a young single woman with no husband or children, I wouldn't be considered ready. If I dared to put on a church hat, I'd be violating an unspoken rule. The older ladies in my neighborhood would be like, "Girl, *bye*." You see, hats signal seniority, stature. Only when you're a seasoned survivor of life's trials and tribulations have you earned the right to wear one. They are so sacrosanct, when photographer and author Michael Cunningham put together a portrait book of black women wearing church hats, he named it *Crowns*.[23]

When I was growing up, across the street from my mother's house lived an older woman we'll call Mrs. Johnson.* This lady had been *through* it. She had moved from Mississippi to Cleveland, raised five kids, and worked for nearly sixty years at the post office — which we considered a very good job because it was a government job. I remember going over to her house just to see her hat collection. Every hat was carefully stored in its own hatbox. I was awed by the boxes' pretty pastel colors, the pristine tissue paper. Like a general showing off his war medals, when an older woman unveils her hat collection, she is revealing her badges of honor. Her hats affirm her veteran status.

I know a different, wealthy older black woman who is something of a matriarchal leader in Brooklyn. She told me about an incident that took place many years ago, when she was shopping in a high-end department store in midtown Manhattan. The saleswoman asked her what she was doing there, then trailed her suspiciously around the sweater department, making it crystal clear she did not belong. So the matriarch bought every single cashmere sweater on the display table. She recently invited me over to see her hat collection. It was a sacred invitation I was honored to receive. As she is getting on in years, she gave me five of her hats, to keep. I am not kidding when I say this gift felt as momentous as receiving a diploma. I have all the hats safely stowed in their hatboxes. They fit perfectly. I am waiting to grow into them.

What I do wear currently is head wraps. For those who don't know, lots of black girls wear them when our hair is not done — meaning we aren't wearing it European style, long and straight, usually thanks to a wig or a weave. I have thick natural hair that goes down to my bra strap, but I never show it in public. On days when I want to give my wig a break or want to let my scalp breathe and still look fashionable, I'll wear a leopard-print turban, styled in a beehive. My natural hair connects me to my childhood—to the time before my mother processed or straightened my hair, before weaves or wigs ever entered the conversation. When my natural hair is exposed, I am in my most innocent, raw, and vulnerable state. Being seen with no makeup on is *nothing* compared to the exposed feeling this brings. As adults, black women have been conditioned to hide this aspect of ourselves. The only people I will allow to see my natural hair are my parents and my brothers. Someone I'm dating right now keeps asking to see me without my head wrap or scarf on, but I just don't feel we are there yet.

Nowadays, fueled by pop culture and social media, there is a movement brewing whereby women are becoming more Afro-centric or "woke," and they're saying, *To hell with wigs and weaves!* They are showing off their natural hair in all its glory, embracing their culture and their authenticity, posting hashtags like #WakandaForever on Instagram. My heart swells with pride for them. But I also believe that the way you wear your hair, what you show or what you conceal, is an extremely personal choice. If you are seeing my natural hair, it means you're my hairdresser, my best friend, or my husband. For me, it is that intimate.

I also feel empowered, stalking the streets of New York City in my leopard head wrap. It offers me more than just protection from the elements, or from vulnerability. It makes me feel regal. In order to keep the cloth from slipping off my head, I have to walk with an elegant gait, my neck elongated, my back ramrod straight, just like the hat ladies in church. So why am I sharing this with you, besides to demonstrate the psychological power of accessories, as this chapter promised? I want to point out that as we are torn apart by cultural, religious, racial, and political divisions in our society, hats connect us. When I see Orthodox Jewish women who cover their heads with wigs, or Muslim women who wear a hijab, when I think of Mrs. Johnson and the Brooklyn matriarch, I feel we all have something deeply personal in common. As novelist Zadie Smith (who wears head wraps) told NPR, "Many, many more women in the world wear something on their heads than don't, and I like to be part of that sisterhood."[24] We are all queens wearing crowns.

THE BOTTOM LINE
KEY TIPS AND TAKEAWAYS FROM CHAPTER 7

- **Unbreakable bonds.** Accessories can reduce stress by making us feel connected to loved ones or community. If you don't have a wedding ring or family heirloom, choose your own meaningful accessory.
- **Wear it on repeat.** By ritualistically wearing or carrying the accessory every day (it need not be jewelry), you increase its psychological power and may come to believe it can calm or protect you.
- **Logomania much?** If you are really coveting luxury labels, you might be trying to compensate for diminished personal power. What can you do today to empower yourself that has nothing to do with acquiring status symbols?

Chapter 8

ARE YOU DRESSING FOR YOURSELF OR FOR SOMEONE ELSE?

Conformity is the only real fashion crime. To not dress like yourself and to sublimate your spirit to some kind of group identity is succumbing to fashion fascism.

—*Simon Doonan*

Clothes can become lightning rods for emotion when we wear them to gain approval or be accepted. Have you ever bought a new, trendy item because your style didn't feel good enough? Have you ever *avoided* wearing something you love or downplayed certain aspects of yourself because you worried they could bring you unwanted attention, mistaken assumptions, or prejudice? When you go too far in either direction—using clothes to fit in, or denying yourself clothes for fear of sticking out—you lose what makes you *you*. And that's when things can get ugly.

As I've mentioned before, my signature style is Minimalist Glam. When I teach at FIT, I go heavy on the *glam*. Being surrounded by creative students, I'm inspired to experiment and push boundaries with my look. My confidence is on full display, my white cape and leopard-print stilettos in regular rotation. When I go home to visit my relatives in Ohio, though...let's just say you *cannot* dress like that in Cleveland. If I dared, the reaction would be swift and decisive. My friends and family would be like, *You're too much. What the hell?* My family does not hold back. So when

I go home, I actively mute my look. I'll wear my hair natural. Flat shoes as opposed to heels. No makeup. No jewelry. Bare nails. Unstructured handbags. I dress down. I even have a specific collection of clothes that I set aside for trips home, featuring lots of sweatshirts, leggings, and (though I normally avoid them) sneakers.

At first glance, this behavior may seem harsh—even self-negating. My cousin Ericka recently said to me, "Dawnn, why do you say you have an 'Ohio self' and a 'New York self'? You're just yourself! Why do you go to such extremes to change? Be who you are!" And I was like, *Girl, you don't even know! You do not understand my family.* I am making a conscious choice to blend in. I don't want to be ostracized. In the field of social psychology, there's a lot of discussion about being in the "in group" versus the "out group." Assimilative wardrobe can function like your membership to some type of club or fraternity. I imagine my family as just that sort of club. And I want to belong, to feel a sense of community. So if the attire requirement is cargo pants and a baseball cap, I am willing to accept that for the sake of social harmony and emotional safety. With full awareness, I am prioritizing those benefits over my desire to self-express through clothes. It helps to know, of course, that I'll have the opportunity to dress to the nines once I get back to my life in New York.

When I travel to Dubai to meet with clients, they all wear the traditional dress, the hijab or the abaya. I see a parallel here. Your opinion on my choice to dress down in Ohio may depend on your cultural perspective. On the one hand, from an individualist point of view, dressing in quieter clothes may seem too self-sacrificing. Unjust. You may think I'm oppressed. On the other hand, you could view it as me honoring the group, the collective. In some Asian and Middle Eastern cultures (and apparently in my family), following the group norm is a sign of respect and solidarity. After all, we adhere to professional dress codes. Why not familial ones?

I'm conflicted about this. I see both sides. And I'm being completely honest here. My decision to tone down my style in Ohio is very much self-protective. I do not want to be criticized for what I wear. For the days when I'm at home, dressing to fit in with my family feels better emotionally than risking provoking their commentary. I value protecting myself emotionally in that situation *more* than I value feeling 100 percent totally amazing in my clothes. Psychologically, for me, in that context, style is a less important consideration than feeling safe and at ease.

It is not uncommon to use fashion to avoid putting yourself in an uncomfortable social situation. Some people in the LGBTQIA+ community deal with this on a daily basis. I recently attended a professional training wherein colleagues and I were presented with a case study. The subject was a young gay man who was a student in New York City, but who grew up in a devoutly religious conservative family in the South. The scenario, as it was presented to us, was that when he was home with his family, he dressed to "pass" as a cisgender heterosexual male, wearing traditionally masculine attire. But when he was living his own life in New York, he made more colorful, gender-neutral, form-fitting, and nontraditional clothing choices. He was not out to his parents.

I would not presume to tell this young man to ditch his source of protection—his traditionally masculine clothes—and risk exposing himself to disparagement, ostracism, pain, heartache, and possibly violence unless and until he chose to do so. Sometimes it's just easier to protect yourself. To choose the lesser of two evils. Sometimes "just be yourself" is easier said than done. Clothing can be armor whether you're in a Middle Eastern country with modesty laws, the LGBTQIA+ community, or my damn family. It can be preferable to pass than to suffer. Perhaps you can't afford *not* to pass. And because clothing plays such a vital role in our relationships, people make these choices every single day. I don't judge them for it.

But there's a caveat to all of this and it is crucial: I may dress down in Ohio, but when I do, I make sure I have the nicest Jordans, Adidas, or Balenciaga sneakers and the crispest Yankees cap around. I find small, subtle ways to please myself, to express my individual style, to personalize my look even as I assimilate—even if no one else notices these touches but me. That's the most important lesson of this chapter: I want you to understand that there are still ways to be yourself, and to make a look your own, while meeting the requirements of the collective, without making yourself vulnerable to bias. Whatever you wear, *there has to be some level of authenticity,* whether it's blatant or subtle. I'm not so concerned with what that level is, as long as it's there — as long as *you feel* you're being genuine to yourself. You just have to find that thread somewhere and weave it in.

The way I modify my style in Ohio, the way the young gay man from the case study dresses when he goes home to the South — all of these behaviors fall under the umbrella of **Fashion Identification Assimilation.** I define this as dressing to blend into your sociocultural situation. Within that larger framework is a behavior I call **Fashion Situational Code Switching.** This is when people (especially minorities) modify their style to get along in certain situations, and then transition back into a different mode of dress in others. Think of it like toggling between two open pages on your Web browser.

So many of us engage in these behaviors without fully realizing it. As I mentioned in chapter 4, I have a travel uniform. When I go to the airport, I usually dress in a very specific style that enables me to assimilate into practically any culture. In my experience, if I go to the airport looking as avant-garde as I do at FIT, people will stare at me. So my uniform (all black, usually a soft turtleneck sweater or button-down, cigarette pants, and black stiletto heels) helps me blend in almost anywhere while looking professional and appropriate. I have found this outfit works wherever I am in the world and suits many occasions. I have worn it to Dubai, to Ukraine, to South Korea. I have worn it during corporate lectures, to client meetings, and at London hotel teas. Simply by donning my uniform, I'm a step closer to assimilating into whatever culture I may find myself in. Code switching and assimilation don't always make me feel incredibly stylish, but they do allow me to feel calm, poised, and protected, whatever the context.

But before I go further, I'd like to tell you about another experience I had with these issues. I celebrated a big birthday a few years ago. Instead of doing my usual thing and hanging out at a rooftop lounge with my girls, I flew to Dubai to hit the clubs and the beach. It was a beyond glamorous way to begin a new year and I loved every minute. My trip home to New York included a planned layover in Oslo. And during that flight, the Norwegian airliner I was on experienced sudden engine failure and started rapidly descending. We had to make an emergency landing in — of all places — Shiraz, Iran. As you can imagine, I had only my party clothes with me: white silk pants, a glittering going-out top, a metallic shirtdress, my (energizing!) tangerine swimsuit. I was wearing a version of my go-to travel uniform: my black floral-print silk blouse and matching trousers from Ann Taylor. When we landed in Iran, my fellow passengers and I had to hand over our passports, and despite reassuring calls from both the US State Department and the local Swiss embassy, I felt rattled and completely out of my element. Among other concerns, I remember thinking, *Oh my God, am I dressed appropriately?*

That's when the airline staffers began handing out blankets, instructing us to cover ourselves in accordance with local laws. I noticed that the woman who handed me the blanket was wearing a silk hijab, and that it was gorgeous. I thought to myself, *If I am being forced to cover up, I'd at least prefer to look like that. I don't want to look like I just rolled out of bed and took the blanket with me!* Once we were off the plane and inside the Shiraz airport, I got to chatting with a twenty-two-year-old Iranian woman who told me she had been arrested a few years earlier for having her neck exposed in public. I was suddenly terribly aware that my blouse had no top button. And the blanket situation only added to my anxiety, making me feel more vulnerable, that I was sticking out like a sore thumb. I worried I was communicating disrespect and inviting disapproval and potential punishment simply by looking like myself.

We were escorted to a Shiraz hotel, where we would wait for over twenty-four hours for the airline to send a new plane to pick us up. After I settled in, I asked the hotel staff to direct me to a nearby boutique, where I bought a modest blouse and a scarf to cover my head. The shopkeeper kindly showed me how to style my head cover the way local women do (another example of Fashion Identification Assimilation). I wore my new clothes back to the hotel and kept them on for the remainder of my stay in Iran. And as soon as I stepped inside the lobby, something remarkable began to happen. The hotel employees—particularly the men—who had pretty much ignored me during the check-in process, were suddenly falling all over themselves to help me. One offered me coffee, and when I explained that I had no money to pay for it, insisted I take it for free. The next day, another said, *Can I help you with your bags? Oh—you wait inside the hotel and I'll tell you when they are ready to board the shuttle bus back to the airport. There's no point in you being outside. Don't worry yourself.* Meanwhile, the rest of the passengers were herded onto the street like cattle to wait.

What exactly was going on here? I was reaping the rewards of the behaviors central to this chapter (Fashion Situational Code Switching and Fashion Identification Assimilation). I adapted my style to better assimilate with or gain acceptance by a sociocultural group. And while my motivation for doing it in Iran was a little bit to Mood Enhance and a lot to avoid imprisonment, it was, to a degree, a familiar feeling. Both behaviors are really about fitting in and conformity. And most of us do this regularly, without even really thinking about it. Yes, even in America, land of the free. For example, when we buy an It bag, we are using fashion to assimilate and gain acceptance. In fact, our psychological reasons for doing it are not fundamentally that different, no matter where we are in the world.

Something else happened as I prepared to board the plane out of Shiraz—and it left me shook. As I was passing through the screening area, about to cross into what was effectively international territory, a female Iranian airport security officer unexpectedly came into my personal space and yanked the head scarf off my head. I am deliberately using the word yanked, not pulled. "You are free!" she said. "Go now! You are free!" She and her colleagues (other women) clasped their hands together in quiet celebration. I empathized with their intentions. I got it. In that moment, for me, covering my head was a choice. For her, every day, it is a legal requirement. She does not have the opportunity to code switch. She's effectively locked into her head covering. And here she was, quite literally stripping me of my need to assimilate once it was no longer mandated. But in part because she made that choice for me, without seeking my permission, I felt defenseless, naked, and exposed. I pulled the head scarf back up and made my way onto the plane. As soon as we were safely up in the air, I let it fall away. I had almost totally forgotten about it by the time I made it back to New York. But as I sit here now, thinking deeply about how we all dress to assimilate and why, I wonder if any of us are truly free . . .

ASSIMILATION NATION: WHY WE ALL DRESS TO FIT IN

Dress codes are a regular aspect of everyday life. Whether explicit (a black-tie wedding) or less clearly defined ("business casual"), it is advisable — and advantageous — to dress "appropriately" for your situation, whatever that means. The thing is, it's not always easy to understand and act on unwritten rules. Repeated nuggets of style advice only add to the noise and confusion: *It is always better to be overdressed than underdressed. Always dress like you're going to meet your worst enemy* (thanks, Kimora Lee Simmons).[1] *Dress for the job you want, not the job you have.* Studies show people who dress skillfully enjoy social and economic advantages.[2] But there are added challenges for women, people of color, minorities, and the marginalized when it comes to meeting this arbitrary standard of "looking appropriate." Does "appropriate" mean we have to modify our natural hair? Show some skin (or else you're boring), but never too much (or else you're a THOT)? Should we avoid hoodies, head wraps, bindis, or any items with overtly racial or religious associations for the sake of safety or social acceptance? To avoid being accused of cultural appropriation? (Much more on this in chapter 10.) Do we have to spend a lot of money to be approved of or accepted?

Sometimes we are compelled to adhere to multiple codes within our individual lives. If you look around, conversations about code switching are happening everywhere. Plenty of public figures have opened up about this issue and the complex emotions that come with it. Comic Dave Chappelle once said on *Inside the Actors Studio,* "Every black American is bilingual. All of us. We speak street vernacular, and we speak job interview. There's a certain way I gotta speak to have access."[3] Jessica Williams, the actress and comic, has said that when she was growing up in California, she never quite fit in—not at her mostly white school and not at her black Baptist church. "I was always told that I acted too white," she told NPR. "All of those things were really damaging. I grew up hearing, 'You're pretty for a black girl,' 'You speak well for a black girl.'"[4] Actress Kerry Washington was raised in the Bronx by a college professor mother and real estate broker father. They lived across the street from a housing project, but she spent her days at the posh Upper East Side Spence School, a private school also attended by Gwyneth Paltrow and Emmy Rossum. Moving between two neighborhoods, two groups of friends, two socioeconomic classes gave Washington a sort of PhD in code switching. "It's almost like being bicultural," she once told the *New York Post's Page Six Magazine.* "I had the benefit of learning how to navigate between cultures fluently at a very early age."[5] Once her star began to rise in Hollywood, Washington recognized fashion as yet another way to gain an edge. She noticed other actresses whose careers were on fire thanks to their status as style trendsetters. "So I sort of developed a new character: Red-Carpet Kerry," she told *Glamour.* "I actually called...a good friend, and literally asked, 'How do you pronounce Hermès?' Red-Carpet Kerry needed to know."[6] Language is fashion and fashion is language.

Whether it's about the way you speak or the way you dress, assimilation and code switching are about communication. Most of us are pros at this, believe it or not. We adapt our body language, our slang, our style, depending on the different social situations we find ourselves in. Have you ever hung out with a friend from a different country and found yourself accidentally mimicking her accent? Have you ever been in an elevator with a powerful executive at your company and suddenly found yourself standing taller, quieting your hands, and choosing your words carefully? Have your co-workers or roommates ever overheard you on the phone with your mom or significant other, and only later did you realize you were talking in a sort of sugar-coated baby voice? Awkward much? Hey, you can't help it! Just because you are code switching doesn't necessarily mean you are being fake. There are many ways to express your authentic self.

When we talk about code switching and fashion, we're talking about dressing to gain acceptance—like my Ohio versus New York look. You switch, and then you switch back. You toggle and shift. You may dress one way at home around your family, another way on nights out with friends, another way on dates, and a totally different way at work. You may even favor one style with your nearest and dearest and another with a new clique you are (even subconsciously) hoping to impress. The impulse to code switch is usually accompanied by thoughts like... *Will my friends/ followers/co-workers think this look is cool? Will guys think this is hot? Oh, I can't wear* that *to meet those people.* Your look, your hairstyle, your mannerisms, your attitude, your swagger, the way you carry yourself—it all varies. But there's nothing really wrong with adapting your presentation to different situations, so long as you are keeping it real in some way. So long as you are in the driver's seat. "Fashion can be so valuable—particularly to women—as it affords them so many choices to construct the public persona they wish to have," fashion critic Robin Givhan told *Thought Economics.* "It really can allow them to determine how people respond to them in that first 15 seconds. If you understand that? It's incredibly powerful."[7] Fashion Situational Code Switching and Fashion Identity Assimilation can be a natural execution of that power. But the public persona you're constructing has to be *your choice* on some level. You have got to be both the designer and the model of your own personal brand. You still have to please yourself even while you are dressing within the parameters set by someone else. You have to be conscious of the code.

CODE SWITCHING AND CONFORMITY: THE EMOTIONAL COST OF FITTING IN

Whether or not a look is successful really comes down to how authentic you feel in it. It is one thing to dress to respect the rules (a corporate dress code requiring a suit) while still maintaining your unique personal style (your favorite jewelry and shoes). It is another to cover up who you are entirely in order to fit in with a crowd or to be asked to remove all aspects of your individuality. Many of us walk this fine line every day. But downplaying your authentic self or hiding your background because people may have a problem with it can really mess with your emotions. There has to be relief in sight, a chance to express your genuine self, an opportunity for individuality. A good analogy would be schoolkids who are required to wear uniforms but personalize them with their own spin on skirt length, hairstyles, socks, shoes, pins, or backpack charms. A little bit of self-expression can make the difference between feeling like a faceless cog in the machine and a fully formed person. Jumping on bandwagons and following trends in order to be liked, or betraying your values in order to conform, usually leads to feelings of inauthenticity, incongruence, and shame. This is what happens when you cause yourself discomfort in order to make *other* people more comfortable; when you bury who you are completely in order to get along in the world. Let's meet someone who exemplifies these issues.

CASE STUDY: MY BOYFRIEND, MY STYLIST

I'm currently working with a client, an introverted, very sweet young woman in her mid-twenties we'll call Jackie.* Jackie was recently dumped by her long-term boyfriend, and when she reached out to me, her self-worth was deflated. Jackie explained that she had been dressing to please her boyfriend for the majority of their years-long relationship. In fact, he had edited her closet and would regularly pick out her outfits. He would say, "I would like you in this, I would like you in that." Jackie is a people pleaser who was raised to believe in traditional gender roles. So her boyfriend playing the part of stylist didn't seem like a problem for her during their relationship. But after he broke up with her, she was left with nothing that defined her identity — or her style — separate from him. Once he was gone, she felt lost, especially when it came to what to wear. She looked at her closet and saw only items he had picked out, shopped for with her, or explicitly approved.

During one of our phone sessions, Jackie was especially anxious, as she planned to attend an upcoming church service at the congregation where her ex was also a member. She was sure she'd bump into him and was desperate to feel confident when she did. I spent some time helping her prepare. We did some role playing. What are you going to say when you see him? I asked. What are you going to wear?

Jackie's first instinct was to wear an outfit he approved of, in hopes of impressing him. She was still locked into her old pattern. She texted me a photo of one particular outfit he liked — a long-sleeve emerald-green body-con minidress accented with a colorful scarf and tan suede high heels. It was a gorgeous look, but it wasn't one she'd chosen herself.

So I said, Let's play this out. Imagine yourself running into your ex while wearing that outfit. How would you feel? And she said, Well, I would feel nervous. And really not my best self because he picked out those clothes, and I'm still dressing for him even though we're not even together. My response? No.

Scratch that. Do you have something in your closet that feels empowering to you? If you saw this guy today, what would make you feel like this confident, badass woman, while still being conservative enough for church? *She owned nothing that fit the bill. Everything that he disliked she had trashed long ago. Everything she still owned was linked to a memory of him. Her closet felt contaminated.*

Style Rx

Though I normally don't encourage needless shopping, in this case I advised Jackie to go out and buy a new outfit, to make a fresh start. As she shopped, she texted me images of options from the store, seeking my approval. It was evident to me that this was her central issue psychologically. She lacked an internal barometer for what she liked; she had spent so long dressing to please someone else.

As she texted me photos of each item she was considering, she would ask, Is this cute? Or is it ugly? *I never answered her. Instead, I would reply with a question of my own:* Would you feel empowered in that? *And several times she returned items to the rack, saying,* Oh no, no. I wouldn't. *As she texted me shots of every new item, I kept asking her,* How do you feel in this? It doesn't matter if it's on-trend. How do *you* feel?

I gave Jackie a rating system to help clarify her reactions to the clothes: Good, Better, Best. *She tried on one piece and texted me that she felt good. I wasn't satisfied.* I'm trying to get you to feel the best, *meaning powerful, I told her. Finally she ended up selecting an outfit that met that criterion for her: black high-waist skinny jeans, gray suede high-heel peep-toe booties, a white oxford shirt with architectural cutouts layered under a long sleeveless gray cable-knit sweater. It was a mix of high-end labels and no-name brands. I asked Jackie to envision running into her ex in her new outfit: How would she feel? She said,* Well, if I saw him, I would feel powerful and I would just casually say hello. I wouldn't care. *Talking through this scenario helped her to connect her sense of strength and preparation with her new clothes. It imbued the clothes with psychological power.*

- - - - - - - - -

It's important to note that Jackie chose pants instead of a skirt. Thanks to her ex's preferences, she tended to wear a lot of dresses and skirts, but she may start to rethink that as a result of our work together. It turns out she felt stronger and less vulnerable in pants. When pants are tight or snug against your body, it can foster a feeling of security. You don't need to worry if your legs are crossed, if you're sweating, if you're exposed. You are freer to be yourself.

Jackie texted me after attending the service and reported that her outfit made her feel confident and secure. She never even saw her ex.

We all want approval. And there are times when we all bow to outside pressure to adapt our looks. Think of your mom forcing you to wear something itchy or formal to a family party or on school picture day. Doing this may bring up feelings of inadequacy. Fashion Situational Code Switching and Fashion Identification Assimilation come at a psychological cost when you change your look because you are pressured to do so in some way, because looking like yourself will be somehow disadvantageous, rendering you unsafe or leaving you feeling unworthy. My advice is to counterbalance this external pressure with small, subtle bits of self-expression. When the motivation to code switch comes from outside forces and not from within, and when you cannot express yourself even in little ways—when every last ember of your individual style is snuffed out by forces beyond your control—that's when emotional problems arise.

My unplanned trip to Iran was just my latest experience with assimilation and code switching in action. It wasn't my first. And I'm not an outlier.

Lawyers dress in certain attire to seem more trustworthy to judges and juries. Politicians do it. (Remember Mitt Romney in his "man of the people" jeans and button-down mode?) Teenagers do it. Wealthy women do it. Superheroes do it. (Clark Kent versus Superman? Classic code switching.) We all modify our dress to ensure our security (emotional or otherwise). The same girl who wears a crop top on a date may wear a turtleneck to meet her boyfriend's parents. The edgy rocker with tattoo sleeves may cover them up under a button-down for a business conference, transforming himself into a clean-cut corporate citizen. On HBO's hit show *Insecure*, Yvonne Orji plays Molly, who works as a corporate attorney. In season two, Molly finds out that her white male colleague earns a higher salary than she does. So she ditches her hot-pink high-fashion dresses and starts wearing traditional black and navy power suits to work. "She realizes that just being good at what she does isn't good enough, so maybe she needs to switch it up a little bit," costume designer Ayanna James told *USA Today*.[8]

When I think about Fashion Identification Assimilation and Code Switching, I also think about the black Ohio state legislator Emilia Strong Sykes. As reported by the *New York Times,* she was searched before entering the statehouse because, the guard told her, "You don't look like a legislator." She now dresses extra-conservatively and is sure to wear her government pin on her lapel — to look the part.[9] I think about the African American Amazon delivery guy who (per *The Atlantic*) wears any branded clothing item he can find — a shirt, a ball cap, a beanie on top of that ball cap — all with the Amazon logo prominently displayed, to avoid getting mistaken for a burglar when he approaches someone's front door.[10] I think about my friend the judge whom I mentioned in chapter 1, who feels at risk on the subway without his robes on. What are the benefits of obeying certain dress codes? What are the consequences of ignoring them?

This issue doesn't affect only minorities. It impacts everyone. I speak with young women who want to feel sexy and beautiful, to celebrate their curves (the way modern marketers tell us we must!), but then are met with harassment on the street or unsolicited dick pics online. As a result, some opt for colorless, baggy clothes. I talk with parents of young kids who see themselves erased. They make wardrobe planning their lowest priority because if they dare to get flashy with fashion, others might assume they are selfish, that they're neglecting their kids to glam up, that their priorities are out of whack. We can all imagine that the mom who shows up on the playground in yoga pants might be welcomed differently from the mom who shows up in a pencil skirt and heels.

Affluent middle-aged women practice Fashion Identification Assimilation when they style themselves with their social groups in mind. Some wear only what they believe will be accepted by the hive mind, hesitant to deviate or self-express for fear of being ostracized. Or perhaps they are just subconsciously attracted to clothes that will meet with group approval. *New York Magazine* took note of a trend that spread like wildfire across Manhattan's Upper East Side and in certain neighborhoods of Brooklyn and Westchester County a few years ago. To this day, if you walk down the street in Park Slope in winter, it seems like every other lady you see is wearing the same $100 Orolay puffer coat from Amazon. The highly specific trend reportedly exploded through word of mouth and insider observation at places like Soul Cycle, Physique 57, and Bloomingdale's.[11] Anthropologist Wednesday Martin wrote about following fashion trends from an anthropological perspective in her book *Primates of Park Avenue.* One day, she told the *New York Post,* she was walking down East 79th Street in Manhattan when a woman deliberately bumped into her with an Hermès Birkin bag—knocking Martin out of the way on an otherwise empty sidewalk. "Something about these arrogant women, who pushed and crowded me like I didn't exist, made me want a beautiful, expensive bag," Martin said. "Like a totem object, I believed, it might protect me from them."[12] Birkin bags can cost six figures. Our human instinct to seek acceptance using style is so strong that even an anthropologist whose *job* it is to study group behavior wanted to buy her way in.

CRACKING THE CODE: HOW TO STAY TRUE TO YOU

Now you might say, Okay Dawnn, I get it. Fashion Identification Assimilation and Code Switching are real! I probably do it! But what the heck does this have to do with what I'm supposed to wear in the year 2020? *I'm* not buying a Birkin bag to fit in with my fancy friends. And I can't do a damn thing about the dress code at my job. Well, first of all, I want you to be aware of how we all assimilate anytime we question our natural instincts to dress or look a certain way in light of how other people may react. This is most obvious when you avoid expressing your race/religion/culture/ethnicity/body shape through style, as you may have to deal with negative stereotypes. But *any* time you succumb to other people's expectations of how you are "supposed" to look—whether it's picking out an outfit to please your mother-in-law or buying something trendy on Instagram—it can bring up feelings of inadequacy and incongruence. So what can you do about it? How do you push back? How do you break free?

As I said earlier in this chapter, I find it helps to start small, to assert and celebrate your true self in little ways. Again, we come back to Focal Accessories. When I was growing up, my mom made a big deal about how I should never leave the house without earrings on. Now I wear them every day as a way to stay connected to her, even if I'm the only one who knows that's why I'm doing it. Hairstyling can be another way to express authenticity when your clothes must be up to code. Like my client Lisa,* from the Case Study in chapter 2, Yara Shahidi, the Harvard undergrad and *Grown-ish* star, rocks her natural hair on red carpets. In doing so, she refuses to assimilate, resisting the pressures of Hollywood beauty standards, which celebrate European-style hair. With her look, Shahidi is challenging the association between straight hair and professionalism. "I think it is a statement saying that I am not going to change for this event . . . that my curls can do it all," she told *Seventeen*. "It's not stemming from insecurities or trying to blend in, rather it's a moment and opportunity to have fun or do something different."[13] As I mentioned in chapter 1, Massachusetts congresswoman Ayanna Pressley wears her hair in Senegalese braids because that makes her feel, she says, like "my most authentic and powerful self."[14] When Alexandria Ocasio-Cortez was sworn in to Congress, she wore a bright red lip and gold hoop earrings, as an homage to Supreme Court justice and fellow Bronx native Sonia Sotomayor, who was advised to wear neutral-colored nail polish to her confirmation hearings to avoid scrutiny. "She kept her red," tweeted Ocasio-Cortez. "Next time someone tells Bronx girls to take off their hoops, they can just say they're dressing like a congresswoman."[15]

Hooray for all of them. For real. But what if you *have* to assimilate? What if you don't live in liberal places like Hollywood or New York City or wield the power of elected office? What if wearing jewelry, lipstick, nail art, head wraps, or hairstyles that nod to your background or community leads to bias, unspoken or obvious? What if wearing anything other than a business suit gets you mistaken for the help? What if code switching and assimilation are not a choice but a requirement, as with the Ross Dress for Less employee I mentioned in chapter 7 who was told to take down her Bantu knots? As she walked out to buy a head scarf to cover her hairstyle, as directed by her white managers, she posted a viral video about her experience, exposing the injustice on social media. Even as she was in the process of assimilating, she asserted herself. Of course, when we confront these issues every day, the circumstances aren't always so obvious or extreme. Bias is often unspoken, unconscious even. When we internalize beauty norms that make us feel like the "other," we aim negativity directly at ourselves. That's why it's so useful to affirm yourself through fashion. Here are some tips to do just that.

Fashion Psychology Tips

How to Keep It Real

It's all in the details: Even if your office dress code is conservative, you can still express your individuality in little ways. Wear your favorite lipstick, nail color/art, headband, jewelry, or even subtle fragrance. Try an elegant coat in a bold color, eyeglasses in funky mixed-material frames like metallic and tortoiseshell, or a shoe with an architectural heel.

Do your own spin on a trend: If everybody in your clique starts wearing cowboy boots and you just can't even, modify. Motorcycle or riding boots won't invite uncomfortable scrutiny, but they won't make you hate yourself either. Think of it as a peaceful protest.

Balance it out: If you couldn't resist a trend, extend its life by keeping the majority of your outfit classic or neutral. If you bought a boxy bright-orange double-breasted blazer, wear it with a gray t-shirt and gray wide-leg pants. Fall for a maroon sequined mock turtleneck and matching maxi skirt? Tone it down and take it casual with a long black cardigan and black slip-on mules. You now own tie-dyed jeans. Peace. Enjoy them for a season and save them for your daughter. It's all about complementing and counteracting: Glitzy meets simple, sparkle meets softness, bright meets neutral, loud meets quiet, yin and yang.

Assimilating got you down? If you spend every day working in an office that requires you to look basic, I feel you. If your efforts to fit in with the other playground moms left you owning so much athleisure you can't even remember what pants feel like, come to Mama. If your relentless trend chasing made your closet look like H&M and Urban Outfitters had a baby and you're not even sure if it's yours, help is on the way. Here is some tried-and-true advice to help you find your way back to you.

Fashion Psychology Exercise

How to Self-Affirm

Here is an exercise I regularly give my clients. It's called an afformation. Popularized by self-help coach Noah St. John, an afformation is simply an **affirmation in the form of a question.**[16]

You may have tried to meditate or do affirmations before. Perhaps you've sat silently and, in your head, repeated a mantra to yourself like, *I am beautiful and everybody loves me.* (Okay, I pulled that one off of Pinterest.) If you're anything like me or Mr. St. John, you'll not only feel ridiculous intoning this to yourself; you'll start coming up with all sorts of evidence that this is not the case!

Fascinatingly, when we flip affirmations around and ask them in the form of a question, we force ourselves to seek out answers—and they tend to be positive ones. Let's try it together. Ask yourself, *Why am I so beautiful and stylish?* Now your brain has to figure out an answer to that question. You might think to yourself, *I am so beautiful because I love my family. I am so beautiful because I am kind to strangers. I am so beautiful because there is only one me. I am stylish because my clothes are simple and streamlined. I am stylish because I look awesome in yellow. I am stylish because that wrap dress makes me feel elegant.*

Call it reframing, inverting, or flipping the script. Changing a sentence into a question forces you to think differently. Will you feel ridiculous doing this at first? Probably! Do I ask clients to do it in front of a mirror every single day for a week? You betcha. But trust me: If you ask yourself these types of questions repeatedly (and write down your responses!), not only will you start to find positive answers; you will also start to believe them.

Again, I go back to a quote from Lisa in chapter 2: "You've just got to find out what you like about yourself." Remember what fuels your purpose on this earth, what matters to you most, and write it down. Knowing and liking who you are is everything. It is the first step to dressing your best.

TREND CHASING: THE RACE WE'LL NEVER WIN

I hate to be a Debbie Downer after all that affirmation, but I want to get real and share something with you. I was once in a professional situation where I felt my higher-ups kept moving the finish line. They would ask me to fulfill a certain job requirement, but as soon as I did, they would meet, invent, and then implement a new policy that seemed designed to test me further, creating new benchmarks for me to satisfy, one after the next. It was clear they didn't want me to be part of their group and they were looking for ways to concretely establish that I didn't belong. They wanted cause to fire me. Instead, I persevered and stayed in that job for three years, fulfilling every new requirement, determined to prove they were wrong about me.

Chasing fashion trends reminds me of that ever-elusive finish line—the endgame that never comes. Fashion is a system set up to make you think, *Oh, if I could just get that latest item, or rock that new look that's blowing up on social media, or cut bangs in my hair, then I'll feel satisfied with myself. My life will improve. I'll become way more outgoing because I'll have going-out outfits! My ex will cry and drool over my Instagram,* and so on. But then a new season of clothes hits the stores, a new trend catches fire and renders the last one obsolete, passé, out of style. So it's on to the next, and round and round we go.

Fashion Situational Code Switching and Fashion Identification Assimilation go hand in hand with chasing trends. Dressing a certain way in order to gain approval from a social group (or likes from followers) makes us feel inadequate because systems (fast fashion, social media) thrive on our never feeling good enough. As Naomi Wolf writes in an updated version of her seminal book *The Beauty Myth,* over the years, women of every age, body type, and skin tone have reached out to her. These women, she writes, are so beautiful they could be models. And yet they all "admitted to knowing, from the time they could first consciously think, that the ideal was someone tall, thin, white, and blond, a face without pores, asymmetry, or flaws, someone wholly 'perfect,' and someone whom they felt, in one way or another, they were not."[17] Insecurity drives our desire to conform. It also drives us to jump on that hype train and buy an endless stream of fashion trends. Too often, this behavior involves trying to please someone other than yourself, by trying to be someone you are not.

Karl Lagerfeld famously said, "Trendy is the last stage before tacky."[18] But I humbly disagree. Despite my warning, trends aren't the enemy. I love trends. Trends are fun! Indulging in one or two a year can keep your wardrobe fresh and fly. What I'm cautioning against is trying to wear *every* trend, especially given the current speed at which they're being dropped. Buying new clothes all the time is a recipe for financial disaster—not to mention a whole mess of incongruence. Have you ever bought something that everyone else seemed to be buying? (Bike shorts, tiny sunglasses, *Little House on the Prairie* dress, I'm talking to you!) Then you get home and realize the purchase severely upset your bank account, or the item that seemed perfect in the store is ridiculously incompatible with the rest of your closet? I'm here to help. Here's a super-speedy way to tell if trends are spicing up your life—or poisoning it.

This quiz is based on research about what makes us conform to social pressure. Which qualities make a person more likely to, as Lisa said, hop on that hype train? What gives someone the confidence to march to the beat of her own drum and resist being too susceptible to trends? And if you don't yet have that confidence, how can you find it?

Fashion Psychology Quiz

ARE TRENDS TAKING OVER YOUR LIFE?

- Are you part of a group of friends, or extended family, or a work posse that communicates regularly, perhaps via group text or Slack or by regularly hanging out and socializing together?
- Do you often feel like the members of your group agree with one another for the most part? And if you have a dissenting opinion, do you tend to keep it to yourself?

- Do you admire this group's status or attractiveness?
- Are you not yet committed to any specific personal style? Are you still exploring, figuring out what your signature vibe is, and open to trying new looks?
- Do you feel scrutinized by your social group, whether in real life or on social media? Do your friends, family members, co-workers, etc. comment regularly on your appearance or style?
- Are you from a family that strongly encourages respect for social standards? Did your parents drill into you the importance of being polite, of having manners, of being respectful, of observing hierarchies, rituals, and traditions?
- Are you from a collectivist culture? Meaning does your culture prioritize the whole group over the individual? Is your identity strongly tied to this culture?

If you answered YES to more than three of these questions, then you may be more likely to purchase an overabundance of trendy or fast-fashion items. It turns out people are more susceptible to conformist behavior when they meet a certain set of criteria. But even if you don't fit this profile, it's helpful to think critically the next time you consider buying into a fashion trend.

Here's a question that comes up for a lot of my clients and friends: What do you do if you've already been caught in the trend trap? A friend of mine owns at least six (!) flowery fast-fashion summer dresses from Reformation. She was (clearly) really into them for a season, but now it's the middle of winter and she feels "over" them. All she sees when she looks at these dresses is wasted money and an overcrowded closet. And now her self-loathing is snowballing. Looking at those dresses makes her feel like she hates *everything* she owns, so she feels the urge to fix her mistake by engaging in retail therapy and buying more stuff she doesn't really need.

I advised this friend to be more intentional when she shops (see chapter 5) going forward. I suggested she look for more minimalist designs that will better stand the test of time and aren't so moment-driven. I also reminded her that she has *learned* from this experience. Those flowery dresses do have value psychologically. So next summer, when she rediscovers them, she won't beat herself up as much. Instead she'll remember our conversation as a turning point—the moment when she decided to start shopping consciously. She may choose to re-wear the dresses, reinvent them with unexpected accessories (combat boots) or outerwear (moto jacket), or she may give herself permission to donate or resell them and move on. Either way, she will have reframed the story she tells herself about them. The next time she sees them she'll say to herself: No surprise there. I already knew those dresses weren't meant to last.

Here's more advice on how to sidestep the trend trap to begin with.

Fashion Psychology Tip

THINK BEFORE YOU BUY:
6 WAYS TO TELL IF A TREND IS RIGHT FOR YOU

Before you pull out the plastic and buy another new and trendy item or outfit, here are six questions to ask yourself. If the garment you're eyeing meets these criteria, then you're *less likely* to wake up with that shopping hangover called buyer's remorse.

1) **Double trouble:** Ask yourself, Do I already own a version of this item or something pretty similar to it? If the answer is yes, put away your wallet.

2) Consider color: What **color** is the trend in? How does that color tend to make you feel when you wear it in general? Happy? Sad?

Anxious? Have you worn the color in the past and received compliments or felt confident? If you've worn the color successfully in the past, even way back in the day (I'm talking childhood), then that's a good indication it will elicit desirable emotions for you.

3) Ask yourself, **Does this feel like me?** Does the new item fit within the framework of your signature style? Does it scream "me," or is it drastically unlike anything else you own, or anything you've ever worn before? I am all for branching out and buying something different—just don't do so impulsively. If you've never worn harem pants before but have been bookmarking photos of them for months, go for it. If you are buying harem pants on a whim because you saw them on an influencer or mannequin or you're having a bad day, you're far less likely to ever wear them.

4) **Where** would you wear this item? Can you think of three situations in which you could actually wear this piece, like to work, to a holiday party, out to brunch, with friends on a night out, for a specific upcoming special occasion? If you can visualize yourself in the look in real life, that's a mark in its favor.

5) **Flattery:** You may love the way something looks on an Instagram model, but if she has a totally different body type than you do, it may not flatter you the same way. If you're not going into a store to try something on, you have to be extra careful to realistically assess how it might fit. I recently bought a swimsuit that looked amazing on Instagram, but the model showing it off had an hourglass figure; I have an athletic build. She was busty. I'm an A cup. Suffice it to say when the package finally arrived and I tried it on, sis did *not* look the same. So here I am now, feeling like crap, with lower self-esteem as a result. It's important that we don't damage our confidence with these online shopping mishaps. What started out as a fun little swimwear mission instead created a whole new psychological problem for me!

6) **Time:** Is this item something you see yourself wearing short-term or long-term? Once this trend is no longer in season, will you still have the confidence to wear it? Do you feel like this garment is going to be something you build an attachment to and love regardless of whether it is still in style or not? Does it have longevity? Is it fast fashion? How disposable is it? Can you honestly say to yourself, even if they come out with something new and fresh, I'm still going to wear this? Will it stand the test of time?

THE BOTTOM LINE
KEY TIPS AND TAKEAWAYS FROM CHAPTER 8

- **Keep it real.** We all dress to fit in and please others sometimes. There is nothing wrong with doing this as long as you weave in some small style element (glasses, shoes, makeup) that makes you feel authentic. You can satisfy outside expectations while still finding ways to celebrate yourself.

- **Affirmations unlock confidence.** We reach for clothes to help us fit in when we are feeling insecure. Try writing down what you love about yourself and document experiences when you feel pride. When you are anxious, reach for your journal, not your credit card.

- **Make trends pass the test.** Critically analyze any new item before you buy it. Can you envision a real-life situation (with a concrete calendar date) in which you'd wear it? Have you been stalking it for months, or is it an impulse buy? Have you seen someone with your body type wear it well? Will it stand the test of time? Raise your standards before you open your wallet.

Chapter 9

SELFIE NATION

All the world's a stage.

— *William Shakespeare*

K im Kardashian may say selfies are dead (possibly because professional photographers take her pics?), but anyone with a social media
account knows that simply isn't true. Do you post pictures and then find
yourself checking a little too often to see how many likes you receive? Is
this preoccupation distracting you from meaningful interactions with
your loved ones, from being productive at work? According to Nielsen, as
of 2018, the average American spent eleven hours a day engaging with
media. (That includes listening to, watching, or reading anything that
comes through a screen.)[1] Anything to which you devote more than half
of your waking hours becomes a formidable psychological force. In this
chapter I share advice on how to utilize social media to serve both your
psyche and your style — and how to sidestep the dangers that can do damage to both. But first let's come to grips with why displaying ourselves on
social media is so enticing to begin with.

According to a Harvard study, the act of disclosing information about
yourself in front of an audience triggers the same reward and pleasure
centers in the brain as those that get activated by eating delicious food,
getting money, or having sex.[2] In its coverage of the study, the *LA Times*
called social media "brain candy."[3] In her groundbreaking *Atlantic* article

"Have Smartphones Destroyed a Generation?" research psychologist Jean M. Twenge writes about the skyrocketing rates of suicide and depression among members of what she calls iGen, the first generation of young people raised with social media: "It's not an exaggeration to describe iGen as being on the brink of the worst mental-health crisis in decades. Much of this deterioration can be traced to their phones."[4] So while these platforms can be fun, inspiring, and, well, social, they can also do real damage to your mental health. It all comes down to how much feedback from your followers matters to you, and how much difficulty you have putting down your phone and living your life.

As a Fashion Psychologist, the first thing I worry about when it comes to social media is your self-esteem. By overdepending emotionally on likes, you're allowing validation from other people to determine your self-worth. Suddenly you're back in middle school and your social network is dictating your confidence level. But don't get down on yourself for this! It's not you, it's Instagram. This is the way the game is played, the way the system is set up. Anytime you post a pic, you are inviting others to judge you; you are putting your emotions in a stranger's hands. When you receive positive feedback, you may experience euphoria, which only leaves you wanting more. And guess what, you guys? That hunger for outside approval is insatiable, because these platforms are designed to allow for infinite followers, limitless likes. How could what you have already possibly be enough?

Furthermore (imagine me putting on my best "Mom" voice here), whether the pic you post is artfully staged, Photoshopped, or the opposite—#nofilter, candid, or silly—you have to be really careful about what you're communicating with your appearance online. People who may want to date you are looking at those photos. So are people who may want to hire you. One day, so will your kids. Then there's the question of comments. Any feedback you read has the potential to live forever—if not on the Internet (because you deleted the post), then in your mind. Criticism cuts deep even if it comes from a hater or a troll or a random stranger you'll never meet. According to Boston College psychology professor Elizabeth Kensinger and other researchers, our memories of negative emotional experiences and painful events are stronger, more vivid, and more impactful in our lives than our memories of positive ones.[5] So there are a lot of potential psychological downsides to the *overuse* of social media.

How does this affect your style? Even if you are not the kind of person who asks your followers to vote on which dress to wear to a party, you may find yourself second-guessing your sartorial instincts, and dressing more in anticipation of your audience's reaction than following your bliss (or your mood!). Imagine if you got a hundred likes the last time you wore a jumpsuit and only twenty-two when you wore jeans and a t-shirt—but at the moment you feel much more authentic in the latter. Are outside influences going to sway you the next time you approach your closet? If you are fashion focused, social media may also exacerbate some of your more compulsive shopping behaviors. Raise your hand if you check Instagram before you go to sleep at night and before you get out of bed in the morning. Come on, we're all friends here. This is a safe space. You may feel compelled to appear in an endless array of new outfits, all for the purpose of receiving likes online. The hashtag #OOTD generated over 270 million Insta hits by my last count. Shopping for the purpose of showing off on social media can become a vicious and costly cycle. New and tempting brands are increasingly infiltrating our feeds.

And once again, when it comes to online self-promotion, women are subject to a different standard. In an article about the pressure on female business founders to present a certain image on social media, Jessica O. Matthews, the CEO of a renewable energy firm, told *Fast Company*, "I know a lot of guys who are seen to be tech geniuses, and they don't shower." For women, she says, that simply would never fly. "I have to make time to build my go-to-market strategy *and* get my weave done. There's no world where anyone's going to be okay with me looking like boo boo the fool."[6]

When you become overreliant on online feedback, when the comments become your mirror, you start living a sort of meta-life. You are no longer present. You begin to imagine how your followers will react to scenes from your life while you're living them out in real time. Watching a sunset, you envision how much better it would look with a filter. As you laugh with a friend, you itch to take a selfie, contemplating the most flattering angle, and start writing the caption in your mind. Does this digitally driven detachment sound familiar? I can't even count the number of clients who have come to me because their confidence has plummeted as they compare themselves to the curated looks and comped lives of influencers.

I want to remind you that these influencers are *paid* to create content. They're presenting a false reality (#WokeUpLikeThis: 1 million posts). In an essay for *Vogue* pointing out this disconnect, Lena Dunham called a love interest's Instagram feed "a time-lapse impression" of his life: "Only the cutest parts, perfectly calibrated."[7] In a Hulu documentary on the Fyre Festival, *New Yorker* journalist Jia Tolentino calls Instagram culture "the performance of an attractive life."[8] Performance is the antithesis of authenticity. You guys, this is entertainment. These social stars are *models*. They may even have teams of professionals styling, setting up, and shooting their photos—the modern-day equivalent of the makeover magicians we talked about way back in chapter 1. They are paid to travel to beautiful locations all around the world and stage all-day photo shoots. They may take shots of eight outfits in a single day and then spread those out and post them over the course of a week, making it appear as though they wear something new and fabulous every single day. This is their job. It's how they earn a living. It isn't real.

But even knowing this, we fall for the illusion over and over again. That's why concepts like digital detox and digital minimalism are so appealing. We want to wean ourselves off of this heady mix of FOMO and fantasy because on some level it feels icky. And yet... social media is also where all your friends are making plans, laughing over inside jokes, sharing heartbreaks and support (or at least sending fist bump emojis). No wonder you feel like a failure when you can't seem to quit.

But are you ready for some emotional whiplash? I love Instagram. Yup, I said it. Even with all the potential drawbacks, I think social media is a positive thing overall. It is an exceptional tool for outfit inspiration, for finding community, for self-empowerment, for the democratization of ideas. The creativity I come across online inspires my style and enriches my life. I just refuse to let it *take over* my life. My goal in this chapter is to help you feel comfortable and confident with your content—and that includes your clothes—before you blast it out to the world for eternity, before you invite feedback from strangers. Instagram is expected to have 2 *billion* users by the year 2023.[9] It is estimated that 95 million photos or videos are posted to the platform every single day.[10] You are not alone in dealing with its benefits—or its hazards. And they're not going away. I'm here to share easy, achievable advice on how to think about—and dress for—your online images. But let's start with this #goal: It's time to win back your own self-approval and dress for yourself first. YOU lead the way, not your followers.

HOW SOCIAL MEDIA IMPROVED MY STYLE

Instagram has opened up the world for me. Already a big international traveler, I get a thrill out of tapping an app on my phone and instantly seeing what people are wearing in India or Australia or Italy. When I was younger and my mom was driving me to modeling school or piano lessons, I would study supermodels in magazines. Now I'm looking at real people. It's amazing. Fashion used to feel inaccessible to me, even when I worked in the industry. But thanks to this platform, I have found acceptance and encouragement from friends and strangers alike. I'm a pretty fearless dresser. I don't hesitate to mix hoodies with high heels or wear my purple wide-brimmed hat with a fuchsia trench, or my gold brocade robe over an all-black ensemble to work.

The average person may not dress as daringly as I do—not even in New York City, and certainly not every day. But I go on social media and see thousands of girls who dress like me—or even *more* adventurously—all the time. I don't even feel edgy anymore! Thanks to Instagram, I now consider a beauty app developer in Atlanta, a lifestyle blogger based in London, an Australian journalist, and a runner-up for Miss India among my closest girlfriends. We like one another's pics, toast one another's career achievements (champagne glass emoji: clink!), and share gossip, insecurities, and copious heart, prayer hand, and fireball emojis. I dress more boldly because they have helped me feel emboldened. This is my community. These are my people. (I also have plenty of loved ones I can touch and speak to, for the record.) The beautiful thing about living a stylish life online is that even though someone out there may hate my outfit, someone else is going to be inspired by it. Maybe I'll start a trend. Maybe you will. That thought delights me. I get to have a voice and I get to control my image, my story.

In her book *Men Explain Things to Me,* Rebecca Solnit writes that it is a quintessential condition of being a woman to have to fight, in some way, to be seen. Every woman "struggles with the forces that would tell her story for her, or write her out of the story, the genealogy, the rights of man, the rule of law. The ability to tell your own story, in words or images, is already a victory, already a revolt."[11] Thanks to social media, we all have the ability to tell our own stories. The key is not letting your online avatar get too far away from the person you actually are in real life.

Here's some more insider info: I use Instagram as my stylist. I have several albums dedicated to other people's outfits that inspire me. I'll give you an example. One day not too long ago, I wanted to illustrate the relaxed, chill mood I found myself in (read: dress comfortably, not push myself too far with fashion). But I still wanted to look cute. I came across an influencer who was wearing a brown faux fur jacket over a black turtleneck, tan satin joggers, and sock booties. She accessorized with sunglasses, a beanie hat, and a small shoulder bag. I loved her glam take on athleisure! And I instantly realized that I already owned many of the elements of her outfit. So I went over to my closet and pulled out my own spin on her look. I own a black hoodie and black joggers. Check. My fur coat is vintage white fox, so though I would still be following her outfit formula, I decided my color scheme would be slightly different: black and white versus her black and brown. (For anyone who's curious, I'm conscious of animal cruelty, so any fur I wear is either vintage or faux.) My accessories also differed slightly: I pulled on steel-toe boots (she wore stilettos) and an Aldo cross-body bag (hers was a Fendi baguette). Then, just like my Insta inspo, I topped off my look with a knit skullcap, sunglasses, and a red lip. I felt comfortable yet fashion forward. I went to teach my class, feeling fresh AF, and my fashion students responded with plenty of compliments. I would not have come up with this look on my own, and yet it wasn't a reach. I still felt like me. I felt awesome.

And just like that, Instagram provided an instant, cost-effective antidote to that *I have nothing to wear* feeling. I categorize my albums of inspiring outfit photos by mood (looks to energize, looks to calm and soothe anxiety, looks to inspire creativity), because I'm an emotional dresser and that works for me. But you can organize yours in whatever way suits your needs. You might compile albums of rainy weather looks, office attire, night out outfits, weekend ideas. Filing, organizing, and re-creating inspirational pics using your own clothes is cheaper than hiring a stylist, easier than using a digital closet app, and way less labor-intensive than a subscription box or rental service (though those are also all excellent tools too). My little digital library is all DIY. It's just another way you can feel empowered to style yourself using technology as opposed to asking—or paying—another person to tell you what to wear.

Fashion Psychology Tip

HOW TO MAKE INSTAGRAM YOUR STYLIST

Only screen-grab, favorite, like, or save pics of outfits composed of clothing elements you already own (or ones that are similar). Instagram has made it all too easy to "shop this look" or "click to buy" or "Like to Know It." You don't need to. Retail therapy is not the answer. As I said in chapter 4, I have a truly minimalistic approach to my wardrobe. I never buy three of the same top. I know every single item I own, so when I see an outfit I like on social media, I can say, *Oh, I have something similar to that!* I'm not going out and buying anything new; I'm shopping my closet. That empowers me.

CASE STUDY: MY SELF-ISH SISTER

- -

Recently I met with two sisters. The older one is in her late twenties and a grad student at Columbia. The younger one is an undergrad in the Midwest, where they grew up. The older sister came to me for help because she fears her younger sister's excessive social media use is having a detrimental effect on her psyche. She says her younger sister obsessively scrolls through pics of influencers, saying, I want to be like them. Anytime the sisters are getting ready to leave the house, the younger one becomes fixated on making herself look "picture-perfect" and photo ready. Instead of looking into a mirror, she looks into her phone's camera and tries out different angles, duck-lipping all the while. According to her older sister, she lives as if she has her own extensive following. (She does not.) She takes hours to get dressed and do her makeup, playing with various filters for ages before she posts anything. Her older sister is concerned that she is constantly bombarded with

*these larger-than-life influencer images and is not aware that this
fixation is taking over. The younger sister is not doing anything to
limit her exposure to social media, nor is she looking to find a
balance between consuming online content and living in reality.
How could this affect her? her worried older sister asked me.*

- - - - - - - - -

As I sat with these young women, two thoughts crossed my mind. I wanted to be open and honest with them about the dangers of the younger sister's habit but also to leave them both feeling empowered with a clear and actionable path forward. I did not want to make social media the enemy; I am a realist. I know it will inevitably remain a part of their lives. My goal was to help the younger, more impressionable sister use the medium in a healthier way.

I'll tell you exactly what I told them: Yes, the younger sister's social media overuse could be a red flag. I explained that the signs of addiction to social media include when it negatively impacts your relationships, when you feel unable to stop using it, or when your usage continues to increase without leveling off.[12] Social media overuse has also been linked to impaired decision making and risky behavior, not to mention depression, anxiety, and a whole host of other mental health woes.[13] I went on to emphasize that comparing yourself to curated influencer images could absolutely have a detrimental effect on your self-esteem.

But I also pointed out that hope is on the horizon: We are now seeing a trend of social media stars opening up about their mental health struggles relating to appearance, from eating disorders to anxiety to acne to addiction. They are shattering the myth of perfection they themselves helped to build. My forecast is that influencers will become increasingly transparent about these issues. But for the younger sister, this wave may not crest soon enough. Here's more of what I told her she could do right now, at this very moment, to mitigate the negative effects of her hard-to-break habit. (Consider this a **Style Rx** for us all!)

How to Have a Healthier
Relationship with Your Self(ie)

■ **Re-populate your feed**

Stop whatever you are doing and think for a minute about the people in your life you can physically touch. Your mom, your sister, your favorite teacher, your coach, your neighbor, your extended family, your friends, their parents, your teammates, your roommates, your co-workers. Think of people you know and admire and who know you on a first-name basis. People whose voices you can hear and whose hand you can shake in real life. Follow some of *them* on social media. Re-populate your feed with those people, so that the simulated reality you scroll through more accurately depicts the real world you live in.

Next, find a few celebrities, street style stars, creatives, or influencers who more closely resemble you—whether in ethnicity, age, or body type (or, ideally, all three). If you aren't sure how to find these people, search hashtags like #plussizemodel or #blackgirlmagic or #petitefashion or #fabover40. Simply plug #streetstyle into Insta's search box and see who pops up. Find someone whose vibe inspires you and see who *they* follow. Make some of these people your influencers. They may inspire you to try new looks and shift your perspective on what's beautiful.

Remember: What you're seeing on your phone is a representation of reality. You can actually change your reality by changing what you see.

■ **Log your screen time**

Download an app that shows you how much time you're spending on social media every day or go to Settings and enable the "ScreenTime" monitor built into your iPhone. (InMoment also does exactly this. AntiSocial compares your screen usage to that of other people in your age and gender bracket so you can compare your usage to that of your peers.) Now take 25 percent of that total time and spend it away from your phone. Do this once a week to start. That itch you feel to check social media is withdrawal, my friend. I'm not suggesting you quit your phone cold turkey. But I do have some ideas for what you can do with that "found" time. Read on.

■ **Go play dress-up in your closet**

I'm serious. Find an afternoon when you have no other obligations, when you're not racing with the clock or under pressure, and use those minutes you're intentionally spending away from your phone to play dress-up the same way you did when you were a little kid. If you need inspiration, go to a park and observe children, read some of your favorite children's books, listen to music you loved as a kid. Let your mind wander. Put on an old prom dress with a pair of cowboy boots and a cardigan. I'm not suggesting you wear that getup to the office tomorrow . . . or ever, for that matter. Donate or sell anything you don't love. The point of this exercise is not only to inspire a closet cleanout; it's to help you tap into and release some of your creative energy.

At a certain age, we all stop playing dress-up. Getting in touch with your inner child opens you up to creativity. And getting those creative juices flowing will help you remix your outfits. You may find the mojo to wear a skinny animal-print belt with an all-black outfit, or bust out those gold pumps you bought for your cousin's wedding and pair them with jeans. Small changes can have a huge impact on how you feel.

■ **Remix your wardrobe**

Here are two easy ideas for unexpected outfits that look equally amazing on the 'gram and IRL.

Create a **monochromatic** base. Find all the pieces you own in a certain color (red, gray, brown), put them together, and see how they look. Next, pull an unexpected piece of outerwear over your shoulders. Imagine a brown halter top, brown high-waist pants, and brown croc-embossed ankle boots all under a luxe camel or tan teddy bear coat. Classic and chic. Or try gray trousers and a gray sweater. Then match your flats to your bag. (It's a royal family styling trick that never fails.) I'm picturing pink loafers or ballet flats and a pink quilted handbag. Accents and extras always pop against a monochromatic background.

■ **Opposites attract**

Mix casual with fancy, silky with soft, menswear with something feminine, or preppy with punk. The most stylish influencers have a flair for the unexpected. They surprise the eye by wearing a sweatshirt with a ball gown skirt or an evening dress with Doc Martens or patent-leather leggings with a woolly turtleneck sweater. There are simple ways to adopt this strategy: Wear gray knit leggings and a gray hoodie with high-heel sandals under a camel coat or trench. Wear a floral-print maxi dress with flat white Stan Smith–style sneakers. Wear an off-the-shoulder body-con top (sexy) with cargo pants (tough). Go black tie and blue jeans: a chambray shirt with a fancy skirt. A velvet blazer and pearl hoop earrings and barrettes on top, relaxed denim on the bottom. Add a colorful shoe and *bam*, watch out world!

A NOTE ON SELF-SATISFACTION

All this solo playtime puts the power back in your hands and not in those of your followers. Get all the likes! Just don't depend on them. Repeat after me: My followers don't run me. So now you might say, Okay, Dawnn, that sounds good. But how do I stop myself from caring about social media feedback? And—most important—how do I stop obsessing over who gives it to me?

Just as I believe in styling from the inside out, I look for *internal satisfaction* first. When I put together an outfit and I like it, I take a minute to feel that good feeling. I acknowledge it, then I name it or label it. I say to myself, *Wow that's a badass look. I didn't even know I could pair X with Y. I must be pretty creative.* I take the time to acknowledge exactly how my look makes me feel: strong or sexy or elegant or polished. I'm not looking for anyone else to activate that feeling for me. I'm always looking for that personal satisfaction first.

By the time I post a pic of an outfit, you better believe I'm already happy with it, and with myself. And I try to leave it there. The reaction that post gets then becomes less important. I'm not saying comments and likes do not affect me. I'm saying I've given myself perspective in advance. I've approved my look before I step out into the public square seeking approval (or opening myself up to disapproval) from others. I strive to please myself first. I look inward first. The trouble starts when we have no clue how we feel about ourselves, when we are unsure whether our look is working, and then we go out on a quest for that information, seeking that approval from people who may not have our best interests at heart. Approve yourself first.

CASE STUDY: TOO HOT FOR TINDER

A few years ago I counseled a French client who worked long hours as a flight attendant. She was actively seeking a romantic relationship via dating apps. And she was dismayed, shocked, and confused by the aggressively sexual and salacious comments she was receiving online from strangers. We sat down together, and I took a look at her profiles and noticed her photos were very suggestive. Many featured her whole body, as opposed to focusing on a close-up of her face. The outfits she wore in the shots showed a lot of skin. She wore bandage dresses and high heels — looks you might wear to go dancing at a club in the early 2000s.

I observed that in her life, she dressed only in extremes. For work, when she was almost fully covered by her airline uniform, she presented as demure and conservative. In her downtime, she

*favored body-con, cleavage, or leg-baring clothes. She seemed to
have only two speeds — modest or scantily clad. And she seemed to
lack awareness that a middle ground could exist. She had no
barometer for what was appropriate once she was out of uniform.
She explained that she felt really stifled and constrained by her
uniform. So the minute she had the chance to ditch it, she wanted
to go all out, to feel as fun, sexy, vibrant, and free as possible. But
her idea of what that looked like was out of sync with the way
others (specifically, potential suitors) perceived her. She was
seeking liberation but ended up still being boxed in, just by a
different stereotype. Her revved-up looks didn't reflect someone
looking to settle down, and that's who she really was.*

Style Rx

*Since this client was primarily coming to me for photo styling
advice, my first goal was to help her achieve a more flattering
appearance within the frame. I pointed out that she was showing a
whole lot of skin in her pics and advised her to offer just a glimpse
of sensuality, as opposed to the whole package. After meeting
several times, we went through her closet, where we discovered a
black boatneck maxi dress with a slit. I advised her to wear it for a
full-body photo, showing a leg, instead of both legs. For a
headshot, we selected a classic white oxford shirt and unbuttoned
it just to her collarbone, not to her cleavage.*

- - - - - - - - -

I have to admit, I was initially surprised to find out this client already
owned several of these middle-of-the-road items. It turned out she would
occasionally wear them to meet up with her family or friends. But they
were in her blind spot. It simply did not occur to her to feature these more
moderate looks in her photos. She didn't think she looked pretty or sexy
in them. She thought they were boring. I tried to help her reframe her

thinking by showing her some social media influencers with subtler, classic, but still feminine style. I suggested she post some of our newer photos to her profile. Not surprisingly, when the client balanced out her look, she received more balanced feedback from guys. She's actually married with a child now. I like to think I had a sliver of something to do with that.

Anyone who has read this far is likely to guess what I'm going to say next. This client suffered from a case of incongruence. The outside she presented online did not, by any stretch, match how she felt inside or her life goals. She's not the only one. Another client—let's call her Grace*— told me recently, "I know these Instagram models spend a whole day working so hard to get one shot. I myself am really good at Facetune [an app that allows you to digitally enhance your selfies]. I love discovering and trying out new beauty apps." Grace is a talented visual artist. She showed me her Insta pics and she looked flawless—slimmer, older than her actual age (early twenties), ethereal thanks to the moody lighting. And she is a beautiful girl, inside and out. But she's also just an ordinary person. The gulf between who she was presenting herself to be online and who she really is set her up for a fall. "I receive lots of compliments online from friends and family on my edited photos," Grace said. "But then I ran into one of my mom's friends in real life and she held the phone up to my face and goes, *Is this really you?!* I guess I have some really good Photoshopping skills...It made me feel awful."

We all yearn for validation and approval. It's a basic human need. But where—and from whom—we seek it is up to us. Meghan Markle gave a talk addressing social media's effect on young people. "You see photos on social media and you don't know whether she's born with it or maybe it's a filter," the duchess told an audience of mental health advocates. "Your judgment of your sense of self-worth becomes really skewed when it's all based on likes."[14] Since becoming a royal, Markle shut down her personal social media accounts, leaving behind nearly 2 million Instagram followers. She described quitting the platforms as "freeing" and said, "Flattery and criticism run through the same filter."[15] It's so true. If you put all your stock in likes, then you also have to believe the haters. When you like yourself first, you become your own fan, your own protector, your own advocate. Be your own filter. Nothing gets by you.

THE BOTTOM LINE
KEY TIPS AND TAKEAWAYS FROM CHAPTER 9

- **Follow real people.** Populate your feed with stylish women who look like you (in terms of age, ethnicity, body type) and others you know in real life. Change your social media input to change your outlook.
- **Make social your stylist.** Like or screen-grab your favorite influencers' outfits, then see if you can replicate them using elements you own.
- **Organize inspo in albums.** Build digital lookbooks of ideal outfits. Organize them by weekend looks, party looks, work ensembles. Or create albums based on emotions you hope to elicit (looks to calm you down, looks to energize you, looks to boost your confidence). Re-create those outfits using items you own.
- **Detox and remix.** Log your daily screen time and aim to take at least twenty-five minutes off a week. Devote that "found time" to playing dress-up in your closet.

Chapter 10

YOUR WOKE WARDROBE

What would America be like if we loved black people as much as we love black culture?

—*Amandla Stenberg*

I can't remember the first time I heard about the Brown Paper Bag Test. It seems like I've always been aware of its message—that because my skin tone was lighter than some, I would be considered more attractive than they are. This concept placed me in a race-based hierarchy of beauty that I had no control over and wanted no part of. The term reportedly originated in Jazz Age New York, at the legendary Cotton Club. In order to be cast as one of the Copper Colored Gals—the beautiful African American dancers who were a big audience draw—the club's (white) owners mandated that your skin tone had to be lighter than a brown paper bag.[1] This is an example of colorism. The concept spread within the black community and persisted throughout the twentieth century, when social institutions like college sororities and fraternities, and even churches, used the test to exclude those with darker complexions. Spike Lee even made this a theme of his 1988 movie *School Daze.*[2]

Beyoncé's father, Mathew Knowles, spoke out about his experience with colorism, noting as recently as 2018 that *he* was subjected to the Brown Paper Bag Test upon entering Fisk University (a private black college in Nashville, Tennessee) in 1972. "When it comes to Black females, who are the people who get their music played on pop radio?" he asked *Ebony's* Jessica Bennett in an interview. Naming Mariah Carey, Rihanna, Nicki Minaj, and his own daughters, Beyoncé and Solange, he asked, "And what do they all have in common?" Bennett observed that they are all lighter skinned. Replied Knowles, "Do you think that's an accident?"[3]

As I grew into adulthood and found my footing in academia, I began to question not just this but *all* beauty standards. Who sets them? Who benefits from them? And what would it take to challenge them? My first thought is to raise awareness that they exist by speaking to students, clients, audiences, and readers like you. The next step is to disassemble these beauty standards, to take them apart and expose them for what they are—social constructs—through thought-provoking examination. Then I wonder, how do we disrupt them?

One idea is to advocate for a more diverse representation of what it means to be "beautiful." This is certainly what I try to do in my practice. When my clients are dismayed because they don't meet the physical beauty standards of their families or communities or of society, this often leads to wardrobe problems. They tend to shop too much or hide themselves in baggy clothes or obsess over their social media images or long for plastic surgery.

When these issues come up, I often tell them about the Brown Paper Bag Test. I also dress to reset expectations and debunk biases. Sometimes when I show up to teach at FIT or to lecture at a museum or other institution, I'll intentionally wear something that looks very "urban," like a hoodie or big, bold earrings, just to throw off my audience and challenge their unconscious belief systems. Whether my audience is made up of college students or older people, I anticipate their expectation that a young black woman in a hoodie will be unprofessional or underqualified. The stereotype that my appearance triggers leads them to assume that perhaps I'm from the hood, that I'm incompetent, that I might be on welfare. But in actuality, my credentials demonstrate that I *am* qualified, and I do an immaculate job with my presentations. So I just go around opening people's minds, and I have fun doing it. These are only a few ways to show beauty standards for what they are: myths. Yes, we carry their weight. They cause us real pain. They can get us down and make us feel bad about ourselves. But I make a big push to help people see themselves from a different perspective. I encourage my clients and students to seek out role models who look like them. This is often the first step in helping them to dress in a way that honors their identity and improves their confidence.

Style lives at the intersection of race, religion, nationality, age, body image, and pop culture. All of these big topics aren't necessarily at the forefront of your mind when you get dressed in the morning. But you (and I) will always instinctively make snap judgments about other people— friend or foe?—based on what they're wearing, on how they look. That's human nature. There are evolutionary, self-protective instincts in play when we do this. "Our evolutionary prehistory shows that we needed many people to help us raise our offspring, so we surrounded ourselves with those who had similar values or who looked like us," writes Hayley Krischer in an article about "mom uniforms" in the *New York Times*.[4] But in certain contexts, like the classroom or the workplace, we might benefit from overriding these instincts. Can you remember a time when you made a knee-jerk judgment about someone based on what they looked like and what they had on, and then had a conversation with them that totally shifted your perception? Their intelligence, humor, or charm may not have changed what their clothes were saying, but these qualities did change how you saw them. It *is* within our power to redefine what "beautiful" means when we look at ourselves and others. On that note, I think of this final section of the book as "How to Dress Woke."

WHAT DOES IT MEAN TO DRESS WOKE?

You may have heard about dressing woke. It certainly has become a buzzword, as more fashion brands align themselves with social movements and activist spokespeople (think Colin Kaepernick and Nike). According to the 2019 "State of Fashion" report, a fashion brand's wokeness increasingly contributes to its success: "Younger generations' passion for social and environmental causes has reached critical mass, causing brands to become more fundamentally purpose-driven to attract both consumers and talent. Consumers...will reward players that take a strong stance on social and environmental issues beyond traditional CSR [Corporate Social Responsibility]."[5] To some, this is yet another cynical marketing ploy or "woke-washing." Others will happily take all the Dove campaigns celebrating "real bodies" or the Savage X Fenty lingerie shows starring pregnant and trans women they can get.

But in the real world, where you and I live, dressing woke may mean different things to different people. It all depends on where you're coming from and what your goals are. Maybe dressing woke means being more intentional with your look. Maybe you want to be more mindful, more attuned to your emotions when you pick out your outfit each day. Or you may decide to consume less fast fashion and shop your closet more, to be less wasteful with your money and with the environment. You may create your own tightly edited Capsule Wardrobe of remix-ready basics to reduce stress and your contribution to landfills. Your goal may be to feel less excessive, less trend-driven, more grounded, more in control, and more comfortable in your own skin.

Others may look outward, feeling more compelled to do what they can to impact culture and society. Dressing woke could mean investing only in fashions that make the world a better place, socially or environmentally. (Check out my list of Favorite Woke Brands on page 240.) Maybe you'll make an effort to buy from brands that use recycled plastics, that upcycle discarded textiles, that are responsibly sourced, are animal-free, or promote ethical manufacturing employment practices. Maybe you'll buy only vintage for similar reasons. You may decide to wash your clothes less frequently or buy clothes from brands like Pangaia (Jaden Smith and Justin Bieber are fans) that are designed to be washed infrequently, in order to cut down on water wastage. Dressing woke may mean supporting designers from a certain community, like Issa Rae and Tracee Ellis Ross did when they hosted award shows wearing only clothes by black designers. Maybe you'll buy more clothes from women-owned companies or designers. You may become a fashion activist, voting with your dollar, like all the shoppers who boycotted Ivanka Trump's clothing line in the wake of Donald Trump's "Grab her by the pussy" comments. Their galvanizing hashtag? #GrabYourWallet. Ivanka's sales subsequently dropped 32 percent.[6] Whatever your cause, dressing woke means you are taking positive, meaningful action when you shop (or abstain from shopping).

But while you are connecting your clothing choices to these broader social issues, dressing woke can also impact you personally — and improve your mental health. Let's spend some time with a client for whom many of these issues intersect.

CASE STUDY: SHOPPING AWAY THE PAIN

My client Grace,* whom you met in the last chapter, grew up in Asia and is now a student in New York City. She worries that she has a compulsive shopping habit and came to me for help. She finds herself buying new clothes from fast-fashion retailers like Forever 21 or H&M every single day. That is not an exaggeration. Her closet can no longer contain her ever-growing wardrobe. Clothes with tags still on them are piled up on her furniture and spill out of her drawers. And still she feels like she has nothing to wear. So she just keeps shopping.

Grace arrived at one of our sessions in a shapeless pastel sweatshirt, black leggings, and beat-up Chuck Taylors. Clearly she was not even wearing the trendy new items she had purchased. She described feeling great when she tries on new clothes in the store, but by the time she gets them home, something has shifted. The clothes lose their magic and her insecurities return. Every time.

Over the course of several sessions, Grace revealed she was struggling with body image issues, low self-esteem due to a breakup, and cross-cultural stress. Her parents, who live in Asia, have been undergoing financial strain. Grace needed to start job hunting soon. She had a lot to worry about. And it was all playing out through her clothes.

"There's a certain image put on me to meet my parents' and my friends' expectations—an ideal type," she said. "When I see photos in Asian fashion magazines, I feel like, This is how I'm supposed to look. It seems like everyone in China is pretty and skinny, or they use beauty apps to edit their Instagram photos to make it appear that way. But I don't look the way society wants me to. When I go back to Asia, people criticize my weight. They say I'm too fat. Or they say things like, 'You look a little bit out of shape; you should go exercise.' But when I'm here in New York, even though I am more the average weight, people criticize my height. [Grace is around five feet tall.] I feel like, Nothing is ever good enough for you guys! As a result, I don't feel like I look good in any of my clothes. So I just keep buying new ones."

Grace compared herself to me and expressed envy. She said that I—as a tall, thin woman—represent her culture's beauty ideal. I took this opportunity to disclose to her that in my Caribbean culture, she—as a thicker, curvier woman—is much closer to meeting the popular beauty standard. I explained that when I go visit family in Jamaica, I am often teased for being too thin. I'm told by relatives, friends, and strangers alike, You need to eat. You're a bag of bones! You're starving yourself! (Not true.) It's not that my community members are trying to hurt me; it's just normal in Jamaican culture to say this stuff to your face. In patois, mauger means skinny. So they'll say, Hey, little Mauger! Or, if you're heavier, Hey, Miss Fatty-Pants! It's meant to be endearing.

When I opened up about this to Grace, she found it helpful. She began to look at her self-image from a different point of view. "When I see the two sides," she said, "it makes me not as sad. It makes me feel like I'm not alone in the world because everybody is insecure about themselves at some point. It makes me feel optimistic, like maybe I could actually be attractive to somebody somewhere." Then eventually, she self-affirmed: "The most important thing is I should be able to figure out who I want to be as opposed to who I 'should' be."

Style Rx

I encouraged Grace to shop only her closet for the next week and to steer clear of stores. Looking at her social media feeds together, we isolated a certain sartorial vibe she was drawn to (a playful hip-hop-inspired street style). We observed how her Instagram idols played with proportion, wearing XXL sports jerseys as dresses with Doc Martens and other bold accessories, or all-black outfits featuring crop tops with joggers and moto jackets. I suggested she edit her existing wardrobe with these outfits in mind and try to develop a consistent aesthetic. Once she had some direction and a specific goal, I was confident she could redirect her energy toward curating what she already owned, and de-escalate her compulsive shopping urges.

As my work with Grace demonstrates, when I sit down with my clients, we almost invariably start talking about how they feel about their looks, their self-esteem, and how this affects the way they present themselves. We focus on their families of origin, exploring how and when they absorbed messages about what it means to be "beautiful." See, these beauty standards are taught to us from a young age by our families and communities as well as by pop culture. The only thing we have control over — as adults — is how we react to them. We can decide who to follow on social *media. We can see marketing for what it sometimes is (an effort to sell us self-loathing in order to separate us from our money). We can do our best to mute those messages. We can put our money where our mouth is.*

- - - - - - - - - -

MY FAVORITE WOKE BRANDS

Slow Factory: Fair trade and 100 percent eco-friendly, this activist fashion brand donates proceeds to humanitarian and environmental causes. Look for their flashy AF (in a good way) endangered species **silk scarf series.**

Girlfriend Collective: A figure-flattering brand of **bralettes and leggings** made from recycled fishing nets and plastic water bottles. Ideal basics to wear to the gym or throw on under a cardigan with statement shoes.

Reformation: As if their **delicate print dresses and jumpsuits with sexy cutouts** weren't already appealing enough, this fire brand tracks its environmental impact and holds itself accountable with public quarterly sustainability reports. Thanks to this thought leader, transparency is trending.

DL1961: The problem with most denim production is it involves damaging dyes and massive water wastage. This **affordable yet trendy jeans brand** is doing something about it. A traditional pair of jeans is made using 1,500 gallons of water. This brand uses less than ten gallons per pair, and 98 percent of it is recycled.

Everlane: These guys offer the most appealing **clean, modern t-shirts, sweaters, button-downs, and essentials** around, and are famous for their humane HR practices. Each factory they work with is evaluated for fair wages, reasonable hours, and environmental impact.

G-Star Raw: Who knew your go-to brand **for hoodies, joggers, and jean jackets** would be the one to develop the most eco-friendly denim ever designed?

Kindred Black: Did I just die and go to **vintage luxury** heaven? The creators of this shopping site call it "an environmentally focused retail project—an unusual curation of luxury lifestyle goods that are eco-responsible, artisan produced, and ethically manufactured." I call it a peerless online marketplace where you can find army-green boilersuits, high-waist swim bottoms and lingerie, vintage Versace tops, velvet gowns, delicate accessories, chic leather bucket bags, and **spot-on styling advice** for how to wear them all.

Patagonia: Its **classic fleeces and utilitarian outerwear** aren't the only offerings that will give you the warm fuzzies. This legendary brand has created an online social platform called Patagonia Action Works to connect customers with local grassroots environmental organizations. At wornwear.patagonia.com you can shop pre-worn items or trade in your own gently used Patagonia gear for store or site credit.

APPRECIATION VERSUS APPROPRIATION

Let's go back to my original definition of Fashion Psychology: the study and treatment of color, beauty, style, image, and shape and their effects on human behavior, while addressing cultural sensitivities and cultural norms. As far as I'm concerned, you can't dress woke without gaining an understanding of certain cultural issues, namely, appropriation, representation, and erasure. It seems like not a week goes by without some new scandal involving a fashion house causing offense because of their inexplicable blind spots. Some recent examples include Gucci releasing a $900 balaclava sweater with a triggering image of blackface and a $790 "Indy

Full Turban" similar to the sacred religious head coverings worn by Sikhs (both of which appeared on its fall 2018 runway, modeled by white people).[7] Zara notoriously released a striped shirt with a gold star that looked shockingly like a symbol of the Holocaust.[8] H&M cast a little black boy to model a hoodie featuring the slogan "Coolest Monkey in the Jungle."[9] Gendered gaffes are also prevalent, even when it comes to messages intended for young children. Old Navy came under fire in 2016 for releasing a *Ghostbusters* t-shirt series that featured the slogan "Ghostbuster in Training" on pink t-shirts intended for toddler girls; the boys' t-shirt just depicted a regular Ghostbuster (presuming boys are born fully accredited in paranormal policing).[10] A Batgirl t-shirt released by Target in Australia listed domestic chores on Batgirl's to-do list. The boys' t-shirt featured the slogan "Like father, like son...Yes, my dad's Batman."[11] Welcome to the patriarchy, kids.

You may think these glaringly offensive items have nothing to do with you or your closet. *I would never culturally appropriate or buy an offensive item, Dawnn*, you might say. *That'll never be me.* But it helps to be sure. I know plenty of worldly, well-intentioned fashionistas who get tripped up on these issues. With my own eyes, I have observed blond Caucasian women wearing cornrows with dashikis (traditional African caftans), or henna hand tattoos, and American tourists posting selfies while wearing turbans with embroidered caftans in the Middle East. I can't help but wonder if they see these things as colorful, disposable accessories to be amusingly donned and then ditched. In general, I don't believe these people are malicious, or intend to hurt anyone by borrowing the sartorial symbols of a culture that is not their own. But when you wear another group's cultural signifiers head to toe, it can create the impression that you see them as a costume. It's demeaning. Being white and wearing a dashiki could be interpreted as problematic; wearing one *with* cornrows or dreadlocks in your hair almost certainly would be. We have a term within the black community, "Christopher Columbus–ing." It's taking something from a marginalized group and renaming it to claim it as your own. Or, as the

Washington Post's Clinton Yates explained, it's "showing up someplace and acting as if history started the moment you arrived."[12]

What's in a name? A lot, as it turns out. When Zara released a $90 women's check miniskirt that was in fact indistinguishable from the *lungi* traditionally worn by men in South Asia, they gave no credit to its origins. The word "Asia" never appeared in its website's display copy. Rather, the garment was renamed and passed off as something original.[13] When Kim Kardashian wore cornrows/Fulani braids—a hairstyle with deep roots in the black community—but called them "Bo Derek braids" (a reference to the iconic blond-and-blue-eyed movie star who wore them in the 1979 movie *10*), she was met with outrage.[14] Black people I know were like, *No, these are cornrows or boxer braids! We grew up with this! These are styles we get as kids!* Kardashian more recently wore traditional Indian bridal forehead jewelry to a Sunday service, prompting one Instagram commenter to remark, "I love how this is from the Indian culture and no recognition [is] given whatso[e]ver."[15]

Remember Miley Cyrus's 2013 makeover from Hannah Montana to twerking, grill-flashing, hand signal–throwing, bandana-wearing, tongue-thrusting *Bangerz* hitmaker? As Dodai Stewart wrote at the time for Jezebel, Cyrus "can play at blackness without being burdened by the reality of it...But blackness is not a piece of jewelry you can slip on when you want a confidence booster or a cool look."[16] Privilege and erasure are at the heart of any discussion about appropriation. It's not that Kim K or Miley Cyrus (or Kesha or Gwen Stefani or Katy Perry or Shailene Woodley) *meant* to offend with their hairstyles or jewelry. Their intent may very well have been homage. But as non-black or -brown celebrities, they have the *privilege* to wear the looks associated with another person's culture, when that person can't necessarily wear looks from her *own* culture without suffering some type of fallout.

Why are certain looks "cutting-edge" when one person wears them but "urban" or "ratchet" or "trashy" or "gangsta" when another does? Who gets the privilege of wearing oversize hoop earrings or nameplate necklaces or North Face puffer coats or tracksuits or baggy jeans or shred-ded skintight jeans or hoodies or Timberland boots or head wraps or ban-danas or elaborate nail art or grills without consequences? Sometimes I wish I could wear those "Bo Derek" cornrow braids because I just want my hair off my face. But what does it signal when I wear them as a black woman? It denotes that I'm ghetto. I'm likely not educated. Maybe I'm into rappers and I smoke weed. I don't have the license to wear this particular hairstyle as I want to. Kylie Jenner, however, can wear it any day of the week and walk into an office or a business meeting and no one is going to think she uses drugs or lacks sophistication. No one is going to fire Kim or Kylie or Gwen, or kick them out of school for wearing these hairstyles.[17] People will think they're stylish.

I read a quote on Instagram (posted by New York City hairstylist Teni-sha F. Sweet) that said, "If you don't understand cultural appropriation, imagine working on a project and getting an F and then somebody copies you and gets an A and credit for your work."[18] Sarah Jessica Parker wears a turban in Abu Dhabi in *Sex and the City 2* and it's fashion. But a Middle Eastern or Indian or other minority woman wearing the same turban in the United States has to worry, *Is someone going to think I'm a terrorist or a Gypsy or a palm reader?* or whatever other stereotypes are associated with wearing a turban. In America, turbans are associated with danger. Com-prehensive research out of Stanford shows we exhibit automatic biases (heightened since 9/11) against those wearing turbans, are more prone to perceive innocent objects held by the turban wearer as weapons, and, in video games at least, shoot at them more frequently simply because they wear turbans.[19] But no one is going to worry that Sarah Jessica Parker might blow up the plane. She actually has the privilege to enter most rooms and spaces dressed any way she likes without people attaching ste-reotypes to her. I know a Middle Eastern young woman who wears a head covering for religious reasons. When she goes out, she thinks twice: *Maybe I should show a bit of my hair or wear more makeup so I seem less threatening?* These are the second thoughts that some people have to consider when they're trying to display their own culture. Others only have to think once.

Privilege is a touchy subject because it puts the people who have it on the defensive. (And, P.S., that's pretty much all of us, since we all benefit from one form of privilege or another.) As activist Janaya "Future" Khan so powerfully explained in a viral video, people have explosive reactions to the word "privilege." They feel defensive because they themselves have almost certainly been marginalized in some way; they too have gone through heartache and trauma at the hands of others. But, as Khan clarifies, "Privilege isn't about what you've gone through; it's about what you *haven't* had to go through."[20] This much I know: In order to work through these issues, we have to hear one another, to see one another's humanity, to acknowledge one another's hurt. We need understanding at every level. As Roxane Gay writes in her book *Bad Feminist,* "We need to stop playing Privilege or Oppression Olympics... We should be able to say, 'This is my truth,' and have that truth stand without a hundred clamoring voices shouting, giving the impression that multiple truths cannot coexist."[21]

On the fashion front, what is someone who loves lots of different cultures to do? Are we as individuals "allowed" to wear only the native styles of our ancestors? Should everybody just shop at the Gap and call it a day? I'm not discouraging anyone from being inspired by other cultures. I don't think we should water down our looks for fear of the thought police. There are super-simple ways to be sensitive without sacrificing style. Personally, I love wearing kimonos. I recently gave a lecture on their history at the Newark Museum. I was fascinated to learn how the garment has evolved over millennia, and how even today in Japan, there are strict rules about how a kimono has to be tied and folded. When I wore a kimono for that lecture, I made it my own. I paired it with black over-the-knee suede boots and minimal accessories. In other words, I didn't wear wooden clogs or style my hair in a *shimada,* the way Karlie Kloss did in a famously appropriative and incendiary 2017 *Vogue* spread.[22] Again, it's culture, not costume.

But the line differentiating the two isn't always clear. Nicki Minaj was slammed for "fetishizing" Asian culture when she performed her song "Chun-Li" (inspired by a video game character) on *Saturday Night Live* in 2018. Notably, Minaj has tweeted that her great-grandfather was Japanese.[23] Some have argued that her self-reported ancestry gives her more of a right to explore (or exploit?) Asian cultural imagery. Other Internet commenters felt that by wearing chopsticks in her hair and a gold dragon on her loincloth, and casting backup dancers of Asian descent, she created a disrespectful, stereotype-heavy mishmash of several distinct cultures.[24] And still other posters, self-identifying as Asian or Asian American, seemed to applaud how Minaj was remixing cultures and highlighting traditional symbols.[25] The debate raged on. Reaction was similarly mixed when Caucasian Utah high school student Keziah Daum wore a cheongsam to her senior prom. It's important to note that her hair, makeup, and accessories were tasteful and subdued. One angry observer tweeted: "My culture is NOT your goddamn prom dress."[26] But the popular opinion in China, per press reports, was to celebrate Daum for her stylish choice.[27]

There is no law on whether or not it's acceptable to wear a cheongsam if you are not Chinese. I believe it depends on how you style it, whether your accessories, hair, and makeup seem over the top in their "ethnicity." It comes down to the spirit in which you wear the garment—and whether that spirit communicates respect versus condescension. There are nuances to consider. Can you see the difference between a teenager's prom dress and Victoria's Secret's 2012 "Sexy Little Geisha" lingerie? (The caption when that teddy was sold online? "Your ticket to an exotic adventure... Sexy little fantasies, there's one for every sexy you.")[28] The line between celebration and appropriation gets crossed when there is the *unacknowledged* or *inappropriate* adoption of the customs, practices, or ideas of one group by members of another, typically more dominant group. Let's underline the words <u>unacknowledged</u> and <u>inappropriate</u>. It comes down to whether you're aware of a look's cultural history, whether you give credit where it is due (as opposed to renaming the style), and how you honor whatever you are borrowing. So borrow away—just be conscious about it.

Fashion Psychology Tip

R-E-S-P-E-C-T: FIND OUT WHAT IT MEANS TO ME

- **Educate yourself** Do a little research into a garment's cultural history before you wear it. I'm not saying pull out a book and read a whole history of boxer braids or the kimono. But google it. Do your due diligence by looking into a style's historical meaning, so you're not walking around inadvertently renaming something. If a brand is repeatedly put on blast for making culturally insensitive mistakes or overstepping in this way, or for putting out offensive images or slogans (however unintentionally), think about whether to support it or spend your hard-earned money elsewhere.

- **Be low-key with your behavior** If you are wearing a spiritually significant item from a culture other than your own, don't behave in a way that's antithetical to that culture's values and customs. Of course, we are all free to do as we wish. As my friends might say, "Who's gonna check me, boo?" But I personally wouldn't wear a hijab to a bar or a bindi with a bikini. I would be careful not to dishonor the symbol.

- **Are you Halloween-ing it?** This tip is about moderation. When you wear cultural items head to toe, it can seem like a Halloween costume. Mix in elements of your own or neutral style.

- **Ponder privilege** Think about whether someone else would encounter bias if she wore the style you're considering. If a member of the culture that originated the look were to wear it, might she suffer for it? If the answer gives you pause, rethink whether the fashion statement is worth it.

YOU BETTER REPRESENT: WHAT IT MEANS TO BE SEEN

When we talk about woke style and beauty standards, it also brings up questions about who has access to fashion. Who is represented in the advertising and images that define what's desirable? What color is their skin? What age are they? What body type? What gender identity? Are they disabled or neurotypical? It's also essential to ask: What is this brand selling and who gets to buy it? Does it offer a full range of sizes or products that serve a spectrum of skin shades?

Access is important. Historically, it wasn't until the Sears catalog came along at the dawn of the twentieth century that many black Americans even had the *opportunity* to dress well. As professor Louis Hyman, who teaches a course at Cornell on the history of shopping, has explained, Jim Crow laws that came about in the late nineteenth century were specifically designed to limit the consumerist opportunities of black people. When they went shopping at their local general store, Hyman says, they had to wait to be served until every white person in the store was served, even if they walked in first. If they protested, they risked their lives. "White shop owners who controlled the credit also controlled what they got, i.e., whether they got the same clothes as white people," Hyman told Jezebel. "They usually didn't."[29] To this day, there are barriers to looking "classy" or "appropriate" or on-trend or up to date. Tom Ford—chairman of the Council of Fashion Designers of America—once said, "Dressing well is a form of good manners."[30] What is implied, then, about the people who can't afford to dress "well" or don't have the body type required to do so or simply find fashion intimidating? Do those people have bad manners? Are they rude? What kind of bias is a statement like that setting up?

Representation is about more than just skin color or socioeconomics. It's about size, age, and all the other isms. When we see women who look like us celebrated for their beauty, it expands our idea of who gets to be considered beautiful. To quote Alex Waldman, co-designer of Universal Standard, a high-end fashion line that ranges from size 00 to 40, "I believe that if we're still talking about plus-size clothing in five years then we will have all failed... It should just be clothing for women," she told Goop in 2018. Waldman envisions a world in which labels like "plus-size" or "size inclusive" become obsolete, in which women of every size can shop together in the same store, in which "no one is waiting outside of the dressing room."[31] When no one is excluded from looking stylish, it doesn't get more woke than that.

But I'm not going to lie to you. Fashion has always been a game of insiders versus outsiders, the haves versus the have-nots. Psychologically, why would you pay a lot of money for something everyone can have? Finite supply and exclusivity drive up demand. Wokeness aims to shift that paradigm. But things are moving slowly. American women spend three times as much on clothing as men, yet only 14 percent of major fashion brands are run by female executives.[32] Out of the seventy-nine designers who showed at New York Fashion Week in February 2018, only nine were black. This in spite of the fact that in 2015, black consumers spent $26 billion on apparel.[33] Research out of the Wharton School of Business at the University of Pennsylvania shows that blacks and Hispanics spend up to 30 percent more than whites of comparable income on visible goods like clothing, cars, and jewelry.[34] Yet they remain underrepresented in the corridors of power in the fashion industry. As Beyoncé wrote in *Vogue*, "If people in powerful positions continue to hire and cast only people who look like them, sound like them, come from the same neighborhoods they grew up in... they will hire the same models, curate the same art, cast the same actors over and over again, and we will all lose."[35]

When we broaden access to fashion and present truly diverse role models, we invite more people to see themselves as fashionable. Brands pay a lot of lip service to these ideas, but they can always do better. Tokenism is not the same as progress. Tyra Banks once talked about a disturbing trend she witnessed in the modeling industry. Like skirt lengths, various races and ethnicities seemed to cycle in and out of fashion. First, Banks said, the Brazilian girls were hot. Then the It girls were from Africa.

During another era, black American models ascended. "There was never a 'white model' season—that was always the default...while us girls of color were transient exotic spices to sprinkle onto the runway when we were in style," Banks said. "Race is not a trend. My skin is not a trend. My body, my booty—not a fashion trend."[36]

So what can *you* do to push the wheels of history forward a little faster? You can shop your values. You can work to self-affirm and lift others up as you climb. You can be sensitive to other people's pain and careful not to add to it. You can dress your best—whatever that means to you—because it will help you hold your head up high. As they say, be the change you want to see in the world. You never know who's watching.

THE BOTTOM LINE

KEY TIPS AND TAKEAWAYS FROM CHAPTER 10

- **Shop your values.** You can choose to buy clothes from companies that promote diversity, inclusivity, and sustainability. Support brands whose ethics match your own.

- **Appreciate, don't appropriate.** If you are borrowing a look that's easily identified as being from a culture other than your own, learn its history. Consider what the reaction could be if someone from that culture were to wear the item or style in public. If you do decide to wear it, balance it out with neutral accessories, hair, and makeup.

CONCLUSION

Don't be eye candy. Be soul food.

— Unknown

Recently I made history. I appeared on NBC News to discuss "the death of the business suit" and the increasingly casual nature of professional dress codes. It was the first time a Fashion Psychologist (or someone with that title anyway) had ever appeared on national TV in the United States. The anchor, Ali Velshi, introduced me as someone who "studies how what we wear affects what we think." I loved that because even though I'm the one invited to give lectures at places like Harvard and approached for guidance by undergrads at the London College of Fashion, I AM still a student. Just like you, I find that my eyes are constantly being opened to the ways attire and emotions interact. When it comes to what to wear or how to be happier, I don't pretend to have all the answers. But after reading this book, you should now have a firmer grasp on the right *questions*. Now that you've read these ten chapters, here is what I hope you'll ask yourself as you shop and get dressed:

Does this make me feel incredible? (Instead of, Is this cool?)

Do I love it? (Instead of, Will they like it?)

Do I need it? (Instead of, Do I want it?)

What do I already have to work with? (Instead of, What new thing should I buy?)

Who made it, with what materials, and how ethically was it sourced and manufactured? (Instead of, What label is it?)

I spent the introduction of this book walking you through my personal history. It wasn't easy and it wasn't always pretty. But as we say good-bye, you begin your own journey toward sharper style and a more centered and confident state of mind. I hope we part ways as two true believers in styling from the inside out. Thank you for being open to my ideas. And for embracing the notion that emotional awareness is essential to good style—because you really need one to have the other.

I hope that after reading this book you feel more and shop less. I hope you make conscious, deliberate style choices that serve you before you consider anyone or anything else. I hope that as you approach your (ideally way less crowded!) closet tomorrow, you'll feel empowered to dress your best, and that doing so makes you feel better than you did yesterday.

As you carefully examine your clothes, they will no doubt bring up memories and associations. Some will be bittersweet, others joyful, others triumphant. Together those clothes represent a portrait of your life. I hope you understand what powerful assets your clothes are, that they can help to heal and protect you. And that by deciding what to wear every day, you have the opportunity to redefine yourself, to channel their magic, whether you decide to use your clothes to feel calmer, stronger, or simply more alive.

You already own the tools to feel better—to feel your best. They're hanging in your closet. But most important, they're within you.

ACKNOWLEDGMENTS

I would like to thank the many people who helped take this book from a dream to a reality. You have blessed me immensely.

Thank you to my editor, Marisa Vigilante, and everyone at Little, Brown Spark, including Tracy Behar, Ian Straus, Jessica Chun, Juliana Horbachevsky, Lauren Harms, and Ben Allen.

Thank you to my collaborator, Suzanne Zuckerman, a talented writer and gifted listener.

Thank you to my agent, Elizabeth Bewley, at Sterling Lord Literistic.

My colleagues at the Fashion Institute of Technology, especially Dr. Paul Clement, Rosa Maria Smith, and Hadassah Perez. All of you inspire me every day. To my students, thank you for bringing your curious minds to the classroom.

Thank you to my former professors and supporting faculty at Bowling Green State University, especially Martha Chandran-Dickerson, Dr. Manuel Pomales, and Dr. Mike Zickar, and my former professors at Teachers College, Columbia University, especially Dr. Gregory Payton.

Thank you to my loyal, hardworking interns: Frank, Jessica, Korona, and Kat.

A big thanks to the many journalists that I've met over the past few years, especially Jennifer Bennour. You have embraced fashion psychology and helped me to share my research and philosophy with people around the world.

And finally, the last and biggest thanks to my family: my father, Coejo;

ACKNOWLEDGMENTS

my mother, Karen; my brother, Jovan; my nannies, Jacqueline and Gail; my uncle Franc; my cousin Audrey; my cousins Loriann, Ericka, Sal, and others. Also to my sorority sisters Rebecca and Carleta, best friend Sierra Narciese, friends Anthony and Martha, and advisors Darryn and Eric.

I love you all.

NOTES

INTRODUCTION: MY STYLE STORY

1. Monnica T. Williams, PhD, "Why African Americans Avoid Psychotherapy," *Psychology Today,* November 2, 2011, https://www.psychologytoday.com/us/blog/culturally -speaking/201111/why-african-americans-avoid-psychotherapy. In this article, Williams quotes from J. Alvidrez, L. R. Snowden, and D. M. Kaiser, "The Experience of Stigma among Black Mental Health Consumers," *Journal of Health Care for the Poor and Underserved* 19 (2008): 874–93.

2. Lindy West, "People Really Don't Like It When You Say It's Okay to Be Fat, Notes Lindy West," *New York Magazine,* The Cut, October 17, 2018, https://www.thecut .com/2018/10/women-and-power-chapter-three.html#lindy-west.

3. Gavin de Becker, *The Gift of Fear, and Other Survival Signals That Protect Us from Violence* (New York: Penguin Random House, 1999), 70.

4. This statistic comes from the Centers for Disease Control, which offers a Fast Fact Web page called "Preventing Intimate Partner Violence," https://www.cdc.gov/violence prevention/intimatepartnerviolence/fastfact.html.

5. Kim K. P. Johnson, Jane E. Hegland, and Nancy A. Schofield, "Survivors of Rape: Functions and Implications of Dress in a Context of Coercive Power," in *Appearance and Power,* ed. Kim K. P. Johnson and Sharron J. Lennon (Oxford: Bloomsbury Academic, 1999), 11–32, retrieved from "Dress, Body, Culture," Bloomsbury Fashion Central, bloomsburyfashioncentral.com.

6. Jo Hartley, "Fashion and Mood: How Clothes Affect Your Emotions," *Sydney Morning Herald,* July 17, 2015, https://www.smh.com.au/lifestyle/fashion-and-mood-how -clothes-affect-your-emotions-20150717-giei1f.html.

7. Cassandra Willyard, "Need to Heal Thyself?" *gradPSYCH Magazine: An American Psychological Association Publication,* January 2012, https://www.apa.org/gradpsych/ 2012/01/heal.

8. Benedict Carey, "Can We Really Inherit Trauma?" *New York Times,* December 10, 2018, https://www.nytimes.com/2018/12/10/health/mind-epigenetics-genes.html.

9. Lawrence V. Harper, "Epigenetic Inheritance and the Intergenerational Transfer of Experience," *Psychological Bulletin* (2005): 340.

10. Liz Phair, Twitter, September 27, 2018. Phair's complete quote: "For those of us contemplating the harms that we're [sic] done to us and that we suffered in silence—the price of growing up female in this culture—I salute you. There is an unacknowledged battle field and we are the undecorated veterans #IBelieveChristineBlaseyFord."

11. Paulo Coelho, Twitter, August 16, 2018.

12. Jennifer Miller, "The Dress Doctor Is In," *New York Times,* April 12, 2018, https://www .nytimes.com/2018/04/12/fashion/fashion-psychologist.html.

13. Sarah Spellings, "Everybody Wants to Know What a Fashion Psychologist Thinks," *New York Magazine,* The Cut, April 20, 2018, https://www.thecut.com/2018/04/dawnn -karen-is-the-academic-behind-fashion-psychology.html.

14. In May 2017 I presented a webinar on Fashion Psychology for Empower Women, an online platform for women's economic empowerment co-developed by UN Women, United Nations Entity for Gender Equality and the Empowerment of Women, https:// www.youtube.com/watch?v=_xG2SntA75w.

CHAPTER 1: FASHION PSYCHOLOGY 101

1. Kenzie Bryant, "What Makes Taylor Swift's $895 Balenciaga Sweatshirt So Controver- sial," *Vanity Fair,* July 23, 2018, https://www.vanityfair.com/style/2018/07/taylor-swift -balenciaga-hoodie-new-york.

2. Alexander Todorov and Janine Willis, "First Impressions: Making Up Your Mind after a 100-Ms Exposure to a Face," *Psychological Science* 17, no. 7 (July 1, 2006): 592–98, https:// journals.sagepub.com/doi/abs/10.1111/j.1467-9280.2006.01750.x?ssource=mfc&rss=1&.

3. Molly Lambert, "Trixie Mattel Says Drag Queens Are Like Swiss Army Knives," *New York Times Magazine,* August 29, 2018, https://www.nytimes.com/2018/08/29 /magazine/trixie-mattel-says-drag-queens-are-like-swiss-army-knives.html.

4. "Renaissance Fashion and Dress Codes," March 5, 2012, Metropolitan Museum of Art, https://www.metmuseum.org/blogs/teen-blog/renaissance-portrait/blog/ renaissance-fashion-and-dress-codes. See also "Social Class and Clothing," *Encyclopedia of Clothing and Fashion* (2005), https://www.encyclopedia.com/fashion/encyclopedias -almanacs-transcripts-and-maps/social-class-and-clothing.

5. Vikas Shah, MBE, "The Role of Fashion in Human Culture," *Thought Economics,* Sep- tember 15, 2012, https://thoughteconomics.com/the-role-of-fashion-in-human-culture/.

6. Lindsay Peoples Wagner, "Everywhere and Nowhere: What It's Really Like to Be Black and Work in Fashion," *New York Magazine,* The Cut, August 23, 2018, https://www.thecut .com/2018/08/what-its-really-like-to-be-black-and-work-in-fashion.html?utm_source=tw.

7. Stephanie Chan, "Leslie Jones Says No Designers Want to Dress Her for 'Ghostbusters' Premiere," *Hollywood Reporter,* June 29, 2016, https://www.hollywoodreporter.com /news/leslie-jones-says-no-designers-907297.

8. David Yanofsky, "The US Is Now Buying More Stretchy Pants Than Blue Jeans," *Quartz,* March 1, 2018, https://qz.com/1218844/the-us-bought-more-yoga-pants-leg gings-and-other-elastic-fabrics-than-blue-jeans-in-2017/.

9. Veronica Webb, "Closet Case: Fashion Psychologist Dawnn Karen Styles from the Inside Out," *The Root,* April 16, 2018, https://theglowup.theroot.com/closet-case-fashion -psychologist-dawnn-karen-styles-fr-1825301103.

10. George Dvorsky, "Why Freud Still Matters, When He Was Wrong about Almost Every- thing," *Gizmodo,* August 7, 2013, https://io9.gizmodo.com/why-freud-still-matters -when-he-was-wrong-about-almost-1055800815.

11. Amy Cuddy, *Presence: Bringing Your Boldest Self to Your Biggest Challenges* (New York: Back Bay Books/Little, Brown and Company, 2015), 174.

12. Cecelia A. Watson, "The Sartorial Self: William James's Philosophy of Dress," *History of Psychology* 7, no. 3 (September 2004): 214, http://www.ceceliawatson.com/Cecelia _Watson/Curriculum_Vitae_files/Sartorial%20Self.pdf.

13. Roland Barthes, *The Language of Fashion* (London: Bloomsbury Academic, 2013), https://www.bloomsbury.com/uk/the-language-of-fashion-9781472505422/.

14. Sharon J. Lennon and Kim K. P. Johnson, *The Social Psychology of Dress* (New York: Fair-

child Books, 2017), https://www.bloomsburyfashioncentral.com/products/berg-fash ion-library/article/bibliographical-guides/the-social-psychology-of-dress.

15. Amanda Woods, "Reporter Tries to Shame 'Struggling' Ocasio-Cortez over Ward-robe," *New York Post*, November 16, 2018, https://nypost.com/2018/11/16/reporter-tries -to-shame-struggling-ocasio-cortez-over-wardrobe/.

16. Rebecca Jennings, "Ayanna Pressley, Alexandria Ocasio-Cortez, and the Year of Victory Red Lipstick," Vox, November 7, 2018, https://www.vox.com/the-goods/2018/11/7/1807 1900/alexandria-ocasio-cortez-ayanna-pressley-red-lipstick-election.

17. Nina Burleigh, "Melania, Ivanka and Ivana Trump Wear High Heels, a Symbol of Every-thing That Is Beautiful and Horrifying about Them," *Newsweek*, August 10, 2017, https:// www.newsweek.com/trump-melania-trump-ivanka-trump-first-lady-stiletto-649286.

18. Kate Bennett, "Melania Trump's Africa Visit and the Message It Sends from America," CNN, October 8, 2018, https://www.cnn.com/2018/10/08/politics/melania-trump-africa -trip-wrap/index.html.

19. Dan Amira, "Hillary Clinton Is Asked What Designers She Wears Moments after Mak-ing Point about Sexism," *New York Magazine*, December 2, 2010, http://nymag.com /intelligencer/2010/12/hillary_clinton_asked_what_des.html.

20. Rosemary Feitelberg, "Melania Trump Says 'Focus on What I Do, Not What I Wear,'" *WWD*, October 6, 2018, https://wwd.com/fashion-news/fashion-scoops/melania-trump -says-focus-on-what-i-do-not-what-i-wear-1202870328/.

21. Vanessa Friedman, "Melania Trump: Out of Africa, Still in Costume," *New York Times*, October 8, 2018, https://www.nytimes.com/2018/10/08/fashion/melania-trump-africa -trip-fashion-fedora.html.

22. Hajo Adam and Adam D. Galinsky, "Enclothed Cognition," *Journal of Experimental Social Psychology* 48, no. 4 (July 2012): 918–25, https://www.sciencedirect.com/science /article/pii/S0022103112000200.

23. Kristen Bateman, "Everything I Learned from a Session with a Fashion Psychologist," StyleCaster, 2016, https://stylecaster.com/fashion-psychologist/.

24. Ann Shoket, "How Power Dressing Moved beyond the High Heel," Thrive Global, October 9, 2018, https://thriveglobal.com/stories/power-dressing-beyond-high-heel -status-symbol-change-fashion-psychology/.

25. Helena Fitzgerald, "All the Lipsticks I've Bought for Women I'll Never Be," *New York Magazine*, The Cut, October 8, 2018, https://www.thecut.com/2018/10/all-the-lipsticks -ive-bought-for-women-ill-never-be.html.

26. Stacy London, "Stacy London on Her Year of Going Broke," Refinery 29, February 2, 2018, https://www.refinery29.com/en-us/2018/02/188983/stacy-london-managing-money -heartbreak.

CHAPTER 2: WHAT'S YOUR STYLE STORY?

1. Naomi Braithwaite, "What Your Shoes Say about You (Quite a Lot, Actually)," The Conversation, March 6, 2015, https://theconversation.com/what-your-shoes-say-about -you-quite-a-lot-actually-38142.

2. Angela J. Bahns, Christian S. Crandall, Fiona Ge, and Omri Gillath, "Shoes as a Source of First Impressions," *Journal of Research in Personality* 46, no. 4 (August 2012): 423–30, https://www.sciencedirect.com/science/article/abs/pii/S0092656612000608.

3. "The 50 Greatest Fashion Quotes of All Time," *Harper's Bazaar*, January 11, 2018, https:// www.harpersbazaar.com/fashion/designers/a1576/50-famous-fashion-quotes/.

4. Stevie Martin, "The Psychological Reason Why We Wear the Clothes We Wear,"

Grazia, March 6, 2015, https://graziadaily.co.uk/fashion/news/psychological-reason -wear-clothes-wear/.

5. Ayalla Ruvio, Yossi Gavish, and Aviv Shoham, "Consumer's Doppelganger: A Role Model Perspective on Intentional Consumer Mimicry," *Journal of Consumer Behaviour*, January 2013, https://www.researchgate.net/publication/264466739_Consumer's _doppelganger_A_role_model_perspective_on_intentional_consumer_mimicry.

6. Roland Barthes, *The Language of Fashion* (London: Bloomsbury Academic, 2004), 90–91.

7. Stephanie Newman, PhD, "Why Your Teen Insists on Dressing Exactly Like Her Friends," *Psychology Today*, September 14, 2010, https://www.psychologytoday.com /us/blog/apologies-freud/201009/why-your-teen-insists-dressing-exactly-her-friends.

8. "What Are Youths' Biggest Clothing Style and Brand Decision Influencers?" *Marketing Charts*, July 30, 2014, https://www.marketingcharts.com/industries/retail-and-e -commerce-44453.

9. Karen Pine, "Happiness: It's Not in the Jeans," University of Hertfordshire, March 8, 2012, www.sciencedaily.com/releases/2012/03/120308062537.htm.

10. Nadene van der Linden, "Unshakeable Calm: Top Tips to Stay Calm with Toxic People," Psych Central, December 15, 2017, https://blogs.psychcentral.com/unshakeable -calm/2017/11/top-tips-to-stay-calm-with-toxic-people/. For more on the Gray Rock Method, see Lindsay Champion, "Try the 'Gray Rock Method,' a Foolproof Technique to Shut Down Toxic People," PureWow, November 6, 2018, https://www.purewow .com/wellness/gray-rock-method.

11. Alexis Conason, PsyD, "Should Therapists Self-Disclose?" *Psychology Today*, May 5, 2017, https://www.psychologytoday.com/us/blog/eating-mindfully/201705/should -therapists-self-disclose.

12. Laura M. Simonds and Naomi Spokes, "Therapist Self-Disclosure and the Therapeutic Alliance in the Treatment of Eating Problems," *Eating Disorders: The Journal of Treatment & Prevention* 25, no. 2 (January 6, 2017): 151–64.

13. Z. D. Peterson, "More Than a Mirror: The Ethics of Therapist Self-Disclosure," *Psychotherapy: Theory, Research, Practice, Training* 39, no. 1 (2002): 21–31.

CHAPTER 3: THE SCIENCE BEHIND SHOPPING

1. Cydney Henderson, "Revolve Apologizes for Sweatshirt Saying 'Being Fat Is Not Beautiful, It's an Excuse,'" *USA Today*, September 12, 2018, https://www.usatoday.com/story/ life/entertainthis/2018/09/12/lena-dunham-responds-fat-shaming-sweatshirt-contro versy/1286151002/. See also Rob Bailey-Millado, "Plus Size Brand Slammed for Using Thin Models to Show How Big Lingerie Is," *New York Post*, May 8, 2019, https://nypost.com/ 2019/05/08/plus-size-brand-slammed-for-using-thin-models-to-show-how-big-lingerie-is/.

2. Alexandra Olson, "Sephora Closes All US Stores for a 1-Hour 'Inclusion Workshop,'" *Time*, June 5, 2019, https://time.com/5601284/sephora-stores-diversity-inclusion -training/. See also Nicole Saunders, "SZA Fronts Fenty Beauty's 'Mattemoiselle' Lipstick Campaign," *Billboard*, December 14, 2017, https://www.billboard.com/articles/news /lifestyle/8070477/rihanna-fenty-beauty-sza-lipstick-campaign-mattemoiselle-pics.

3. Barbara McMahon, "Wonder Why You've Tons of Clothes but Nothing to Wear? The Answer Lies in Your Mind, Says a Top Psychologist," *Daily Mail*, August 26, 2018, https:// www.dailymail.co.uk/femail/article-6100191/amp/What-does-reveal-wardrobe -emotional-history.html.

4. Research commissioned by technology company Akamai and conducted by Forrester Consulting. "Akamai Reveals 2 Seconds as the New Threshold of Acceptability for

eCommerce Web Page Response Times," September 14, 2009, https://www.akamai
.com/us/en/about/news/press/2009-press/akamai-reveals-2-seconds-as-the-new
-threshold-of-acceptability-for-ecommerce-web-page-response-times.jsp.

5. Ray A. Smith, "A Closet Filled with Regrets," *Wall Street Journal*, April 17, 2013, https://
www.wsj.com/articles/SB10001424127887324240804578415002232186418.

6. Statista Research Department, "U.S. Apparel Market Statistics & Facts," January 7,
2019, https://www.statista.com/topics/965/apparel-market-in-the-us/.

7. Matthew Frankel, "How Does the Average American Spend Their Paycheck? See How
You Compare," *USA Today*, May 8, 2018, https://www.usatoday.com/story/money
/personalfinance/budget-and-spending/2018/05/08/how-does-average-american
-spend-paycheck/34378157/.

8. Imran Amed, Anita Balchandani, Marco Beltrami, Achim Berg, Saskia Hedrich, and Felix
Rölkens, "The State of Fashion 2019: A Year of Awakening," *The Business of Fashion*, November 2018, https://cdn.businessoffashion.com/reports/The_State_of_Fashion_2019.pdf.

9. United States Congress, Joint Economic Committee, "The Economic Impact of the
Fashion Industry," February 6, 2015, https://maloney.house.gov/sites/maloney.house
.gov/files/documents/The%20Economic%20Impact%20of%20the%20Fashion%20
Industry%20—%20JEC%20report%20FINAL.pdf.

10. The Business of Fashion Team, "A Fashion Education That Meets Market Needs," *The
Business of Fashion*, October 22, 2018, https://www.businessoffashion.com/articles
/education/a-fashion-education-that-meets-market-needs.

11. Alexandria Sage, "Fashion Trends in an Uncertain Economy," Reuters, April 27, 2008,
https://www.reuters.com/article/us-fashion-recession/fashion-trends-in-an-uncertain
-economy-idUSN2721944120080427.

12. Sheila Marikar, "The Transformational Bliss of Borrowing Your Office Clothes," *New
York Times*, October 12, 2018, https://www.nytimes.com/2018/10/12/business/rent
-the-runway-office-clothes.html.

13. Deborah J. Vagins, "The Simple Truth about the Gender Pay Gap," American Association of University Women, Fall 2018, https://www.aauw.org/research/the-simple
-truth-about-the-gender-pay-gap/.

14. Emma Johnson, "The Real Cost of Your Shopping Habits," *Forbes*, January 15, 2015,
https://www.forbes.com/sites/emmajohnson/2015/01/15/the-real-cost-of-your
-shopping-habits/#f481b7a1452d.

15. "Average Cost of Clothing per Month Will Surprise You," Credit Donkey, November
15, 2017, https://www.creditdonkey.com/average-cost-clothing-per-month.html.

16. Alexandra Schwartz, "Rent the Runway Wants to Lend You Your Look," *The New
Yorker*, October 15, 2018, https://www.newyorker.com/magazine/2018/10/22/rent
-the-runway-wants-to-lend-you-your-look.

17. Vanessa Friedman, "The Biggest Fake News in Fashion," *New York Times*, December 18,
2018, https://www.nytimes.com/2018/12/18/fashion/fashion-second-biggest-polluter
-fake-news.html.

18. Suzanne Zuckerman, "We Asked a Financial Therapist for Money Advice—and It Was
Fascinating," PureWow, March 15, 2018, https://www.purewow.com/money
/what-is-a-financial-therapist.

19. Apocryphal quotation attributed to Will Rogers, Will Smith, Edward Norton, and
various others.

20. Sarah O'Brien, "Consumers Cough Up $5,400 a Year on Impulse Purchases," CNBC,
February 23, 2018, https://www.cnbc.com/2018/02/23/consumers-cough-up-5400-a
-year-on-impulse-purchases.html.

21. Alina Dizik, "Shopping a Sale Gives You the Same Feeling as Getting High," BBC, November 24, 2016, http://www.bbc.com/capital/story/20161123-shopping-a-sale-gives -you-the-same-feeling-as-getting-high.

22. Carmen Nobel, "Neuromarketing: Tapping into the 'Pleasure Center' of Consumers," *Forbes,* February 1, 2013, https://www.forbes.com/sites/hbsworkingknowledge/2013/02/ 01/neuromarketing-tapping-into-the-pleasure-center-of-consumers/#5642fece2745.

23. Liraz Margalit, PhD, "The Psychology of Choice," *Psychology Today,* October 3, 2014, https://www.psychologytoday.com/us/blog/behind-online-behavior/201410/the -psychology-choice.

24. Jameela Jamil, Twitter, January 19, 2019, https://twitter.com/jameelajamil/status/1086 721920039448577?lang=en.

25. Sangeeta Singh-Kurtz, "The Body-Positive Skincare Trend Is Driven by Women's Fear of Aging," Quartzy, November 4, 2018, https://qz.com/quartzy/1445782/the-body -positive-skincare-trend-is-driven-by-womens-fear-of-aging/.

26. Catherine Kast and Suzy Weiss, "Victoria's Secret Only Hires Super-Skinny Models— and That's a Problem," *New York Post,* November 5, 2018, https://nypost.com/2018/11/05 /victorias-secret-only-hires-super-skinny-models-and-thats-a-problem/.

27. Hilary George-Parkin, "Size, by the Numbers," *Racked,* June 5, 2018, https://www .racked.com/2018/6/5/17380662/size-numbers-average-woman-plus-market.

28. Marisa Dellato, "Retailer Trends on Twitter for Showing Off Size Diversity," *New York Post,* November 7, 2018, https://nypost.com/2018/11/07/retailer-trends-on-twitter-for -showing-off-size-diversity/.

29. Heidi Zak, "An Open Letter to Victoria's Secret," ThirdLove, November 19, 2018, https:// www.thirdlove.com/blogs/unhooked/thirdloves-open-letter-to-victorias-secret.

30. Imran Amed, Johanna Andersson, Achim Berg, Martine Drageset, Saskia Hedrich, and Sara Kappelmark, "The State of Fashion, 2018: Renewed Optimism for the Fashion Industry," McKinsey, November 2017, https://www.mckinsey.com/industries/retail/ our-insights/renewed-optimism-for-the-fashion-industry.

31. Praveen Adhi, Tiffany Burns, Andrew Davis, Shruti Lal, and Bill Mutell, "A Transfor- mation in Store," McKinsey, May 2019, https://www.mckinsey.com/business-fun ctions/operations/our-insights/a-transformation-in-store?cid=eml-web.

32. Daphne Howland, "27% of Apparel Sales Are Now Online," RetailDive, July 2, 2018, https://www.retaildive.com/news/27-of-apparel-sales-are-now-online/526941/.

33. Dhani Mau, "In 2018, Holiday Shoppers Are Losing Trust in Social Media, Prefer Retailers with Physical Storefronts," Fashionista, November 1, 2018, https://fashioni sta.com/2018/11/holiday-shopping-trends-statistics-2018.

34. Lauren Thomas, "Black Friday Pulled in a Record $6.22 Billion in Online Sales: Adobe Analytics," CNBC, November 28, 2018, https://www.cnbc.com/2018/11/24/black-friday -pulled-in-a-record-6point22-billion-in-online-sales-adobe.html.

35. Martinne Geller and Kate Holton, "Firing Fake Pineapples, Pernod Uses 'Influencers' to Drive Sales," Reuters, July 3, 2018, https://www.reuters.com/article/us-pernod-ricard -marketing-influencers-idUSKBN1JT1OZ.

36. Vikram Alexei Kansara, "Amid 'Retail Apocalypse,' the Future of Commerce Is Com- munity," *The Business of Fashion,* December 1, 2017, https://www.businessoffashion.com/ articles/video/amid-retail-apocalypse-the-future-of-commerce-is-community?source =emailshare.

37. Lisa Fickenscher, "How High-End Department Store Reps Use Social Media to Rake in Millions," *New York Post,* November 5, 2018, https://nypost.com/2018/11/05/how-high -end-department-store-reps-use-social-media-to-rake-in-millions/.

38. Zameena Mejia, "Kylie Jenner Reportedly Makes $1 Million per Paid Instagram Post—Here's How Much Other Top Influencers Get," CNBC, July 31, 2018, https://www.cnbc.com/2018/07/31/kylie-jenner-makes-1-million-per-paid-instagram-post-hopper-hq-says.html.

39. Lucy Tesseras, "A Third of Brands Admit to Not Disclosing Influencer Partnerships," *Marketing Week*, November 14, 2018, https://www.marketingweek.com/2018/11/14/influencer-marketing-partnerships/.

40. Sapna Maheshwari, "Are You Ready for the Nanoinfluencers?" *New York Times*, November 11, 2018, https://www.nytimes.com/2018/11/11/business/media/nanoinfluencers-instagram-influencers.html.

41. Yuyu Chen, "The Rise of 'Micro-Influencers' on Instagram," *Digiday*, April 27, 2016, https://digiday.com/marketing/micro-influencers/.

42. Gillian Fournier, "Mere Exposure Effect," Psych Central, 2018, https://psychcentral.com/encyclopedia/mere-exposure-effect/.

43. Shanelle Mullin, "The Science of Familiarity: How to Increase Conversions by Being Completely Unoriginal," CXL, October 1, 2015, https://conversionxl.com/blog/science-of-familiarity/.

44. Dennis Payne, "How Many Contacts Does It Take Before Someone Buys Your Product?" *Business Insider*, July 12, 2011, https://www.businessinsider.com/how-many-contacts-does-it-take-before-someone-buys-your-product-2011-7.

45. David DeSteno, Leah Dickens, Jennifer S. Lerner, and Ye Li, "Gratitude: A Tool for Reducing Economic Impatience," *Psychological Science*, April 23, 2014, https://journals.sagepub.com/doi/10.1177/0956797614529979.

46. Kit Yarrow, "12 Ways to Stop Wasting Money and Take Control of Your Stuff," *Money*, November 20, 2014, http://money.com/money/3070984/overspending-overconsumption-stuff/.

47. James Hamblin, "Buy Experiences, Not Things," *The Atlantic*, October 7, 2014, https://www.theatlantic.com/business/archive/2014/10/buy-experiences/381132/.

48. Seung Hwan Lee and June Cotte, "Post-Purchase Consumer Regret: Conceptualization and Development of the Ppcr Scale," *Advances in Consumer Research*, Association for Consumer Research, 2009, 456–62.

49. "The Smell of Commerce: How Companies Use Scents to Sell Their Products," *The Independent* (UK), August 16, 2011, https://www.independent.co.uk/news/media/advertising/the-smell-of-commerce-how-companies-use-scents-to-sell-their-products-2338142.html.

50. N. R. Kleinfeeld, "The Smell of Money," *New York Times*, October 25, 1992, https://www.nytimes.com/1992/10/25/style/the-smell-of-money.html.

CHAPTER 4: A DIFFERENT WAY TO GET DRESSED

1. Walter Isaacson, *Steve Jobs* (New York: Simon & Schuster, 2011), 361–62.

2. Michael Lewis, "Obama's Way," *Vanity Fair*, October 2012, https://www.vanityfair.com/news/2012/10/michael-lewis-profile-barack-obama.

3. Eugene Kim, "Here's the Real Reason Mark Zuckerberg Wears the Same T-Shirt Every Day," *Business Insider*, November 6, 2014, https://www.businessinsider.com/mark-zuckerberg-same-t-shirt-2014-11?r=UK.

4. Craig Bloem, "Why Successful People Wear the Same Thing Every Day," *Inc.*, February 20, 2018, https://www.inc.com/craig-bloem/this-1-unusual-habit-helped-make-mark-zuckerberg-steve-jobs-dr-dre-successful.html.

5. Joel Hoomans, "35,000 Decisions: The Great Choices of Strategic Leaders," *Leading Edge Journal,* Roberts Wesleyan College, March 20, 2015, https://go.roberts.edu/leadingedge /the-great-choices-of-strategic-leaders.

6. John Tierney, "Why You Need to Sleep on It," *New York Times,* August 17, 2011, https://6thfloor.blogs.nytimes.com/2011/08/17/why-you-need-to-sleep-on-it/.

7. Liraz Margalit, PhD, "The Psychology of Choice," *Psychology Today,* October 3, 2014, https://www.psychologytoday.com/us/blog/behind-online-behavior/201410/the -psychology-choice.

8. Alison Beard, "Life's Work: An Interview with Vera Wang," *Harvard Business Review,* July–August 2019, https://hbr.org/2019/07/lifes-work-an-interview-with-vera-wang.

9. Eliza Brooke, " 'The True Cost' Is a Jarring Look at the Human Casualties of Fast Fashion," May 28, 2015, Fashionista, https://fashionista.com/2015/05/the-true-cost.

10. Vanessa Friedman, "The Biggest Fake News in Fashion," *New York Times,* December 18, 2018, https://www.nytimes.com/2018/12/18/fashion/fashion-second-biggest-polluter -fake-news.html.

11. Amanda Mull, "There Is Too Much Stuff," *The Atlantic,* May 24, 2019, https://www .theatlantic.com/health/archive/2019/05/too-many-options/590185/.

12. Elizabeth Paton, "Burberry to Stop Burning Clothing and Other Goods It Can't Sell," *New York Times,* September 6, 2018, https://www.nytimes.com/2018/09/06/business/ burberry-burning-unsold-stock.html.

13. Bryanboy, Twitter, October 30, 2018.

14. Mary Lynn Damhorst, "In Search of a Common Thread: Classification of Information Communicated through Dress," *Clothing and Textiles Research Journal,* January 1, 1990, https://journals.sagepub.com/doi/abs/10.1177/0887302X9000800201.

15. Dorothy U. Behling and Elizabeth A. Williams, "Influence of Dress on Perception of Intelligence and Expectations of Scholastic Achievement," *Clothing and Textiles Research Journal,* June 1, 1991, https://journals.sagepub.com/doi/abs/10.1177/0887302X 9100900401.

16. Arianna Huffington, "Introducing 'The Psychology of What We Wear to Work,'" Thrive Global, October 10, 2018, https://thriveglobal.com/stories/introducing-the-psycho logy-of-what-we-wear-to-work/.

17. Maria Pasquini, "Tiffany Haddish Wears Famous Alexander McQueen Dress for the 5th Time during David Letterman Sitdown," *People,* May 16, 2019, https://people.com /style/tiffany-haddish-rewears-alexander-mcqueen-dress-5th-time-david-letterman/.

18. Lauren Adhav, "Here's Why You Always Reach for the Same Shirt in Your Closet," *Cosmopolitan,* January 22, 2019, https://www.cosmopolitan.com/style-beauty/fashion /a25940043/fashion-psychologist-explains-stripes-meaning/.

19. My August 2018 session with editor Tony Rotunno can be viewed on YouTube: https:// www.youtube.com/watch?v=uEOh1z0dME8.

20. Nick Hobson, PhD, "The Anxiety-Busting Properties of Ritual," *Psychology Today,* September 25, 2017, https://www.psychologytoday.com/us/blog/ritual-and-the-brain/2017 09/the-anxiety-busting-properties-ritual.

21. Janet Singer, "Symptoms of OCD," Psych Central, October 8, 2018, https://psychcen tral.com/lib/symptoms-of-ocd/.

22. "Vivienne Westwood: Everyone Buys Too Many Clothes," *The Telegraph,* September 16, 2013, http://fashion.telegraph.co.uk/news-features/TMG10312077/Vivienne-West wood-Everyone-buys-too-many-clothes.html.

23. David Gelles, "Eileen Fisher: 'When Was Fashion Week?'" *New York Times,* October 5, 2018, https://www.nytimes.com/2018/10/05/business/eileen-fisher-corner-office.html.

24. Elizabeth Segran, "This Women's Clothing Brand Is Made for Professional Women Who Hate to Shop," *Fast Company*, March 31, 2016, https://mmlafleur.com/press/fast-company?utm_source=facebook-instagram&utm_medium=paidsocial&utm_campaign=Prospecting&utm_term=NC-1%25LAL_Top10%25LTV_W_21+.

25. "The 50 Greatest Fashion Quotes of All Time," *Harper's Bazaar*, January 11, 2018, https://www.harpersbazaar.com/fashion/designers/a1576/50-famous-fashion-quotes/.

26. Silvia Bellezza, Francesca Gino, and Anat Keinan, "The Red Sneakers Effect: Inferring Status and Competence from Signals of Nonconformity," *Journal of Consumer Research* 41, no. 1 (June 2014): 35–54.

27. Matthew Hutson and Tori Rodriguez, "Dress for Success: How Clothes Influence Our Performance," *Scientific American*, January 1, 2016, https://www.scientificamerican.com/article/dress-for-success-how-clothes-influence-our-performance/.

CHAPTER 5: MOOD MATTERS

1. Amy Cuddy, *Presence: Bringing Your Boldest Self to Your Biggest Challenges* (New York: Back Bay Books/Little, Brown and Company, 2015), 198–206.

2. Katya Wachtel, "La DressCode: The Banker's Guide to Dressing and Smelling Like a Winner," *Business Insider*, December 15, 2010, https://www.businessinsider.com/ubs-dresscode-clothes-bank-2010-12#ties-length-perfection-and-letting-it-have-a-siesta-is-key-13.

3. Barbara L. Fredrickson, Tomi-Ann Roberts, Stephanie M. Noll, Diane Quinn, and Jean M. Twenge, "That Swimsuit Becomes You: Sex Differences in Self-Objectification, Restrained Eating, and Math Performance," *Journal of Personality and Social Psychology* 75 (1998), https://www.ncbi.nlm.nih.gov/pubmed/9686464.

4. Allison Dryja, "Try These Powerful Tools to Stop Emotionally Eating," MindBodyGreen, https://www.mindbodygreen.com/0-15554/try-these-powerful-tools-to-stop-emotional-eating.html.

5. Jeryl Brunner, "Happy Birthday, Oprah Winfrey! We Celebrate with 35 of Her Most Inspiring Quotes," *Parade*, January 29, 2019, https://parade.com/453846/jerylbrunner/happy-birthday-oprah-winfrey-we-celebrate-with-35-of-her-most-inspiring-quotes/.

6. Steve Greene, "'2 Dope Queens' Podcast Says Goodbye with Michelle Obama Conversation," *IndieWire*, November 14, 2018, https://www.indiewire.com/2018/11/2-dope-queens-podcast-ends-michelle-obama-episode-1202020663/.

7. "17 Dolly Parton Quotes on Success That Will Inspire You," *Southern Living*, May 15, 2017, https://www.southernliving.com/culture/dolly-parton-quotes-success.

8. "Lady Gaga Opens Up about Sexual Assault and Mental Health in Vulnerable Elle Women in Hollywood Acceptance Speech," *Elle*, October 16, 2018, https://www.elle.com/culture/celebrities/a23813974/lady-gaga-opens-up-about-sexual-assault-and-mental-health-elle-women-in-hollywood-acceptance-speech/.

9. Carly Stern, "'Matching Pajama Sets Is Key to Productivity': Alexandria Ocasio-Cortez Insists Having a LOUNGE Uniform Can Make You Perform Better at Work, as She Shares Her Skincare Routine and Love of Oat Milk," *Daily Mail*, January 28, 2019, https://www.dailymail.co.uk/femail/article-6641769/Alexandria-Ocasio-Cortez-shares-skincare-routine-importance-matching-pajamas.html.

10. "Beyoncé Is Sasha Fierce," Oprah.com, November 13, 2008, https://www.oprah.com/oprahshow/beyonces-alter-ego/all#ixzz5XF5KBavc.

11. Jessica Prince Erlich, "How I Get It Done: QVC Star Josie Maran," The Cut, October 2, 2018, https://www.thecut.com/2018/10/how-i-get-it-done-josie-maran.html.

12. "PTSD Clinical Practice Guideline: What Is Exposure Therapy?" American Psychological Association, https://www.apa.org/ptsd-guideline/patients-and-families/exposure-therapy.

13. Rei Kawakubo, *Interview,* October 13, 2015, https://www.interviewmagazine.com/fashion/rei-kawakubo-1.

14. Liz Higgins, "Marriage Is Not a Big Thing, It's a Million Little Things," Gottman Institute Relationship Blog, July 24, 2017, https://www.gottman.com/blog/marriage-not-big-thing-million-little-things/.

15. Vikas Shah, MBE, "The Role of Fashion in Human Culture," *Thought Economics,* September 15, 2012, https://thoughteconomics.com/the-role-of-fashion-in-human-culture/.

16. Hannah Betts, "Brave Face," *The Weekend Australian,* October 29–30, 2016, https://www.theaustralian.com.au/weekend-australian-magazine/brave-face-hannah-betts-on-how-fashion-is-armour/news-story/bf9c3b1f39faf90cbb5d63a4b80045dd.

17. Henry Navarro Delgado, "Joyous Resistance through Costume and Dance at Carnival," *The Conversation,* July 30, 2018, https://theconversation.com/joyous-resistance-through-costume-and-dance-at-carnival-98890.

18. Tiffany Ayuda, "How the Japanese Art of Kintsugi Can Help You Deal with Stressful Situations," NBC News, April 25, 2018, https://www.nbcnews.com/better/health/how-japanese-art-technique-kintsugi-can-help-you-be-more-ncna866471.

CHAPTER 6: COLORS IN CONTEXT

1. Abby Gardner, "Meghan Markle Broke Royal Protocol with Her Nail Polish at the British Fashion Awards," *Glamour,* December 10, 2018, https://www.glamour.com/story/meghan-markle-dark-nail-polish-british-fashion-awards-2018.

2. Adrian Furnham, MD, and Raj Persaud, MD, "Does the Color Red Hold the Secret to Attraction?" *Psychology Today,* February 14, 2016, https://www.psychologytoday.com/us/blog/slightly-blighty/201602/does-the-color-red-hold-the-secret-attraction.

3. Natalie Wolchover, "How Eight Colors Got Their Symbolic Meanings," Live Science, September 27, 2011, https://www.livescience.com/33523-color-symbolism-meanings.html.

4. Manny Fernandez, "Crime Blotter Has a Regular: Yankees Caps," *New York Times,* September 15, 2010, https://www.nytimes.com/2010/09/16/nyregion/16caps.html.

5. Justin Block, "The 10 Most Gang-Affiliated Hats in Sports Today," *Complex,* August 2, 2013, https://www.complex.com/sports/2013/08/most-gang-affiliated-hats-sports-today/.

6. Erik Ortiz, "Pictures of Trayvon Martin's Hoodie and Bloodied Clothes Released by Prosecutors," *New York Daily News,* July 12, 2012, https://www.nydailynews.com/news/crime/pictures-trayvon-martin-hoodie-bloodied-clothes-released-prosecutors-article-1.1113426.

7. Kaitlyn Folmer, Matt Gutman, Candace Smith, and Seni Tienabeso, "Trayvon Martin Shooter George Zimmerman Called Overzealous 'Soft Guy' with a 'Little Hero Complex,'" ABC News, July 12, 2012, https://abcnews.go.com/US/trayvon-martin-shooter-george-zimmerman-called-overzealous-soft/story?id=16762044.

8. Linton Weeks, "Tragedy Gives the Hoodie a Whole New Meaning," NPR, March 24, 2012, https://www.npr.org/2012/03/24/149245834/tragedy-gives-the-hoodie-a-whole-new-meaning.

9. Thomas Gilovich and Mark G. Frank, "The Dark Side of Self- and Social Perception: Black Uniforms and Aggression in Professional Sports," *Journal of Personality and Social Psychology* (1988): 74.

10. "Men and Women Really Do See the World Differently," Live Science, September 4, 2012, https://www.livescience.com/22894-men-and-women-see-things-differently.html.

11. "Facts about Color Blindness," National Eye Institute, February 2015, https://nei.nih.gov/health/color_blindness/facts_about.

12. Maureen Healy, "The Color of Emotion," *Psychology Today*, December 4, 2008, https://www.psychologytoday.com/us/blog/creative-development/200812/the-color-emotion.

13. Julie Miller, "How 20-Year-Old Queen Victoria Forever Changed Wedding Fashion," *Vanity Fair*, April 3, 2018, https://www.vanityfair.com/style/2018/04/queen-victoria-royal-wedding.

14. Dr. Valerie Steele, "Pink: The History of a Punk, Pretty, Powerful Color," Special Exhibitions Gallery, the Museum at FIT, 2018, http://www.fitnyc.edu/museum/exhibitions/pink.php.

15. Rachel Adelson, "Hues and Views: A Cross-Cultural Study Reveals How Language Shapes Color Perception," American Psychological Association, *Monitor on Psychology* 36, no. 2 (February 2005), https://www.apa.org/monitor/feb05/hues.

16. Jeanne Maglaty, "When Did Girls Start Wearing Pink?" Smithsonian.com, April 7, 2011, https://www.smithsonianmag.com/arts-culture/when-did-girls-start-wearing-pink-1370097/.

17. Belinda Luscombe, "The Science of Dating: Wear Red," *Time*, October 25, 2010, http://healthland.time.com/2010/10/25/the-science-of-dating-wear-red/.

18. N. Guéguen and C. Jacob, "Clothing Color and Tipping," *Journal of Hospitality and Tourism Research* 38, no. 2 (2010): 275–80.

19. Steven Young, "The Effect of Red on Male Perceptions of Female Attractiveness: Moderation by Baseline Attractiveness of Female Faces," *European Journal of Social Psychology* (2015): 45.

20. Cassandra Auble, "The Cultural Significance of Precious Stones in Early Modern England" (MA thesis, University of Nebraska–Lincoln, 2011), https://digitalcommons.unl.edu/cgi/viewcontent.cgi?article=1039&context=historydiss.

21. Surya Vanka and David Klein, "Color Tool: Cross-Cultural Meanings of Color," Proceedings of the Human Factors and Ergonomics Society Annual Meeting, October 1, 1995, https://journals.sagepub.com/doi/abs/10.1177/154193129503900510?journalCode=proe.

22. Sharbari Bose and Jaimie Mackey, "12 Hindu Wedding Ceremony Rituals and Traditions, Explained," *Brides*, April 22, 2018, https://www.brides.com/story/hindu-wedding-ceremony.

23. Suzanne Degges-White, PhD, "Dressing for (Sexual) Success," *Psychology Today*, May 31, 2016, https://www.psychologytoday.com/us/blog/lifetime-connections/201605/dressing-sexual-success.

24. Andrew J. Elliot and Daniela Niesta, "Romantic Red: Red Enhances Men's Attraction to Women," *Journal of Personality and Social Psychology* 95, no. 5 (2008): 1,150–64, https://www2.psych.ubc.ca/~schaller/Psyc591Readings/ElliotNiesta2008.pdf.

25. Antonia Blumberg, "Why These 6 Religious Groups Wear What They Wear," Huffington Post, August 18, 2015, www.huffpost.com.

26. "Christie's Asian Art Collecting Guide," May 22, 2019, https://www.christies.com/features/Chinese-robes-collecting-guide-7813-1.aspx.

27. Vanessa Friedman, "The Power of the Yellow Vest," *New York Times*, December 4, 2018, https://www.nytimes.com/2018/12/04/fashion/yellow-vests-france-protest-fashion.html.

28. Ellen Conroy, *The Symbolism of Colour* (London: William Rider & Son, 1921), 24.

29. Jerome Silbergeld and Michael Sullivan, "Chinese Jade," *Britannica*, https://www.britannica.com/art/Chinese-jade.

30. Rachel Jacoby Zoldan, "Your 7 Chakras Explained—Plus How to Tell If They're Blocked," Well + Good, August 2, 2018, https://www.wellandgood.com/good-advice/what-are-chakras/.

31. Ingrid Gaischek, Daniela Litscher, Gerhard Litscher, and Lu Wang, "The Influence of New Colored Light Stimulation Methods on Heart Rate Variability, Temperature, and Well-Being: Results of a Pilot Study in Humans," *Evidence-Based Complementary and Alternative Medicine*, November 28, 2013, https://www.ncbi.nlm.nih.gov/pmc/articles /PMC3863570/.

32. Jaymi McCann, "Want a Good Night's Sleep? Find Out Which Colors You Should Use in the Bedroom (and Avoid) for a Decent Kip," *Daily Mail*, May 16, 2013, https://www .dailymail.co.uk/news/article-2325476/Want-good-nights-sleep-Find-colours-use -bedroom-avoid-decent-kip.html.

33. John M. Grohol, PsyD, "Can Blue-Colored Light Prevent Suicide?" Psych Central, July 8, 2018, https://psychcentral.com/blog/can-blue-colored-light-prevent-suicide/.

34. "Vishnu," BBC, August 24, 2009, https://www.bbc.co.uk/religion/religions/hinduism /deities/vishnu.shtml.

35. Quinn Hargitai, "The Strange Power of the Evil Eye," BBC, February 19, 2018, https:// bbc.com/culture/story/20180216-the-strange-power-of-the-evil-eye.

36. Kendra Cherry, "The Color Psychology of Blue," Very Well Mind, May 6, 2019, https:// www.verywellmind.com/the-color-psychology-of-blue-2795815.

37. Evan Andrews, "Why Is Purple Considered the Color of Royalty?" History.com, July 15, 2015, https://www.history.com/news/why-is-purple-considered-the-color-of -royalty.

38. Linda K. Alchin, "The Color Purple," Elizabethan Era, May 16, 2012, http://www .elizabethan-era.org.uk/color-purple.htm.

39. Stephen M. Silverman, "Prince Sued for Painting House Purple," *People*, March 21, 2006, https://people.com/celebrity/prince-sued-for-painting-house-purple/.

40. Jocelyn Spottiswoode, "Pink Prisons in Switzerland to Calm Inmates," *The Telegraph*, September 11, 2013, https://www.telegraph.co.uk/news/worldnews/europe/switzer land/10302627/Pink-prisons-in-Switzerland-to-calm-inmates.html.

41. Isabel Jones, "Pretty in Passenger-Seat Pink: Why Are Women in Power-Adjacent Positions Flocking toward the Feminine Hue?" *InStyle*, July 2, 2018, https://www.instyle .com/news/melania-trump-meghan-markle-passenger-seat-pale-pink.

42. Amy Chavez, "Japan's National Obsession with the Color Pink," *Japan Times*, July 5, 2013, https://www.japantimes.co.jp/community/2013/07/05/our-lives/japans-national -obsession-with-the-color-pink/#.XRzLq8h7lN0. See also Max Lakin, "Real Men Wear Pink (And Not Just Brooks Brothers Button-Downs)," *Wall Street Journal*, April 5, 2018, https://www.wsj.com/articles/real-men-wear-pink-do-you-have-the-guts-1522936348.

43. Sarah Lindig, "Famous Words of Fashion's Greatest: Part Two," *Harper's Bazaar*, July 11, 2014, https://www.harpersbazaar.com/fashion/designers/a2818/50-famous-fashion -quotes-part-two/.

44. Suzy Menkes, "Fashion's Poet of Black: YAMAMOTO," *New York Times*, September 5, 2000, https://www.nytimes.com/2000/09/05/style/IHT-fashions-poet-of-black-yamamoto.html.

45. Emilia Petrarca, "What 10 (More) People Wore to Their Interviews with Anna Wintour," The Cut, September 21, 2017, https://www.thecut.com/2017/09/anna-wintour -interview-outfit.html.

46. Marisa Iati, "Why Did Women in Congress Wear White for Trump's State of the Union Address?" *Washington Post*, February 6, 2019, https://www.washingtonpost.com /history/2019/02/05/why-are-women-lawmakers-wearing-white-state-union/?nore direct=on&utm_term=.4c33e27dd75b. Caroline Kenny, "Democratic Women Wear White to Trump's Address," CNN, March 1, 2017, https://www.cnn.com/2017/02/28 /politics/democratic-women-wear-white-donald-trump-speech/index.html.

47. Ella Alexander, "Carolina Herrera: Why the White Shirt Still Rules," *Vogue*, February 13, 2013, https://www.vogue.co.uk/article/carolina-herrera-white-shirt-collection-inter view-film-exclusive.

48. According to renowned architect and feng shui expert Anjie Cho, "the element of Earth is related to earthy colors like brown, orange, or yellow and the feng shui bagua areas of Abundance, Health, and Knowledge." https://www.anjiecho.com/holistic-spaces -blog/2014/5/23/find-feng-shui-balance-with-the-five-elements.

49. Bobby Schuessler, "The Fashion-Person Outfit That's Already Ruling 2019," *Who What Wear*, January 27, 2019, https://www.whowhatwear.com/brown-outfits.

CHAPTER 7: POWER ACCESSORIES

1. Jonathan Van Meter, "The Awakening of Kim Kardashian West," *Vogue*, April 10, 2019, https://www.vogue.com/article/kim-kardashian-west-cover-may-2019.

2. Melissa Minton, "Why Elizabeth Taylor Once Burned All of Her Designer Clothes," *New York Post*, Page Six Style, October 31, 2018, https://pagesix.com/2018/10/31/why -elizabeth-taylor-once-burned-all-of-her-designer-clothes/.

3. Sarah Lindig, "Famous Words of Fashion's Greatest: Part Two," *Harper's Bazaar*, July 11, 2014, https://www.harpersbazaar.com/fashion/designers/a2818/50-famous-fashion -quotes-part-two/.

4. Nicolas Guéguen, "High Heels Increase Women's Attractiveness," *Archives of Sexual Behavior*, November 2015, https://www.ncbi.nlm.nih.gov/pubmed/25408499.

5. "The Kick-Ass Shoe Quotes to Live Your Life By," *Marie Claire*, January 4, 2019, https:// www.marieclaire.co.uk/fashion/shoe-quotes-the-25-best-of-all-time-61098.

6. Chakra Anatomy, https://www.chakra-anatomy.com/solar-plexus-chakra.html.

7. Delia Ephron and Nora Ephron, *Love, Loss, and What I Wore* (New York: Dramatists Play Service, 2008), 39–40.

8. Lynn Douglass, "Lady Gaga Buys 55 Items from Michael Jackson Auction, Says She'll Archive All," *Forbes*, December 5, 2012, https://www.forbes.com/sites/lynndou glass/2012/12/05/lady-gaga-buys-55-items-from-michael-jackson-auction-says-shell -archive-all/#67bdb5019b0c.

9. Peter Born, "The (Un)Death of Celebrity Fragrance," *WWD*, September 9, 2015, https:// wwd.com/beauty-industry-news/fragrance/celebrity-fragrance-falters-10212061/.

10. Emily Kirkpatrick, "Kris Jenner's New $16K Bag Lets People Know She's 'Rich as F——,'" *New York Post*, Page Six Style, December 26, 2018, https://pagesix.com/ 2018/12/26/kris-jenners-new-16k-bag-lets-people-know-shes-rich-as-f-k/.

11. Judith Thurman, "The World's Oldest Crown," *The New Yorker*, March 12, 2014, https:// www.newyorker.com/culture/culture-desk/the-worlds-oldest-crown.

12. Philippa Morgan, "Everything You Need to Know about the Making of Rihanna's Nefertiti-Inspired Hat," *Vogue Arabia*, October 31, 2017, https://en.vogue.me/fashion/ rihanna-nefertiti-hat-vogue-arabia-november-2017-issue/.

13. Marijn Meijers and Rob Nelissen, "Social Benefits of Luxury Brands as Costly Signals of Wealth and Status," *Evolution and Human Behavior* 32, no. 5 (September 2011): 343–55, https://www.sciencedirect.com/science/article/abs/pii/S1090513810001455.

14. L. N. Chaplin and D. R. John, "Growing Up in a Material World: Age Differences in Materialism in Children and Adolescents," *Journal of Consumer Research* 34, no. 4 (2007): 480–93.

15. Derek D. Rucker and Adam D. Galinsky, "Desire to Acquire: Powerlessness and Compensatory Consumption," *Journal of Consumer Research* 35, no. 2 (August 2008): 257–67, https://insight.kellogg.northwestern.edu/article/desire_to_acquire.

16. Christian Jarrett, "The Psychology of Stuff and Things," *The Psychologist* 26 (August 2013): 560–65, https://thepsychologist.bps.org.uk/volume-26/edition-8/psychology-stuff-and-things.

17. Alessandra Galloni, "Interview: 'Fashion Is How You Present Yourself to the World,'" *Wall Street Journal*, January 18, 2007, https://www.wsj.com/articles/SB116907065754279376.

18. Robin Givhan, "Seriously, Prada, What Were You Thinking? Why the Fashion Industry Keeps Bumbling into Racist Imagery," *Washington Post*, December 15, 2018, https://www.washingtonpost.com/arts-entertainment/2018/12/15/seriously-prada-what-were-you-thinking-why-fashion-industry-keeps-bumbling-into-racist-imagery/?noredirect=on&utm_term=.2fd0611ce52b.

19. Stacia Brown, "What the Black Church Taught Me about Lipstick," The Cut, November 6, 2018, https://www.thecut.com/2018/11/what-the-black-church-taught-me-about-lipstick.html.

20. Jacob Bogage, Alex Horton, and Eli Rosenberg, "A White Referee Told a High School Wrestler to Cut His Dreadlocks or Forfeit. He Took the Cut," *Washington Post*, December 22, 2018, https://www.washingtonpost.com/sports/2018/12/21/referee-high-school-wrestler-cut-your-dreadlocks-or-forfeit/?utm_term=.a430d9aad373.

21. Nadra Nittle, "Bantu Knots Are the Latest Natural Hairstyle at the Center of a Workplace Dispute," Vox, December 20, 2018, https://www.vox.com/the-goods/2018/12/20/18150268/bantu-knots-ross-dress-for-less-natural-hairstyles-workplace.

22. Michael Cunningham and Craig Marberry, *Crowns: Portraits of Black Women in Church Hats* (New York: Penguin Random House, 2000), excerpted in *Time,* http://content.time.com/time/photogallery/0,29307,1874131,00.html.

23. Ibid.

24. Terry Gross, "Novelist Zadie Smith on Historical Nostalgia and the Nature of Talent," *Fresh Air,* NPR, November 21, 2016, https://www.npr.org/2016/11/21/502857118/novelist-zadie-smith-on-historical-nostalgia-and-the-nature-of-talent.

CHAPTER 8: ARE YOU DRESSING FOR YOURSELF OR FOR SOMEONE ELSE?

1. Suzannah Ramsdale, "The 57 Fashion Quotes to Live by *Every* Single Day," July 4, 2018, *Marie Claire UK,* https://www.marieclaire.co.uk/fashion/the-40-best-style-quotes-of-all-time-122453.

2. Andrew M. Penner and Jaclyn S. Wong, "Gender and the Returns to Attractiveness," *Research in Social Stratification and Mobility* 44 (June 2016): 113–23.

3. Dave Chappelle appeared on *Inside the Actors Studio* on February 12, 2006. See https://www.youtube.com/watch?v=bTQYXRoIzhI.

4. Terry Gross, "Comic Jessica Williams on 'The Daily Show' and Learning to 'Never Be Average,'" *Fresh Air,* NPR, July 25, 2017, https://www.npr.org/2017/07/25/539240567/comic-jessica-williams-on-the-daily-show-and-learning-to-never-be-average.

5. Suzanne Zuckerman, "Kerry Washington: In the Heights," *New York Post, Page Six Magazine,* September 20, 2008.

6. Cindi Leive, "Kerry Washington Talks Her New Marriage, Scandal Style, and Her Real-Life Gladiators," *Glamour,* September 3, 2013, https://www.glamour.com/story/kerry-washington-glamour-inter.

7. Vikas Shah, MBE, "The Role of Fashion in Human Culture," *Thought Economics,* September 15, 2012, https://thoughteconomics.com/the-role-of-fashion-in-human-culture/.

8. Anika Reed, "How Issa Rae's 'Insecure' Navigates the Workplace with Style," *USA*

Today, September 9, 2017, https://www.usatoday.com/story/life/2017/09/09/how-issa
-raes-insecure-navigates-workplace-style/645655001/.

9. Christine Hauser, "How Professionals of Color Say They Counter Bias at Work," *New York Times*, December 12, 2018, https://www.nytimes.com/2018/12/12/us/racial-bias -work.html.

10. Austin Murphy, "I Used to Write for *Sports Illustrated*. Now I Deliver Packages for Amazon," *The Atlantic*, December 25, 2018, https://www.theatlantic.com/ideas/archive/ 2018/12/what-its-like-to-deliver-packages-for-amazon/578986/.

11. Katy Schneider, "The Unlikely Tale of a $140 Amazon Coat That's Taken Over the Upper East Side," *New York Magazine*, March 27, 2018, http://nymag.com/strategist/2018 /03/the-orolay-amazon-coat-thats-overtaken-the-upper-east-side.html.

12. Maureen Callahan, "Inside the Bizarre Life of an Upper East Side Housewife," *New York Post*, May 24, 2015, https://nypost.com/2015/05/24/inside-the-bizarre-life-of-an-upper -east-side-housewife/.

13. Kelsey Stiegman, " 'Blackish' Star Yara Shahidi Got into Every School She Applied To," *Seventeen*, April 10, 2017, https://www.seventeen.com/celebrity/interviews/a46309/ yara-shahidi-interview/.

14. Anne Branigin, "Black Hair Matters: The Affirmative Power of Politicians Like Ayanna Pressley and Stacey Abrams," *The Root*, December 3, 2018, https://theglowup.theroot .com/black-hair-matters-the-affirmative-power-of-politician-1830750951?utm _medium=sharefromsite&utm_source=theroot_email&utm_campaign=bottom.

15. Alexandria Ocasio-Cortez, Twitter, January 4, 2019, https://twitter.com/aoc/status/10 81284603850174467?s=21.

16. Noah St. John, "Afformations: Better Than Affirmations? Part 1," from the blog of self-help author Steven Aitchison, https://www.stevenaitchison.co.uk/afformations -better-than-affirmations-part-1/.

17. Naomi Wolf, *The Beauty Myth* (New York: HarperCollins, 2002), 1.

18. Kelsey Garcia, "Karl Lagerfeld's Most Outrageous Quotes," *Elle*, February 19, 2019, https:// www.elle.com/culture/books/g7696/karl-lagerfeld-world-according-to-karl-quotes/.

CHAPTER 9: SELFIE NATION

1. "Time Flies: US Adults Now Spend Nearly Half a Day Interacting with Media," Nielsen, July 31, 2018, https://www.nielsen.com/us/en/insights/article/2018/time-flies-us-adults -now-spend-nearly-half-a-day-interacting-with-media/.

2. D. I. Tamir and J. P. Mitchell, "Disclosing Information about the Self Is Intrinsically Rewarding," *Proceedings of the National Academy of Sciences*, May 22, 2012, 109.

3. Deborah Netburn, "Facebook, Twitter, Other Social Media Are Brain Candy, Study Says," *Los Angeles Times*, May 8, 2012, https://www.latimes.com/business/la-xpm-2012 -may-08-la-fi-tn-self-disclosure-study-20120508-story.html.

4. Jean M. Twenge, "Have Smartphones Destroyed a Generation?" *The Atlantic*, September 2017, https://www.theatlantic.com/magazine/archive/2017/09/has-the-smartphone -destroyed-a-generation/534198/.

5. Alina Tugend, "Praise Is Fleeting, but Brickbats We Recall," *New York Times*, March 23, 2012, https://www.nytimes.com/2012/03/24/your-money/why-people-remember -negative-events-more-than-positive-ones.html. See also Roy Baumeister, Ellen Bratslavsky, Catrin Finkenauer, and Kathleen D. Vohs, "Bad Is Stronger Than Good," *Review of General Psychology* 5, no. 4 (2001): 323–70. Andrea Thompson, "Bad Memories Stick Better Than Good," *Live Science*, September 5, 2007, https://www.livescience .com/1827-bad-memories-stick-good.html.

6. Carrie Battan, "The Instagram Trap: Social Influence Is Helping Women Build Brands — as Long as They Follow the Rules," *Fast Company*, April 22, 2019, https://www.fastcompany.com/90324013/what-its-like-to-be-a-female-founder-in-the-instagram-era.

7. Lena Dunham, "Can a Good Man Mistreat You during Sex — If That's What You Desire?" *Vogue*, March 18, 2019, https://www.vogue.com/article/can-a-good-man-mistreat-you-during-sex-lena-dunham.

8. Sam Adams, "With Hulu and Netflix's Fyre Festival Docs, Instagram Influencers Get Their *Gimme Shelter*," *Slate*, January 16, 2019, https://slate.com/culture/2019/01/fyre-festival-docs-netflix-hulu-review-which-to-watch.html.

9. Emily McCormick, "Instagram Is Estimated to Be Worth More Than $100 Billion," Bloomberg, June 25, 2018, https://www.bloomberg.com/news/articles/2018-06-25/value-of-facebook-s-instagram-estimated-to-top-100-billion.

10. Guy Trebay, "On Instagram, Who's Who When It Comes to Followers," *New York Times*, January 10, 2019, https://www.nytimes.com/2019/01/10/fashion/pitti-uomo-instagram-florence-italy.html.

11. Rebecca Solnit, *Men Explain Things to Me* (Chicago: Haymarket Books, 2014), 78.

12. Mark Griffiths and Daria Kuss, "6 Questions Help Reveal If You're Addicted to Social Media," *Washington Post*, April 25, 2018, https://www.washingtonpost.com/news/theworldpost/wp/2018/04/25/social-media-addiction/?noredirect=on&utm_term=.863458995120.

13. Dar Meshi, Anastassia Elizarova, Andrew Bender, and Antonio Verdejo-Garcia, "Excessive Social Media Users Demonstrate Impaired Decision Making in the Iowa Gambling Task," *Journal of Behavioral Addictions* 8, no. 1 (2019), https://akademiai.com/doi/10.1556/2006.7.2018.138.

14. Sarah Young, " 'Your Sense of Self-Worth Becomes Skewed': Meghan Markle Discusses the Effect of Social Media on Mental Health," *The Independent* (UK), October 30, 2018, https://www.independent.co.uk/life-style/meghan-markle-social-media-mental-health-self-worth-new-zealand-a8608331.html.

15. Olivia Petter, "Royal Tour: Meghan Markle Says It's 'Freeing' to Be off Social Media," *The Independent* (UK), October 20, 2018, https://www.independent.co.uk/life-style/meghan-markle-prince-harry-royal-tour-social-media-freeing-bondi-beach-sydney-a8593286.html.

CHAPTER 10: YOUR WOKE WARDROBE

1. Gabriela Mernin, "99 Problems: Shades of Belonging," *New York Daily News*, November 3, 2016, https://www.nydailynews.com/new-york/education/examining-paper-bag-test-evolved-article-1.2844394.

2. Dr. David Pilgrim, "Brown Paper Bag Test," Jim Crow Museum of Racist Memorabilia, February 2014, https://www.ferris.edu/HTMLS/news/jimcrow/question/2014/february.htm.

3. Jessica Bennett, "Exclusive: Mathew Knowles Says Internalized Colorism Led Him to Tina Knowles Lawson," *Ebony*, February 2, 2018, https://www.ebony.com/entertainment/books/exclusive-mathew-knowles/#axzz56JUbaNKn.

4. Hayley Krischer, "The New Mom Uniform of Park Slope," *New York Times*, January 16, 2019, https://www.nytimes.com/2019/01/16/style/clogs-no-6-moms.html.

5. Imran Amed, Anita Balchandani, Marco Beltrami, Achim Berg, Saskia Hedrich, and Felix Rölkens, "The State of Fashion 2019: A Year of Awakening," *The Business of Fashion*, November 2018, https://cdn.businessoffashion.com/reports/The_State_of_Fashion_2019.pdf.

6. Maxine Bédat and Michael Shank, "Every Purchase You Make Is a Chance to Vote with Your Wallet," *Fast Company*, April 5, 2017, https://www.fastcompany.com/40402079/every-purchase-you-make-is-a-chance-to-vote-with-your-wallet.

7. For Gucci's racially offensive runway show, see Chris Perez, "Gucci Slammed for Sweater That Appears to Resemble Blackface," *New York Post*, February 7, 2019, https://nypost.com/2019/02/07/gucci-slammed-for-sweater-that-appears-to-resemble-blackface/. See also Layla Ilchi, "Gucci Accused of Cultural Appropriation over 'Indy Turban,'" *WWD*, May 16, 2019, https://wwd.com/fashion-news/fashion-scoops/gucci-indy-turban-cultural-appropriation-backlash-1203132880/.

8. Emanuella Grinberg, "Retailer Pulls Shirts Reminiscent of Holocaust," CNN, August 28, 2014, https://www.cnn.com/2014/08/27/living/zara-pulls-sheriff-star-shirt/index.html.

9. Lauren Thomas, "H&M Slammed as Racist for 'Monkey in the Jungle' Hoodie," CNBC, January 8, 2018, https://www.cnbc.com/2018/01/08/hm-slammed-for-racist-monkey-in-the-jungle-hoodie.html.

10. Ana Colon, "Two More Retailers Come Under Fire for Sexist Children's T-Shirts," Refinery 29, September 1, 2016, https://www.refinery29.com/en-us/2016/09/121889/target-old-navy-sexist-girls-t-shirts.

11. Elle Hunt, "Batgirl 'Housework': Target Removes 'Sexist' T-Shirt and Apologizes," *The Guardian*, August 31, 2016, https://www.theguardian.com/world/2016/aug/31/batgirl-housework-target-removes-sexist-t-shirt-and-apologises.

12. Clinton Yates, "Columbusing Black Washington," *Washington Post*, October 8, 2012, https://www.washingtonpost.com/blogs/therootdc/post/nouveau-columbusing-black-washington/2012/10/08/62b43084-10db-11e2-a16b-2c110031514a_blog.html?utm_term=.ea1b2ab37806.

13. Michelle Gant, "Zara's New Mini Skirt Accused of Cultural Appropriation," *New York Post*, February 4, 2018, https://nypost.com/2018/02/04/zaras-new-mini-skirt-blasted-for-cultural-appropriation/.

14. Danielle Gray, "Kim Kardashian Slammed for Calling Cornrows 'Bo Derek Braids,'" *Allure*, January 29, 2018, https://www.allure.com/story/kim-kardashian-called-cornrows-bo-derek-braids-lol-come-on-girl.

15. Melissa Minton, "Kim Kardashian's Sunday Service Look Called Out for Cultural Appropriation," *New York Post*, Page Six Style, April 5, 2019, https://pagesix.com/2019/04/05/kim-kardashians-sunday-service-look-called-out-for-cultural-appropriation/.

16. Dodai Stewart, "On Miley Cyrus, Ratchet Culture, and Accessorizing with Black People," Jezebel, June 20, 2013, https://jezebel.com/on-miley-cyrus-ratchet-culture-and-accessorizing-with-514381016.

17. Julia Jacobs and Dan Levin, "Black Girl Sent Home from School over Hair Extensions," *New York Times*, August 21, 2018, https://www.nytimes.com/2018/08/21/us/black-student-extensions-louisiana.html.

18. Tenisha F. Sweet, Instagram, May 31, 2019, https://www.instagram.com/p/ByHbEOIAbw4/.

19. "Turban Myths: The Opportunity and Challenges for Reframing a Cultural Symbol for Post-9/11 America," Stanford Peace Innovation Lab, September 9, 2013, https://online.wsj.com/public/resources/documents/TurbanMyths.pdf.

20. Janaya "Future" Khan, Now This News, October 22, 2018, https://nowthisnews.com/videos/politics/activist-janaya-future-khan-on-redefining-privilege.

21. Roxane Gay, *Bad Feminist: Essays* (New York: HarperCollins, 2014), 19.

22. Cady Lang, "The Internet Is Sounding Off about Karlie Kloss's Japan-Themed *Vogue* Shoot," *Time*, February 15, 2017, https://time.com/4671287/karlie-kloss-vogue-backlash/.

23. The complete quote is "Since the barbz wanna b ratchet, I will tweet ONLY in Japanese for the next WEEK! To honor my great grandfather!!! Mwahhahaahaa *evil laugh.*" Nicki Minaj, Twitter, May 20, 2012, https://twitter.com/nickiminaj/status/204453861371559937?lang=en.

24. Michael Harriot and Maiysha Kai, "Was Nicki Minaj's SNL Performance Cultural Appropriation?" *The Root*, May 21, 2018, https://theglowup.theroot.com/was-nicki-minajs-snl-performance-cultural-appropriation-1826198535.

25. Nick Reilly, "Nicki Minaj Accused of 'Cultural Appropriation' after SNL Performance," *NME*, May 21, 2018, https://www.nme.com/news/music/nicki-minaj-accused-cultural-appropriation-saturday-night-live-performance-2321789.

26. Nicole Rojas, "Student Wears Traditional Chinese Dress to Prom, Sparks Cultural Appropriation Debate," *Newsweek*, April 30, 2018, https://www.newsweek.com/students-traditional-chinese-dress-prom-sparks-debate-over-cultural-906297. See also Megan McCluskey, "Teen Defends Her Chinese Prom Dress after Cultural Appropriation Backlash," *Time*, May 2, 2018, https://time.com/5262748/chinese-prom-dress-cultural-appropriation/.

27. Sean Rossman, "Chinese Are OK with Utah Teen's Controversial Cheongsam Prom Dress," *USA Today*, May 4, 2018, https://www.usatoday.com/story/news/nation-now/2018/05/04/chinese-ok-utah-teens-controversial-cheongsam-prom-dress/580062002/.

28. Jenna Sauers, "And Here We Have a 'Sexy Little Geisha' Outfit from Victoria's Secret," *Jezebel*, September 26, 2012, https://jezebel.com/and-here-we-have-a-sexy-little-geisha-outfit-from-victo-5946583.

29. Maria Sherman, "How the Sears Catalog Revolutionized African American Shopping under Jim Crow," *Jezebel*, October 17, 2018, https://pictorial.jezebel.com/how-the-sears-catalog-revolutionized-african-american-s-1829802142.

30. Andrew D. Leucke, "10 Essential Quotes about Men's Style," *Esquire*, January 21, 2015, https://www.esquire.com/style/mens-fashion/a32357/10-essential-quotes-about-mens-style-012115/.

31. "Meet Universal Standard: The Women Creating Clothes for Every Body," *Goop*, November 2018, https://goop.com/work/career/meet-universal-standard-the-women-creating-clothes-for-every-body/?utm_source=social-email&utm_medium=social-earned&utm_campaign=onsite-share-button.

32. Marc Bain, "Women's Labor, Ideas and Dollars Prop Up the US Fashion Industry, but Men Still Run It," *Quartzy*, May 23, 2018, https://qz.com/quartzy/1285516/a-fashion-industry-study-finds-that-while-women-prop-it-up-men-run-it/. See also Helena Pike, "Female Fashion Designers Are Still in the Minority," *The Business of Fashion*, September 9, 2016, https://www.businessoffashion.com/community/voices/discussions/how-can-fashion-develop-more-women-leaders/less-female-fashion-designers-more-male-designers.

33. On the number of designers showing at the February 2018 New York Fashion Week, see http://nyfw.com/designers/r. See also Crystal Tate, "Meet the Nine Black Designers Showing at New York Fashion Week," *Essence*, February 12, 2018, https://www.essence.com/fashion-week/new-york-fashion-week/nine-black-designers-showing/; "African-Americans: Demographic and Consumer Spending Trends," 10th ed., Research and Markets, September 2016, https://www.researchandmarkets.com/research/2p5kjz/africanamericans.

34. "Conspicuous Consumption and Race: Who Spends More on What," Knowledge @ Wharton, May 14, 2008, https://knowledge.wharton.upenn.edu/article/conspicuous-consumption-and-race-who-spends-more-on-what/.

35. Beyoncé Knowles, "Beyoncé in Her Own Words: Her Life, Her Body, Her Heritage," *Vogue*, August 6, 2018, https://www.vogue.com/article/beyonce-september-issue-2018.

36. Lindsay Peoples Wagner, "Everywhere and Nowhere: What It's Really Like to Be Black and Work in Fashion," *New York Magazine*, The Cut, August 23, 2018, https://www.thecut.com/2018/08/what-its-really-like-to-be-black-and-work-in-fashion.html?utm_source=tw.

INDEX